"To discover wisdom in the heart of confusion is the most precious gift. To have Irini Rockwell deliver this message is our greatest fortune. With precision and warmth, Rockwell shows us that shadows only occur when we turn away from the light, our own natural brilliance. This wonderful book shows us how to turn back into it."

—Andrew Holecek, author of *The Power and the Pain*

"In an act of sustained devotion, Irini Rockwell has preserved and elucidated Chögyam Trungpa's teaching of the Five Wisdom Energies, making them accessible and pertinent to anyone doing spiritual practice today. With elegance, skill, and experience born of her own practice with them, she has written the indispensable handbook for applying the Five Wisdoms to your own life and work."

—Diane Musho Hamilton Sensei, Boulder Mountain Zendo

"Highly accessible and profound. Based on the Buddhist understanding of the five wisdom energies, it offers a wonderful example of applied contemplative psychology, with many useful instructions on how to liberate our egocentric emotions and confusion into the egoless emotions and wisdom of the Buddha."

—Han F. de Wit, author of *Contemplative Psychology* and *The Spiritual Path*

"This presentation of the Five Wisdoms is clearly the fruit of years of working with people. Recognizing these wisdoms in our lives, including their possible shadow aspects, yields both the recognition of who we are and the potential to let go of unhelpful behavioral patterns."

—Mauk Pieper, head of research and development at Venwoude Training in Personal Leadership, the Netherlands

"Through her lucid explanation of the Five Wisdoms in action, Irini Rockwell offers a beautiful and powerful vehicle to navigate the complex subtle energies of our lives. Her insights serve as luminous guideposts that invite us into a more engaged relationship with each moment, within and without."

—Barrett C. Brown, PhD, executive director, Integral Sustainability Center, MetaIntegral Foundation

"Irini Rockwell offers us many possibilities from her practical and deep understanding, so we are able to rediscover the wisdom qualities in our lives."

—Sebo Ebbens, PhD, founder, Centre for Contemplative Practices

"Irini Rockwell has made a great compassionate gesture to digest and present one of the greatest wisdom fruits of Tibetan Buddhism—the teachings on the Five Wisdom Energies—in a way that is accessible, meaningful, and workable. She rightly refers to it as 'a human path.' She has made a great contribution to bring these higher teachings down to earth and into the hearts of people."

—SYDNEY LEIJENHORST, KenKon, Integral Life and Training Centre, Wageningen, the Netherlands

"Irini brings a clarity and accessibility to this arcane subject, making it directly relevant and understandable for contemporary dharma practitioners and those interested in personal growth."

—JOHN CHURCHILL, Samadhi Integral, Massachusetts

"A very precise, practical, and profound exploration of the Five Buddha Families leading to the discovery of our inherent sanity and basic goodness. A great manual to bring out the best of who we are."

—CATHERINE PAGÈS ROSHI, head teacher, Dana Sangha, Paris

"*Natural Brilliance* is a welcome tour guide to developing leadership practices because it reveals five innate energies all leaders can access. Irini Rockwell shows that it is actually easy to live in sustainable ways by applying the five wisdoms for Purpose, Priority, People, Place, and Planet."

—MARILYN HAMILTON, PhD, author of *Integral City*

"*Natural Brilliance* is all it promises to be and much more. Irini's writings plug us into deeper dimensions of reality that are always there, patiently awaiting our return."

—ANOUK BRACK, founder of Experience Integral for Sustainability Leadership, Cultivating Leadership Presence and Intuitive Intelligence at the University of Wageningen, Netherlands

"Irini Rockwell has helped many people worldwide to uncover their courage, dignity, and strength. This text shines with its own 'natural brilliance.'"

—DR. SONYA JONES, author of *Small Claims, Large Encounters*

Natural Brilliance

Natural Brilliance

A Buddhist System
for Uncovering Your Strengths
and Letting Them Shine

Irini Rockwell

SHAMBHALA · Boston & London · 2012

Shambhala Publications, Inc.
Horticultural Hall
300 Massachusetts Avenue
Boston, Massachusetts 02115
www.shambhala.com

9 8 7 6 5 4 3 2 1

First Edition
Printed in the United States of America

⊗ This edition is printed on acid-free paper that meets the
American National Standards Institute z39.48 Standard.
✿ Shambhala Publications makes every effort to print
on recycled paper. For more information please visit
www.shambhala.com

Distributed in the United States by Random House, Inc.,
and in Canada by Random House of Canada Ltd

Library of Congress Cataloging-in-Publication Data
Rockwell, Irini Nadel.
Natural brilliance: a Buddhist system for uncovering your
strengths and letting them shine / Irini Rockwell.—1st ed.
p.   cm.
Includes bibliographical references.
ISBN 978-1-59030-932-2 (pbk.: alk. paper)
1. Spiritual life—Buddhism. I. Title.
BQ7805.R64 2012
294.3'444—dc23
2011024987

This book is dedicated to my Buddhist and Shambhala teachers,
Chögyam Trungpa Rinpoche, Khenpo Tsultrim Gyamtso Rinpoche, and Sakyong Mipham Rinpoche,
who exist solely to bring out the wisdom in everyone.

And to all sentient beings, who are my teachers who inspire me moment to moment.

Contents

Preface

AFTER WRITING MY FIRST BOOK, *The Five Wisdom Energies: A Buddhist Way of Understanding Personalities, Emotions, and Relationships*, I felt I had no more to say. What more was there? I had presented the five wisdom energies quite fully, and that was to be my contribution. However, the more life went on, the more I experienced a deepening awareness of the Five Wisdoms teachings. There was certainly more to say.

Five Wisdoms @ Work, the two-year personal and professional development training that I created, became a primary vehicle for embarking on a deeper journey. The more I taught, the more I realized how much more there was to teach. I was basking in the feast of learning that comes from the rich personal experiences participants and I were having in the training. Writing in juxtaposition with experiential work is like rubbing sticks together to ignite the fire of insight. Bringing awareness to all experiences creates a bonfire of collective wisdom.

My first book presented the Five Wisdoms using psychological language and atmospheric description. The book focused on how the Five Wisdoms can be experienced in our lives, giving an understanding of energy, personality, emotions, relationships, creative process, and working with others. In this book I continue to pursue my primary goal: to show the immediate applicability of the Five Wisdoms in life and work.

For me this work is very fruitional. It brings together my training in and understanding of mind/body disciplines, dance and movement, creative process, psychotherapy, meditation, Buddhism, leadership training, and an integral perspective. Moreover, I have seen this work transform people's lives, whether it be to give them greater awareness of themselves, bring out more emotional intelligence, make a breakthrough in their primary relationship, or see their energy in a work situation. I invite you to embark on this adventure of discovery with the Five Wisdoms.

Acknowledgments

THE TEN-YEAR PERIOD between the publication of my first book and this one has been rich. First, there was a two-year book tour combined with teaching at Buddhist and personal growth centers and educational institutions from California to Istanbul. Then, in order to bring out more depth, I created Five Wisdoms @ Work (now called Wisdoms@Work), a two-year personal and professional development training.

At times my travels have been fraught with global disturbances: disastrous fires in California, unsettling terrorist bombs in Istanbul, and a major blizzard in New York City. Life! As well, I saw the difficult situations people find themselves in every day, and how the Five Wisdoms work can bring people very quickly into deep personal awareness.

My Buddhist and Shambhala practices have also deepened. The breadth and depth from which these teachings are born and the immeasurably skillful way in which my teachers have presented them, ha continually rained blessings upon me. I am showered by insights. I feel immeasurable gratitude to my teachers Chögyam Trungpa Rinpoche, Khenpo Tsültrim Gyamtso Rinpoche, and Sakyong Mipham Rinpoche.

Another primary influence has been the leadership training in a variety of communities. Susan Skjei and Mark Wilding founded the Authentic Leadership at Naropa University in Boulder, Colorado. Michael Chender, David Sable, Susan Skjei, and others founded Authentic Leadership in Action (ALIA) Institute in Halifax, Nova Scotia, now directed by Susan Szpakowski. These programs, which attract people from all over the world, deeply explore questions of authenticity, skillful communication, and effective action.

I have also made strong connections with people in the Integral community spawned by Ken Wilber and others. In particular, Ken-Kon Integral Life Training Center in the Netherlands, directed by Sydney Leijenhorst, has hosted several cycles of the two-year training. Sydney and I also have Tibetan Buddhism in common, and a shared commitment to embodied teachings. I greatly appreciate his contribution to the graphics. The other team members at KenKon are Berry Trip, Monique Volkers, Diane Schaap, and Francesco Melita. Other centers, also in the Netherlands, are Experience Integral, directed by Anouk Brack and Ric Hoevers, and the trainers at Venwoude, including Mauk Pieper, Chahat Corten, Leon Grass, Lena Huisman, Sujata van Overveld, and Pauline Botden. I feel very privileged to have been hosted by these very professional and creative people.

In education, the Naropa University has always been a primary inspiration to me. I also appreciate the tremendous amount of creative energy that The National Institute for School Development in the Netherlands has stimulated. I want to thank Sebo Ebbens and An van Bolhuis who made it possible for me to train the trainers at this very professional institution.

At each program or longer training, participants have revealed themselves to the group, bringing warmth and intimacy to our collective endeavor. As well, I am indebted to them for sharing their experiences in order to shed light on yet another facet of these vast teachings.

Without the support of a worldwide community of like-minded people with a shared vision—to lead a life worth living—I would not have the courage or the resources to present this material in the way I do. Together we have explored the potential, relevance, and value of the wisdoms in our everyday lives and work.

I feel we have all written this book. Everywhere I went, every person I met, every display of Mother Nature, every situation I encountered, spoke to me. And I was listening, and taking notes. During this period I saw myself move from being a teacher to being a trainer, not so much interested in downloading what I know, to creating arenas of learning and exploring for others. This has allowed me to listen even more fully.

At a very personal level, I have met with deaths. Dissolving the relationship with my husband brought me into the deepest transformational shift of my life. Attending my stepmother at her deathbed gave me the profound experience of embracing death. That sense was echoed as my sister passed away. Death also is our teacher.

Particularly precious to me has been the growing understanding and mutual appreciation I have with my children Julian Nadel and Karuna Rockwell (formally Chandra Rockwell). In being completely themselves, they continually offer their particular intelligence and intuition to everyday situations. My close relationship with my father, now twice widowed, has also become a touchstone from which I draw comfort and an appreciation for the celebration of life. At my tango class, he surrenders his cane and starts to dance. Or, at the mention of tango, he conjugates it in Latin. At age ninety-five, he continues to delight me.

I want to thank those who have given me material comfort by hosting me in their homes, and those who have given this project financial support: Tom Melcher, Dai En Hi Fu Roshi, Susan Edwards, Judith Skinner, Steve Smaha, the van Otterloo family, Jessica Winslow, Sol Rueben, and John Neumeier.

Lastly, much appreciation goes to my editors and other staff at Shambhala Publications: Eden Steinberg, Beth Frankl, and Ben Gleason. The patience and integrity with which they produce a book is inspirational.

Natural Brilliance

Introduction
Moving toward Wisdom

WE LIVE in a remarkable age. This is a time of abundance and opportunity that could scarcely be imagined even a few generations ago. Our access to information, material goods, and communication is unprecedented in human history. Yet few of us seem truly satisfied with our lives. Our levels of stress, fatigue, conflict, and confusion appear equally unprecedented.

Just think. Fundamentally we have the same body and mind as our ancestors who plowed fields with an ox or a horse and used simple hand tools. In days gone by, one lifetime saw relatively few technological changes. Perhaps someone discovered a better way to harvest wheat or store vegetables. Gradually life has become more complex, and the human learning curve has become much, much steeper.

We find that we must learn something new each day or even several times a day. Advanced technology and globalization are continually challenging us to keep up. And we think we can beat the system. In fact, technological advancements have speeded up life to the point of a technological tsunami, leaving us killing ourselves in a vain attempt to find inner peace.

The speed of life pushes us forward to beat the clock, but has it occurred to us that we might be trying to win at the wrong game?

In our increasingly complex lives, we have more opportunities and want to take advantage of them all, so we move through our lives with greater and greater speed. In the onrush of life, as well as in our desperate attempts to escape from it, we seldom stop to consider what we are doing. Putting the cart before the horse, we madly try to accomplish one thing after another. We have wings to fly, rockets to go into outer space, but in a sense we don't really know our destination. Many of us feel we're going around in circles. This is precisely the Buddhist definition of a life without wisdom.

TURNING THINGS AROUND

When we get right down to it, what most of us really want more than anything—more than the newest smartphone, job promotion, or getaway vacation—is inner peace. The radical message of the Buddhist tradition comes down to this: the peace and fulfillment we are seeking are present in us right now. They have never really left us—and can never leave us.

1

How could this be true? we ask. If calm and clarity are always within me, why do I feel so stressed and burdened by my life?

Challenging life situations create tremendous confusion and pain. Faced with conflicts in relationships, job pressures, illness, and more, we become fearful, aggressive, or we just shut down. Our habitual ways of doing things and our attempts to find happiness actually create a pervasive anxiety, which leads to our becoming perpetually self-protective and self-absorbed. We walk around with the mind-set, "I don't think much of myself, but it's all I think about."

The good news is that we can rediscover our inherent wisdom, clarity, warmth, and intelligence—our natural brilliance. There is a different type of advanced technology, an inner technology, for doing this. It is described in a set of profound teachings from the Buddhist tradition called the Five Wisdoms.

WHAT IS WISDOM?

What do we mean by "wisdom"? It's important to distinguish between knowledge and wisdom. Simply said, we accumulate knowledge, but we discover wisdom within us. Knowledge has an object, a body of facts, information to acquire, and it relates to something outside ourselves. Wisdom, on the other hand, is a state of being. We become wise; we don't acquire wisdom. Another essential quality of wisdom is this: it is always experienced in the moment.

Our education system focuses primarily on the acquisition of knowledge rather than the discovery of wisdom. To connect with our inherent wisdom, we need a fundamentally new method: a contemplative approach, an inner journey.

Why would we want to start an inner journey? Perhaps we think this kind of thing is for the extraordinary few, "spiritual people," not for us. From the Buddhist point of view, the inner journey is not for special people, it's for all of us. The spiritual journey is nothing more and nothing less than the human journey.

DO YOU WANT A MORE MEANINGFUL CONNECTION TO LIFE?

Contemplate these questions:

- What do you turn to in times of distress, when you feel most vulnerable?
- What are your deepest values? Do you align yourself with them, live by them?
- What if you had the confidence that your wisdom is always at work within you and you could call on it at any moment?
- Could your deeper self be a beacon to direct everything you think, feel, say, and do?
- Is the deeper journey worth the effort? Can you make it a priority in your life?

The journey we're talking about is not to someplace far away; it is to someplace within. After we get started, we find that taking this kind of journey is completely natural. When we have absolute confidence in this journey and are willing to put some effort into it, our wisdom is at hand. Up until now, we have turned away from our deepest potential because it does take effort, like mining for gold. Yet to turn away from this potentiality is to deny the best within us. We have the opportunity to bring out the best of who we are. Let's do it! Certainly our world needs this of us.

> We are not human beings having a spiritual experience. We are spiritual beings having a human experience.
>
> —TEILHARD DE CHARDIN

DISCOVERING WHO WE ARE

If we all stopped to think about what we really want, without a doubt we would say we want to be happy or fulfilled or enlightened—free from the oppression we feel about our lives. Habitually we dream of something external to ourselves that will give us happiness or fulfillment: more money, a fancier car, a bigger house, a more fulfilling relationship. But what we find is that our desire for external objects of gratification can never be sated. There's always the next thing, the better thing, to reach for. It's clear that if we seek happiness this way, it will always elude us.

If we stop to reflect, we will probably see that the times when we have really felt our best are when we have been truly relaxed and deeply satisfied for no specific reason at all. We have felt a sense of timelessness and spaciousness. We have felt a warmth and clarity that have arisen spontaneously. Yes, we might say that it was because we were on vacation, far away from the worries of our daily life. But if we see it this way, we miss the point. Though the external circumstances can be a factor, we also need to acknowledge that these qualities of being—stillness, satisfaction, warmth, and peace—exist within us, not outside of us.

The Five Wisdoms are a set of teachings that help us to realize all this. These teachings help us to uncover the inner riches we already possess and make them more accessible in our daily lives—in our relationships, in our careers, and more.

Briefly put, the Five Wisdoms are a way of understanding human dynamics. They describe five qualities or "energies" inherent in people, places, and situations. These qualities are:

1. Spaciousness
2. Clarity
3. Richness
4. Passion
5. Activity

At the deepest level, we each possess the full array of these wisdom qualities in perfect balance. However, in daily life, each of us tends to express certain qualities more than others. In part 1 you'll learn how to identify your dominant wisdom qualities and explore how they manifest in your life and relationships.

One of the essential insights of the Five Wisdoms teachings is that we don't discover wisdom by avoiding pain and confusion. Wisdom isn't a matter of transcending difficulty or somehow "getting over" the messy and uncomfortable aspects of life. In reality, our pain and confusion are the fertile ground of our wisdom.

As we explore the Five Wisdoms teachings, we'll see that there is clarity in our confusion and dysfunction. Negative states of mind are two-sided: they express our bewilderment, but they are also a cry, a demand, for deeper insight. We'll see that each of the five wisdom qualities has an enlightened aspect and a confused aspect, and we'll put this information to use in moving ourselves closer to our natural brilliance.

WISDOM IS ALREADY HERE

At some point we realize there is really no journey at all: wisdom is already here, right now. It is characterized by a sense of spaciousness, clarity, and warmheartedness. You may not feel these qualities at this moment, but they are always available to you nonetheless. This natural wisdom has a sustaining power: when we are connected to it, we have more strength and stability in dealing with the vicissitudes of our lives.

In embracing all of who we are—with gentleness and loving-kindness—we realize we are basically good. At the deepest level, we are healthy, whole, clear-sighted, and deeply loving. That sense of basic goodness becomes a wellspring of potent energy.

Our natural wisdom helps us to finally understand that pain is not our enemy, it is our teacher. We can stop struggling against challenges. Having the courage to embrace our pain is empowering. Our wisdom is like the vast open sky, which always resides beyond the clouds, even when hurricanes are bombarding the ground below.

WE ACCESS OUR GOODNESS AND WISDOM WHEN WE COME TO JUST BEING RIGHT HERE

- Settle into your chair and just breathe.
  - Drop your agenda and ignore any distractions.
  - Be aware of your upright posture and your breath going in and out.
- As thoughts arise, acknowledge them as the natural intelligence of mind.
  - However, do not follow them, but let them dissolve.
  - Come back to just being and breathing.
- Rest in basic being for a few minutes and return to what you were doing.
  - Let the stillness of mind and body infuse your activities.

Learning to just be—accessing our wisdom—can be that simple. However, life is complex, so we need a way to meet that complexity. We need the Five Wisdoms. They reveal to us our particular style and the many qualities we have to work with life's challenges. Rather than saying, "Stop the world. I want to get off," we can let the Five Wisdoms be our guide to riding life's energies. We can learn to ride a cyclone. What fun! And in the center of the cyclone there is stillness. We can learn to find that still point under any circumstance. We can remember to come out of the whirlwind and into that stillness again and again.

> It is wisdom which is seeking for wisdom. . . . It is the readiness of the mind that is wisdom.
>
> —SHUNRYU SUZUKI ROSHI

ABOUT THIS BOOK

I've written this book to be interactive. There's explanatory text as well as many exercises for you to use to explore these teachings for yourself. Most of the exercises can be done on your own, though some require a group.

Part 1, "Wisdom Energy in People, Places, and Situations," gives both a conceptual and experiential understanding of the five wisdom qualities in ourselves, others, situations, and surroundings. Part 2, "The Five Wisdoms Applied," is about bringing the wisdoms into action: we cultivate the best of who we are and bring that into specific areas of our life, including intimate relationships, work life, and more. Chapters 7 to 12 are a generic exploration of leadership, whether to empower ourselves to lead ourselves or to lead others. Chapter 13 focuses on the two professional arenas where the Five Wisdoms have had their greatest impact: education and the serving professions. As well, chapter 3 is of specific interest to artists as it explores expression.

On the one hand, the Five Wisdoms teachings are simple and practical, and on the other hand, they are very profound. How much we get from them is largely up to us. We may be asking, "How can the wisdoms help me in my day-to-day life?" or "How can I bring an enlightened perspective to experience?" Since we all have our capacities and propensities, each of us will glean what we find most relevant. The more we invest, the more we will reap.

Finally, the Five Wisdoms will mean nothing if we just read about them. For them to be of any real value, we need to work with them in our daily lives, bring them into our daily experience. Let's go ahead and put our wisdom to work!

Part One

Wisdom Energy in People,
Places, and Situations

1

Five Wisdom Qualities

THE FIVE WISDOM QUALITIES are about us, personally and interpersonally: what we think, feel, say, and do. They describe different styles of perceiving and interacting with our world. These teachings give us a map of our inner world of thoughts and emotions as well as an approach to understanding our ways of behaving and relating to others. In short, the Five Wisdoms offer a model of human dynamics.

Each energy style expresses itself in the form of certain personality traits, some of which we might call dysfunctional or neurotic, and some of which we consider constructive or wise. Both troublesome emotions and pleasant ones arise out of a common energetic matrix.

The Five Wisdoms reveal the subtle energetic dimension of the basic elements of our experience: body, emotions, mental activity, and sense perceptions. The Five Wisdoms also manifest in aspects of the physical world—the landscape, architecture, interior design. When we gain more awareness, we begin to align with our inner wisdom and the wisdom around us. Ultimately the Five Wisdoms are teachings about bringing out the best of who we are and seeing the world with new eyes.

Let's briefly look at the central characteristics of the five wisdom qualities, both how we might get stuck in them and how they can make us shine.

THE FIVE WISDOMS (WITH THEIR TRADITIONAL NAMES)

SPACIOUSNESS (BUDDHA)

At its best: Open and peaceful. Residing in the present moment. The state we might experience during meditation practice or sitting contentedly under a tree. A sense that everything is OK.

At its worst: Not caring about anything; ignoring and denying reality; wanting to be left alone. Apathy and inertia. Oblivion.

CLARITY (VAJRA)

At its best: Perceptive, highly intelligent, and able to see things as they are. Mental clarity that demands nothing of others.

At its worst: Opinionated, self-righteous, and controlling. Convinced of being right and knowing how things should be. Imposing one's opinions on others.

RICHNESS (RATNA)

At its best: Resourceful, satisfied, and generous. The feeling that comes from enjoying a meal in the company of friends and family. Deeply satisfied and utterly fulfilled.

At its worst: Low self-esteem, greed, puffed-up pride, and feeling overwhelmed.

PASSION (PADMA)

At its best: Empathic, compassionate, caring, and warm. Intuitive, emotional. Thrives in relationship.

At its worst: Obsessively wanting to posses someone or something—a significant other, a job, a dress, or simply life at its best. Grasping and clingy.

ACTIVITY (KARMA)

At its best: Effective, productive, and swift; acting for the benefit of others.

At its worst: Power-hungry, manipulative, competitive, and envious; living in overdrive.

In Tibetan Buddhism a mandala is a graphic depiction of the full spectrum of the five energies existing in relationship with one another. They are associated with specific colors, which hold the essence of the energy. It is a way of taking an integral perspective in everything we think, feel, say, and do.

EXPRESSING THE FULL RANGE OF OUR ENERGETIC QUALITIES

Our personality or disposition, our habits and tendencies, all make us an open book. It is not hard to sense different qualities in people: a demanding child, a seductive lover, a sharp-tongued boss. Each person and situation has a perceivable energy: a person has "presence," or a place has "atmosphere." An event might be characterized as "intense" or a person as "mellow." For example, Molly is sluggish, Pete is antsy, and Francois is self-absorbed. The day is muggy, last night there was a thunderstorm, and now we are going into a lively air-conditioned restaurant. Donna and Steve are struggling in

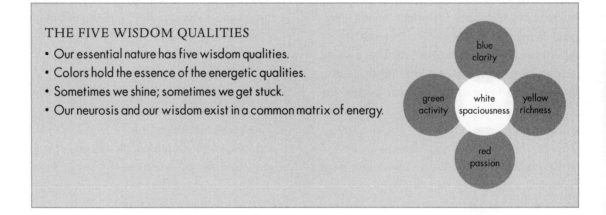

THE FIVE WISDOM QUALITIES
- Our essential nature has five wisdom qualities.
- Colors hold the essence of the energetic qualities.
- Sometimes we shine; sometimes we get stuck.
- Our neurosis and our wisdom exist in a common matrix of energy.

their relationship, and the energy is frozen between them; Jazmine and Justin are in love, and they can't stop touching each other. The ambient tone of places could be soft rolling hills or jagged peaks, winter or summer, a cozy living room or a busy airport. We could find ourselves in a variety of situations: a lively party, a deadly boring board meeting, or a tense courtroom.

Here are two couples, one more energetically attuned, with a fuller spectrum of color, than the other. Dorothy and Gerald's marriage is quite traditional. They live much as their parents and grandparents did: in a small house in a suburban neighborhood. He works a nine-to-five job; she stays home and takes care of the house and children. They both have a lot of buddha energy, keeping life simple and routine. They both work hard (karma). Their world is fairly shut down, uncomplicated, and survival oriented: two-dimensional but content in a simple way.

In contrast, Isabella and Jake live in the city where they both attended the university. She studied psychology and he architecture. They share many things together, such as tango (padma) and backpacking (buddha/karma), and they recently began to meditate (buddha). They are personable (padma), active (karma), and, having similar views (vajra), engage in promoting an ecologically friendly world. They have a good balance of the energies. They are vibrant.

WHERE ARE THE FIVE WISDOM ENERGIES?

- In our inner world of:
  thoughts   emotions
  breath   sense perceptions

- In our self-expression through:
  body   posture   movement
  facial expressions   mannerisms
  word choices   tone and tempo of our voice
  attitudes   decisions and actions
- In the external world, manifesting as:
  colors   landscapes
  shapes   seasons
  elements   environments

There is a natural progression to acquainting ourselves with these energetic qualities. The more experiences we have where they illuminate situations, the more authentic they seem. We see the particular style of our confusion or intelligence in the moment. We both know about them and experience them. They come into our being and give us a new language for understanding and expressing our experience. Finally they become part of us and reflect in what we think, feel, say, and do.

To summarize, first we learn about these energetic qualities, then we contemplate them as they are reflected in life experiences, and finally we embody and apply them.

Though we have the potential to embody all the energies and can display different energies in different areas of our lives, we come into this life with our unique propensities. We show one or two energies particularly clearly, though the others are always at play. Then we create a life around those (subconscious) choices and eventually become entrenched in that way of being. In so doing, we limit ourselves. Therefore, it takes a significant amount of awareness to begin to see our energetic mix and begin to embrace *all* that we are.

It's difficult to let go of the habitual patterns by which we have operated our whole life. In my own life, I have displayed a lot of padma energy and so I thought of myself as someone who would always be in a primary relationship. Relatively late in life, though, I became single. From a padma perspective, this was like a death sentence. Though it took some time, I came to understand that as a single person, I was able to become emotionally intimate with more people since I had time for more people. To my amazement, this growing sense of richness in relationships (ratna) was tremendously liberating and joyful.

WHAT DO WE MEAN BY ENERGY?

To understand the Five Wisdoms, we need to understand energy. There is an underlying premise that energy pervades our existence and is constantly in flux. The energetic dimension opens the door to a subtle level of being, which cannot be understood conceptually. Energy is not what is physical: tangible, concrete, or solid like a table or chair that we can see and name. It is also not what we think, our concepts. Here are some commonly used words that describe energy: *quality, ambiance, radiance, vibration, resonance,* or *tone*. Note that the last three are primarily used in music.

When we become attuned to energetic display in an unbiased way, without the filters of like, dislike, or disinterest, we experience the world directly. The wisdom qualities of spaciousness, relaxation, and warmth allow this to happen. We break down the barrier between ourselves and "other": we dissolve duality. With *maitri* (a Sanskrit word meaning "loving-

kindness"), we intermingle and resonate with life in and around us. Energy is not bound by form, so inner and outer are interdependent and interpenetrate. Just as sound has a vibration, resonance, and tone, so does energy. We experience ourselves and phenomena as inseparable and interwoven. The salient point is that the outer environment affects our inner experience, either clarifying or distorting it, and our state of mind colors our experience of the environment.

THE DYNAMIC WORLD OF ENERGY

- Energy is the basic vitality of our existence, the vibrant aspect of being.
- It is experienced intuitively.
- As our natural power or strength, we can align with it or diminish it.
- Wisdom energy is a positive life force; confused energy sabotages it.
- We experience ourselves and primal phenomena as inseparable and interwoven.
- We are in an energetically reciprocal relationship with our world.

Direct experience—being "tuned in"—is the only way to understand the energetic dimension of reality. We detect or sense energy with what I have termed our psychophysical barometer: we feel or intuit energy both mentally and physically. We can gauge the atmospheric condition, tone, or energetic feel of people, places, and situations through our senses and by using our intuition. We can learn to "read" energy.

Energetic resonance—the unfiltered direct

experience of ourselves and our world—is a fundamental principle of the Tantric tradition of Tibetan Buddhism but shared by many cultures. For instance, feng shui is the study of how powerful energy spots in landscapes and building structures can enhance the energy. In many cultures there is reciprocity among spirituality, art, and everyday functioning. People in these cultures are more tuned in to the felt experience of reality.

UNDERSTANDING OUR PSYCHOPHYSICAL BAROMETER

- We are affected by the energy around us whether we are aware of it or not.
- With awareness we can gauge the atmospheric condition in a given situation.
- Life is constantly challenging us to say yes or no, to open or close.
- When open and welcoming we feel spacious and full of possibility.
- When closed and withdrawn, we feel stuck, dense, and claustrophobic.

COMING INTO THE ENERGY OF THE MOMENT

- What is your energy right now? The ambient tone of the room you are in?
- What do you know? What do you feel, intuit?
- Can you sense these as distinct and different experiences?

We might feel that the energetic dimension of reality is not important enough to bother with, but energy affects us whether we are aware of it or not. Unconsciously, we sense things and react to them all the time. What are the consequences of not tuning in to energetic reality? If we are aware of the energy, we can ride it. If not, we become a slave to it. As well, reality would have no vibrancy.

Tuning in to this more subtle level of our existence expands our experience exponentially. In particular, our willingness to stay with whatever arises—likable or disagreeable—opens us to a vivid encounter with life. Having accessed more depth, we become the best of who we are with a more authentic and enlivened relationship to everyone and everything. Though these ideas may initially seem foreign, we could still feel some attraction to them. Our curiosity is sparked because these five energetic qualities begin to resonate with us. They ring true.

PRACTICAL USES OF THE FIVE WISDOM ENERGIES

When we learn to identify and understand the distinctive energetic qualities, we discover new ways of working with everyday situations. We can get away from rejecting our neurosis (or someone else's) and instead use it. Soon we start to see unevolved areas as dynamic growth areas—and that any situation is workable.

When we accommodate the parts of ourselves that we like the least and energies in others that feel threatening, we are allowing the full spectrum of human experience to display itself. One of the essential lessons of the five wisdom energies is that in embracing our confusion, we discover that our wisdom is right there. When we are familiar with the characteristics of each energy style, we immediately know where the sanity is and where the neurosis is. We can align ourselves with the sanity, with the wisdom aspect. At that point we have discovered the best within us, our unique brand of brilliance. We discover we have great liberty to be who we are, and we can celebrate that.

BRINGING OUT THE BEST OF WHO YOU ARE

- Recollect three times in your life when you felt the best of who you are.
- What outer circumstances made that possible?
- What qualities in you began to shine?

Here is one of my favorite analogies: As a frequent flier, I never cease to be amazed that up there, above the clouds, the sun is always shining—twenty-four hours a day. Too often we forget this, see only the clouds and become convinced that they are real. We make the clouds solid and identify with them. However, with an attitude of unconditional loving openness, we can begin to see the clouds as transparent and illusory. In fact, we can fly right through them, though the ride might get a little bumpy. When we identify with the sun, we are touching our intrinsic wisdom.

A FIVE WISDOMS QUESTIONNAIRE

Use the following self-reflective questionnaire to reveal your characteristics and tendencies. Because you are a mix of colors, you could choose more than one answer. This is just a first step in asking the questions that will reveal yourself to yourself.

1. What is your style of dress?
   - simple lines, solid colors, or geometric patterns
   - rich, colorful, lots of ornamentation
   - flashy, colorful, sexy
   - plain, functional, muted colors
   - simple, muted colors
2. What kind of landscape or environment do you prefer?
   - high mountains or cities and orderly interiors
   - tropical jungles, dense forest, and shopping malls and richly decorated interiors
   - gardens, flowering meadows, and rolling hills and warm, cozy interiors
   - big, busy cities and functional interiors
   - great plains, deserts, and snowfields and sparsely furnished interiors
3. At what time of day do you feel at your best?
   - dawn
   - late afternoon
   - dusk, twilight
   - morning
   - no particular one
4. Which sense perception is your favorite?
   - sight
   - smell and taste
   - hearing
   - touch (physical connection)

- no particular one

5. What do you desire?
   - to know
   - to have it all
   - to feel
   - to do
   - to just be

6. Which of these activities is most natural to you?
   - learning something and then teaching it to others
   - appreciating people and situations, hosting and embracing others
   - having exciting interactions and communicating deeply
   - creating and doing projects
   - just being

7. Which emotions feel most familiar to you?
   - anger, impatience, irritation with confusing situations and overly emotional people
   - greed and pride fed by a poverty mentality
   - clinging passion and comparison to others
   - jealousy fed by paranoia and competitiveness
   - ignorance or denial fed by insecurity

8. What do you fear?
   - emotional intimacy
   - not having enough
   - boredom, mediocrity, rejection
   - failure
   - intrusion

9. What does your stuckness look like?
   - mind becomes tied in knots by convoluted logic

- self-pity, neediness, hunger for more, or overwhelmed
- obsession, unfulfilled desires, addiction to intensity
- overdrive leading to exhaustion, depletion
- indifference, ambivalence, denial

10. What do you do to take care of yourself when you are upset?
    - take some space and have patience until I come to clarity
    - seek confirmation from others and reconnect to my own richness
    - seek confirmation from others that I am lovable and feel lovable
    - remember to slow down
    - realize that nothing is a big deal

11. How are you most often when you are with others?
    - detached and logical
    - the center of attention
    - intimate and emotional
    - active, making things happen
    - spacious, simple

12. What is your best interpersonal style with friends and coworkers?
    - clear minded
    - embracing and appreciative
    - empathetic and communicative
    - direct, straightforward
    - accommodating

13. How do you get stuck in your relationships?
    - by insisting on being right; by being intolerant, opinionated, critical, and sharp
    - by being possessive, overbearing, and demanding too much time and attention

- by being clinging then rejecting, exhibiting a love/hate dynamic, trying too hard to please
- by being businesslike, confrontive, controlling
- by being aloof, not caring, spacing out

14. What capacities or mental abilities do you have?
    - holding the overview, facility with logic and reasoning, using structures and patterns
    - comprehensive and thorough
    - intuitive and able to discriminate fine points
    - turning thought into action without hesitation
    - spacious and accommodating

15. What is your learning style?
    - intellectual, using analysis, abstractions, and general principles
    - amassing information, doing research
    - intuitive, using imagery, creative expression, and empathetic communication
    - by doing, trial and error
    - repetition using simple, basic concepts, sleeping on it, osmosis

16. What is your style of thinking and use of language?
    - clear, orderly, and precise
    - thorough, circular, comprehensive, elaborate
    - individualistic, intuitive, creative, feeling-based, using analogy and metaphor
    - speedy, matter-of-fact, pragmatic, could be manipulative
    - simple, slow

17. What ways of knowing do you feel comfortable with?
    - seeing the big picture and its details
    - retaining large amounts of information
    - from the heart, intuitive, by association
    - seeing how things work
    - by just being

18. Which of these do you concern yourself with?
    - boundaries, making things right, having discipline
    - wanting to encompass everything and everyone
    - communication, self-image, pleasure
    - making sure things get done
    - nondoing

19. Where do you get preoccupied?
    - trying to make things the way I think they should be
    - wanting to possess
    - not knowing where I stand in relationships
    - needing to get it done
    - sticking my head in the sand, getting absorbed

20. When do you feel most productive?
    - knowing the answers, being right
    - being resourceful
    - making relationships and genuine contact
    - planning and managing
    - making things simple

21. When do you feel most ineffective?
    - not feeling right or perfect
    - feeling inadequate, inferior, unworthy
    - feeling incomplete, lonely, and depressed
    - feeling incompetent, performance anxiety

- not certain who I am
22. What is your defense mechanism or coping strategy?
    - sticking to my own view, distancing myself
    - arrogance, amassing anything spiritual or material
    - wanting to please, ingratiating
    - taking control
    - shutting down, tunnel vision
23. What does your leadership look like at its best?
    - calming or pacifying situations; giving the overview in simple terms; giving clarity, meaning, and understanding
    - recognizing people's potential so their richness is revealed, offering resources, seeing the richness of diversity, being generous
    - making heart connections, being tuned in to others, having a sense of playfulness, sharing in playful creativity, bringing out people's passions
    - knowing what to do, knowing when to do and refrain from doing, making things happen, taking action fearlessly and with a sense of ease, being able to say no
    - being and letting be, being flexible and accommodating
24. What do you like in teamwork?
    - clear communication
    - more information
    - personal connection
    - speedy efficiency
    - on-the-spot brainstorming
25. What do you need from your supervisor?
    - specific direction
    - networking leads
    - confirmation and encouragement
    - an action plan
    - independence
26. What is the essential quality of your wisdom?
    - insightful clarity
    - equanimity
    - intuitive discrimination
    - all-accomplishing action
    - all-encompassing space

Note, if you haven't done so already, that the five possibilities are in this order: vajra, ratna, padma, karma, and buddha. Make a tally of how many you had in each energy. What did you find out? Are you more aware of how the energies are in your life? the ways you manifest and interact with others? when you shine and when you get stuck?

Unfolding ourselves to ourselves is never boring. We are all such rich mixtures of energies. We can reveal ourselves as multidimensional and very colorful. When we miss the opportunity to be fully in the world, we miss our life.

2

Meet Some Friends

Lᴇᴛ'ꜱ ʟᴏᴏᴋ ᴀᴛ ꜱᴏᴍᴇ ᴘᴇᴏᴘʟᴇ who may seem like acquaintances as a way of seeing how the qualities could manifest in real life. To bring out their very distinctive features, I am creating characters who are the epitome of each energy. In real life we would not see such a stark contrast among them, as the energies are always combined rather than monodimensional. I have used men's names for my two characters whose energies manifest more masculine qualities (whether in a man or a woman) and women's names for the two whose energies manifest more feminine qualities. Buddha does not have a gender, so I arbitrarily gave it a man's name.

To give an integral perspective, the descriptions are presented in the five modes: (1) physical, (2) emotional/expressive, (3) mental, (4) quality/essence, and (5) activity. Simply put, they are body, speech, mind, quality, and action (BSMQA). We look at these more deeply in chapter 10, "Unbiased Perception."

CLARK: VAJRA CLARITY

Bᴏᴅʏ, ᴛʜᴇ Pʜʏꜱɪᴄᴀʟ Mᴏᴅᴇ

At age forty-five, Clark has a slim, wiry figure. His body is somewhat stiff and rigid. His chest thrusts forward slightly and is held tightly. He has sharp, distinctive features: a broad forehead, penetrating eyes, and thin lips. His style of dress is simple: elegant with clean-cut lines and predominantly blue, solid colors. His ties have geometric shapes with bold colors. He exudes a dignified strength.

He lives alone in a high-rise apartment with lots of windows, monochromatic colors, and smooth, metallic textures. It is both spacious and orderly. He has high-end furniture with simple, elegant lines. Many photographs, both his own and others', are on the walls. During the evenings or on weekends, he listens to the brilliant and clear music of composers such as Mozart, Bach, and Edgard Varèse. This taste is also reflected in his office: a refined environment in which the mind can open to its own intelligence.

As an architect, Clark employs a contemporary style with clearly delineated spaces and a sense of refinement. He loves to see how things line up and are connected. He likes using glass, mirrors, and lighting to create spaces with sharp contrasts.

Clark loves the mountains, particularly in the winter, when the air is crisp and fresh and sunlight on the snow dazzles the eye. For recreation, he goes skiing, but he also loves to play chess.

His health concerns manifest as headaches and back problems, for which he sometimes sees a chiropractor or gets a shiatsu massage. He eats simple food but often has a poor appetite. His drink is a dry martini.

Speech, the Emotional/Expressive Mode

Clark's speech is precise, with good enunciation and diction. He is very rational, following a train of thought point by point with no superfluity. He sometimes speaks in simple, clear statements and sometimes gives complex, elegantly constructed arguments. He can often miss the emotional undertone of situations. He has a quick-tongued, cutting wit and loves wordplay.

On an emotional level, he has a sense of distance, reserve, and cool detachment. He has a strong sense of boundaries and decorum. He does not get caught in emotional upheavals: he tends to ignore his own disturbing or confusing emotions and is not very empathetic toward such emotions in others. Instead, he is able to see clearly what is going on and pacify the situation, preventing the energy from escalating. He is reasonable and dependable. In personal relationships he prefers platonic to romantic ones, being warm and gentle rather than hot and passionate. He is like a big brother to many who seek his counsel, but he has a fear of emotional intimacy. With friends, he tends to philosophize, wanting to know their worldview.

In working with his colleagues, he demonstrates a sense of inquisitiveness, often asking the right questions to bring clarity to a project. However, he can also be compulsive, perfectionist, and overly analytical. This can lead to being critical, self-righteous, opinionated, and authoritarian. "I know" becomes "I'm right." When he thinks things are not as they should be, he can withdraw into cold anger or lash out with a ruthless, blaming hot anger.

He hates being surprised, confused, or overwhelmed by irrational or chaotic circumstances. Then his energy becomes constricted and solidified. He panics when he doesn't understand and exhibits a neurotic compulsion to clarify things. This leads to a tense alertness and strong need for control. Unambiguous answers are his security.

Mind, the Mental Mode

Clark has a clear mind with an intellectual brilliance, sharp and precise. His primary mode of operating is to use his facility for logic and reasoning. He radiates a sense of "I know." He has a passion to know, to understand, to learn. Perspicacity, an acuteness of discernment or perception, rules his behavior. Unexplored areas are anathema to him, so he is always searching for the newest ways to do architecture. He exhibits a strong attention to detail and is fascinated by new techniques. He is thorough, methodical, and systematic.

In all his business relationships, he has a strong sense of ethics and integrity, and can take an unbiased perspective. He is trustworthy, responsible, and accountable. He understands the importance of discipline and order. All these qualities help his architecture firm land many big projects. Clark has quickly risen to the top of his firm and is most comfortable in this position of power, which keeps others at a distance. He is the one who can have an overview, seeing the advantages and disadvantages of moving in any particular direction. His ability to clearly see how things are helps to defuse conflicting views on how to proceed. Others turn to him for the final answer.

Occasionally things have not gone well for Clark. His logical mind sometimes becomes overly convoluted and ties itself into knots. Overfed by intellectual constructs and analyses and an excessive attention to details, he makes things more complicated than necessary. A compulsion to systematize takes over as he tries to make things the way they should be. His concern for boundaries hardens into a protective stance, and he loses connection to what is happening. At those times he feels less than the perfect person he wants to be, is driven by "shoulds," and his confidence sinks. In interactions he becomes defensive, impenetrable, uptight, and detached.

Quality

Having seen Clark's body, speech, and mind (BSM), we can get a sense of his dominant quality of energy. In its open, brilliant, and pure state, vajra energy is crystal clarity. It is associated with the color blue, the element water, and the sense of sight. Vajra energy reflects its surroundings like a calm, clear pool of water, without distortion or bias. Thus, vajra wisdom is mirrorlike: it sees things as they are.

When their energy is frozen, vajra people are ideological, opinionated, authoritarian, critical, narrowly moralistic, dogmatic, rigid, and self-righteous. They need to convince everyone that theirs is the correct view, which leads to a chronic feeling of anger and resentfulness. They can harden into a withdrawn cold anger or a lashing-out, blaming hot anger. They enjoy conflict as a way of connecting with others and love to outsmart their opponents. They never admit they are wrong. Their belief system becomes rigid and tight. They develop the arrogance of "I know it all."

Action

A calm, even quality is the epitome of vajras' potential for sane action. They can bring everyone around to a common ground so they can work together. When there is a maze of solidified hostility on two or more sides, they can cut through the fixed positions to find the points of agreement. They see through neurotic manipulation and stop it cold. They see chaos and conflict but do not exacerbate the discord by adding their own mental baggage to the situation. They clean up messes and create order. They bring harmony by clearly seeing the obstacles to it. Other people are drawn to the vajras' astute judgment.

People with a preponderance of this energy make great mediators, facilitators, and leaders. They act in the world as diplomats, scientists, surgeons, dentists, watchmakers, engineers, and computer programmers. In terms of a religion or spiritual path, the philosophical and intellectual aspects attract them.

Cultures that have a well-defined vision and a strong sense of propriety and decorum belong to the vajra family. A good example is the

Japanese affinity for visual order, precision, a highly refined sense of decorum, an extremely cultivated aesthetic, and collective principles that override individual will. The Scandinavian countries, Germany, German Switzerland, and England also have strong vajra qualities.

ANECDOTES

The following are some humorous twists on vajra energy.

As we know, there is a lot of vajra energy at country borders with security and customs officials. They go by the book; no foolery allowed. Years ago my father was working at a Turkish hospital and was assigned the task of importing some lab mice. So the lab mice arrived, but customs officials could find no category for mice. The rule was that if a particular animal was not mentioned, the customs fee would revert to the first animal on the list. That happened to be *aslan,* which means "lion"! The mouse that roared!

Another American doctor in Turkey was faced with the problem of an American woman about to die who wanted to be buried in the United States. Transporting a dead body by plane is prohibitively expensive. What to do? He hooked her up to a life-support system and sent her on the plane as a "live" passenger. She promptly died on arrival. No rules were broken.

Coming home from Italy once, I was carrying a peacock feather that I had been given, which became quite the conversation piece as I traveled on trains, planes, and so forth. However, I was detained at the Canadian border. I waited and waited as the customs officer went through a two-inch-thick manual looking for peacock feathers to determine whether mine could come into the country. No peacock feathers. Finally, he just let me through.

GABRIELA: RATNA RICHNESS
BODY, THE PHYSICAL MODE

The first thing one notices about Gabriela is a sense of fullness and grounded physicality. She is rather plump, quite fleshy, with a soft peach-colored complexion. Her features are full: large brown eyes and eyebrows and a big mouth with sensual lips. Her long curly brown hair has blond highlights. She dresses in warm, vibrant colors—deep reds and shades of orange and yellow—often with floral prints. She prefers long skirts or pants with full, sometimes billowy tops. Jewelry is an obsession. She has many boxes as well as hanging racks of earrings, bracelets, and long, colorful necklaces. She loves scents, so a fruity or exotic smell always surrounds her. Her favorite vacation spots are on a tropical isle or the Mediterranean coast. She is a true believer in the siesta.

Gabriela lives with her husband and three children in a large house in the suburbs. She loves to decorate, so the house exudes her energy. It has an open floor plan where each room graciously flows into another. She prefers big, overstuffed furniture. The fabrics of the furniture, pillows, wall hangings, window treatments, and rugs have warm colors and rich textures. Plants are everywhere. Warm, indirect lighting creates a soft glow. Potpourri baskets give the air a luscious smell.

Her greatest enjoyments are gardening and cooking, so she takes great delight in her large vegetable and flower garden. She likes the physicality and earthy sensuality of gardening and loves to cook delicious wholesome meals for her family and friends. Gabriela is a very nurturing mother, not only to her own children but to all their friends. Her house is full of activity, as it has become a place where neighborhood children congregate, so it is most often quite messy. The family has three dogs and two cats, who get a lot of attention from everyone.

As far as health is concerned, Gabriela dealt with an eating disorder in her teens, since she would eat comfort food to excess. In middle age, she has had some high blood pressure problems. She has been advised to lose weight and do things that will allow her to relax, such as getting massages and meditating. She loves aromatherapy and has many aromatic bath oils. Because of the high intensity of her emotions, at times she also suffers from insomnia.

SPEECH, THE EMOTIONAL/ EXPRESSIVE MODE

Gabriela tends to be verbose in her speech and often digresses. She has a strong, loud voice that comes from deep inside her belly, but it can also be soft. If so inclined, she could have been an opera singer. Her speech has a lot of modulation dictated by emotional content. She speaks from her heart and is very sensitive to emotions in herself and others. She loves to tell stories and anecdotes from her life to make a point. Gabriela is warm and nurturing and well loved by her extended family and friends. She is the person they go to when they want someone with whom to talk about their emotional problems. When hosting a dinner party, she is

at her best: at the center of her world and the principal object of attention.

At times Gabriela takes a downward spin, often with worries over money. She is perpetually concerned with how much she has, how much she is worth. Expansion feels good; contraction feels painful. She can be possessive and territorial. When she loses her sense of richness and resourcefulness, she feels insecure, insubstantial, and helpless. "I don't have enough; I'm not good enough; I don't count" become her mental tapes. She becomes emotionally exaggerated and intense. She feels needy and self-pitying and feeds off others' energy. Often she turns to her husband to seek reassurance, affection, and approval or goes on a shopping binge to feel more substantial and confirm her self-worth.

She does not show her vulnerable side to her friends. Instead, she will boost herself up with a false pride but still feels hollow inside. She covers her insecurity by being ostentatious and overbearing. At these times, others feel suffocated and oppressed by her energy. Sometimes she is generous to a fault. She needs to feel needed. The combination of neediness and pride can create a perpetual drama of hurt feelings and emotional outbursts. Too proud to give in, Gabriela can hold grudges.

MIND, THE MENTAL MODE

Most of the time, Gabriela feels expansive and fulfilled. She has a sense of equanimity and appreciates everyone and everything without discrimination. She sees herself as someone who is fundamentally hospitable and generous. She includes, accommodates, embraces, and offers whatever she has. She brings richness out in others by appreciating them wholeheartedly. She continually taps her inner resources—life experience, intelligence, and skills. She has a positive sense that the world is full of possibility and whether good or bad, happy or sad, all is the richness of life.

In school, she was known for being comprehensive and thorough in any written or oral presentation. She wants to encompass whatever it is completely, so she is capable of retaining large amounts of information, particularly around her two pet passions: gardening and cooking. She has been asked to do a television show on cooking but declined, as caring for her family is her priority. Surfing the Net after everyone else has gone to bed or when she has insomnia is a favorite pastime.

Though she is no longer involved, she was a fervent Catholic as a teenager. She loved the sense of devotion, the ritual, and the prayers. This played a large part in getting her through her feelings of worthlessness.

Her emotional cycle is somewhat predictable. She can feel fantastically rich and full but then becomes overwhelmed. Then she feels she can't keep up with it all, can't cope. She feels empty, burdened, and discouraged: she just can't meet the richness of her world. Connecting to her own richness—which is independent of people, things, or activities "out there"—is what brings her back to equanimity.

Quality

Ratna exudes a golden yellow energy that encompasses and enriches everything. Its wisdom quality is equanimity, a sense of such deep satisfaction and fulfillment that there is nothing more to desire. The world is abundant and plentiful. It is associated with earth and the sense perceptions of taste, smell, and sensual touch.

People in their wisdom can be expansive, full of potential, and resourceful. They are hospitable, generous, and give sustenance like the good earth. They recognize the potential in people and bring out their richness. They appreciate cultural, ethnic, and generational diversity. They love creating ambience and texture and tend to be sensual.

This energy can also turn into greedy territoriality and puffed-up pride. Ratnas can be self-important, arrogant, ostentatious, and oppressive. They can be greedy, insatiable, and overindulgent. They tend to be emotionally needy, possessive, and flounder in a poverty mentality.

Action

The ability to enrich and appreciate the world is ratna's potential for sane action. The sense of abundance and resourcefulness makes people with this energy excel in many fields. They could own and create the bountiful environment of a health food store or flower shop. Their love of smell and taste makes them great cooks. Their sensitivity and sense of inclusion make them skillful team members or leaders. With those same qualities, they could became therapists, social workers, or Peace Corps volunteers. They are attracted to the grandiose, so they could become opera singers or write epic novels.

We see ratna energy in the tropics: lush, bountiful gardens with smells and colors that entice the senses. The baroque period captures ratna energy, as do cultures where there is a sense of opulence and sensuality such as the Roman and Ottoman Empires. The Catholic Church and Tibetan Buddhism have strong ratna qualities. The epitome of ratna energy is consumerism, with its feeling that one never has enough. It is also exemplified by massive, solid, or elaborate architecture.

ANECDOTES

His Holiness the Sixteenth Karmapa, a revered Tibetan Buddhist teacher, was visiting New York City. Chögyam Trungpa Rinpoche, Tibetan Buddhist teacher and founder of Naropa University in Boulder, Colorado, the first Buddhist-inspired university in North America, asked one of his senior students, Sara Capp, to take him shopping. So he and several of his monks visited a few major department stores and looked around. His Holiness felt materials and looked at jewelry. After a couple of hours, they left. Sara was mortified. She went to Trungpa Rinpoche and said, "Rinpoche, they didn't buy anything!" Rinpoche laughed and said, "He doesn't need to buy anything; he owns it!" This points to ratna's supreme wisdom in seeing the abundance of the world as not separate from us.

I was once teaching in Amsterdam on Queen's Day. The day's major event is to have a nationwide yard sale, on the streets. People set out everything they are willing to pass along, and others come and pay them a little something for it. My hostess had the dinning room table full of found treasures that evening. I asked, "Why is this the way to celebrate?" and

I heard back, "Well, we have always been traders." So it's just taking delight in commerce: goods to sell and goods to buy. I was also told that the same artifacts might end up on the street the next year. Round and round they go. The day ends with much feasting and beer drinking, and parties that last far into the night.

FELICITY: PADMA PASSION

BODY, THE PHYSICAL MODE

Felicity has a well-proportioned, youthful body with well-toned musculature and is of medium height. Her wavy light brown hair falls to her shoulders when down, though she often wears it up, casually clasped with a hair ornament. She has an oval-shaped face, large brown eyes, a small upturned nose, full sensual lips, and straight white teeth. Her complexion is like liquid warm bronze. As a dancer, she is at ease in her body. She often wears one of her favorite scents: wild rose or gardenia. She is very attentive to her appearance and thus is always well groomed and ready for the world.

Felicity's biggest indulgence is clothes. She has excellent taste with a sense of elegance and refinement, though she mostly wears more casual clothes with warm colors and soft textures that reveal the lines of her body and flow as she moves. She also has a taste for the exotic. However, with a closet full of fashion, she often cannot decide what to wear, feeling she lacks the best outfit or jewelry for the occasion. So she perpetually shops for clothes and accessories and does clothes swaps with her girlfriends.

At age twenty-five, Felicity is well launched in her dance theater career. The very creative group of artists she works with do multimedia theatrical performances in which she does both improvisational and choreographed movement. The group rehearses every day in a loft space, teaches some classes, and goes on performance tours. The members of her group are all very dedicated to their work, and their passion for creative expression radiates in their performances. Being fully embodied and open to the immediacy of each moment, Felicity is a strong performer with an unselfconscious charisma. In the company, she is highly visible and sometimes outrageous.

Felicity and her musician boyfriend live in a little apartment on a street full of small restaurants and shops in a large city. They express their artistic sensibility in every corner of their living space, which is adorned with mementos from their travels and art given to them by friends. It is often cluttered and somewhat dirty. Mostly they go out to eat, so the small kitchen contains only breakfast and snack foods. Many of their friends live close by and often drop in.

SPEECH, THE EMOTIONAL/ EXPRESSIVE MODE

Though not always conscious of it, Felicity draws attention wherever she goes: she is full of life, attractive, engaging, charming, and playful. Her easygoing manner radiates warmth and magnetizes others. She has a never-ending desire to captivate and grasp the most pleasurable people and situations. Her sense of pleasure and promise draws others to her. She can also play coy and seductive, looking at you not directly but with a sideways glance. It is hard to resist loving her; being around her makes you

love yourself. Since she greatly enjoys touching, she does so to get someone's attention, make a point, or have an extended hug. Naturally at ease with expressing herself beyond words and concepts, she often takes expressive stances or exhibits facial expressions. Her voice is quite modulated, as she is often talking about how she feels.

As a teenager and young adult, Felicity had a difficult time. She was often confused, insecure, and very emotional. Addicted to intensity, she was perpetually falling in love, being consumed by it, and becoming chameleonlike to please the object of her affections. She was often manipulative to get what she wanted and then obsessively clung to the other person, only to move on when the relationship got mundane. When it ended, she would become heartbroken, desolate. This made her more confused as to who she was. Both in her relationships and as a dancer, jealousy arose when she did not get what she wanted: the guy or the part in a dance piece. To fit in with her friends, she took recreational drugs. Loving to dance, flirt, and have intimate talks, all-night parties on Ecstasy became the norm. Living intensively as she does, she has a hard time settling and thus has insomnia.

Several years of process-oriented group therapy, which included creative expression working directly with the immediacy of experience, were helpful. In this environment, Felicity found she could learn about herself without too much conceptual overlay. She was able to see her repetitive patterns that sabotaged her best interests and opened to new possibilities. Once she found a stable partnership with a live-in boyfriend, life started to go better. He gave her both closeness and spaciousness, allowing what she most needed: merging and individuality.

Felicity is a good friend and delights in intimate connections: she listens deeply and penetrates to the heart in an intuitive way. She can dissolve boundaries and make genuine contact, drawing out others, engaging them, and reaching the most intimate places. Her own difficulties taught her a lot about empathy and compassion.

Mind, the Mental Mode

Felicity knows with her heart, relying on intuition rather than intellect. She has hunches, gut feelings about things. Her mind is flexible: if something is not working, she is on to the next thing. Her more fluid thought process, which is not logical in a linear way, can shift gears and make leaps with impulsive daring. She can be versatile, eclectic, and idiosyncratic.

She can see the essence of things, sensing both the big picture and the minute particulars. This is very helpful in her professional work, since it gives her a keen sense of what is and isn't working in her company's performance pieces. She can describe what she sees in a sense-oriented way, being specific and concrete.

In general, Felicity has inherent joy and feels the world is endlessly hospitable, and, in truth, she always seems to get what she wants. She has a way of lubricating situations to her advantage. The dance theater world in which she has found herself is perfect for her: they tell stories and portray dreams using innuendo, imagery, analogy, and metaphor.

Quality

Padma glows with the vitality of red energy. Its sanity is a finely tuned intuition that discriminates subtle experiences without bias. Padmas' inherent nature is to feel the intensity and preciousness of each moment. They have an ability to communicate very accurately with the world because it is so immediate to them. It is associated with fire and the sense perception of hearing.

People can be engaging, magnetizing, charming, and flirtatiously sensual. They radiate warmth, listen deeply, and speak from the heart. They love to express themselves and prefer to communicate beyond words and concepts. They can have poise and charisma.

Padmas' confused quality is insecurity. They cling obsessively to what gives pleasure, are manipulative, overly emotional, and perpetually seek confirmation. Their personal feelings can override everything else. They search for perfection—being picky and fussy and making petty comparisons—and become irritable when they don't find it. They hold on to a moment of intensity so tightly that they kill it. They have difficulty making decisions, because choosing one option means forgoing all the others.

Action

Padmas have the ability to live outside societal norms because of their naturally unconventional tastes. They become artists, adventurers, and leaders of tours to exotic places. Because of their love of people, they can be insightful and intuitive therapists, social workers, and teachers. Naturally expressive, they could be visual artists, dancers, actors, and musicians.

Padma environments and architecture are pleasure oriented, with soft, concave, receptive spaces; attention to color; and a warm, inviting quality. We think of southern France and Italy, the South Seas, Bali, California, and Hawaii. Fresh air, flowering meadows, rolling hills, and delightful restaurants invite us to relax and indulge our senses.

ANECDOTES

Here's an anecdote that epitomizes padma's quest for pleasure at all costs. It was midnight at the end of a high school prom. I sat in the hotel lobby waiting for my daughter and her friend. A young girl in a short "practically nothing" dress and high, high heels came in and collapsed into a big chair. When asked, "So, how was it?" she responded with "Oh, it was fabulous, just fabulous. . . . Marv and I had a wonderful time—and we get to go next year!" "Oh, really? How is that?" "Marvin flunked out." I'm sure her reaction to global warming would be, "Oh, great, I get to wear my summer clothes!"

In the medieval-like covered market of Istanbul, bargaining is standard practice. Sebnem, my close childhood friend, and I have gone to the same jeweler and rug dealer for over three decades. From her I have learned how to bargain, a true art. The ritual goes like this. First there is an exchange of pleasantries, with which the Turkish language is replete, as we are served Turkish coffee or tea. The conversation then turns to asking about our families: who is sick, who got married, how the children are, who is not talking to whom, and so on. Af-

ter a while, the shop owner asks, "What can I do for you today?" After we state our desires, he shows us, in a very leisurely way, what he has. More than anything, he wants to please us, so there is always something special—a jewel in the bottom drawer, a particularly precious rug in the back room—that the owner feels is just right for us. Is this all a con? Sure. Is it fun? You bet. So bags of jewels are oohed and aahed over, or one rug after another is rolled out with a grand sweep of the hand until there is a pile on the floor. Trying to select becomes dizzying, but we do. Then, the price. We have known each other for years. There is loyalty involved. Why wouldn't the owner give us a good price? So everyone is satisfied when the deal is made. This little event, which could take upward of two hours, is dramatically different from seeing the price tag and whipping out our credit card, let alone buying online. I realized it was actually a delightful way to do business. It definitely has an Old World charm, and it has nothing to do with conducting business efficiently.

In the many places Sebnem and I have traveled over a lifetime, we have used Turkish as our secret language. At a dinner party in San Francisco, we talked about everyone at the table, right in front of them. We were caught off guard one time when taking a taxi from Paris to Versailles. After we'd spent the ride having a most intimate conversation in the backseat, the taxi driver addressed us in Turkish on arrival.

During several visits to Warsaw, I was delighted by the Polish people's vibrancy, creativity, and sense of fun. However, when you look around you, it is all too evident that this city was flattened by Hitler and rebuilt by the communists. I asked whatever had happened to people's padma energy. I was told that it went underground; art and culture could be shared and enjoyed only in secret. People spoke in code. Even radio broadcasts would contain messages delivered in code. Books were passed around in secrecy. Padma so loves to be secret.

STEVE: KARMA ACTIVITY

Body, the Physical Mode

Steve is thirty-seven, about five and a half feet tall, and of somewhat tight musculature. His short brown hair is parted on the left and combed back. He has brown eyes, a straight nose, and slender lips. His clothes are simple, clean-cut, in drab greens and browns, and appropriate to his work life. He can dress up or down.

He lives in an apartment that is functional, without extraneous decor. He married young and divorced at the age of thirty-five, so he now lives alone. He mostly eats out, on the run, while either on his cell phone or stopping for a quick meal with a work colleague. His refrigerator contains leftover takeout food, snacks, and breakfast food. He drinks many cups of coffee a day and has a mixed drink or glass of wine every evening. Over the years, he has gained excess weight, primarily due to eating out. For a break from his workday, he plays a pickup game of soccer in the late afternoon.

Shortly after graduating from college, Steve started a database company of computer programmers. Over a ten-year period, the firm has grown from two employees to thirty-five employees and contract workers. As the company's president, Steve shows strong en-trepreneurial skills. He oversees all projects, having a good feel for the client's needs and his employees' capabilities. With Steve's clear sense of direction, his company has been able to offer more and more services, utilizing the best technology, hiring top-performing employees, and keeping up with the pulse of the times. Steve and his administrative staff know what to do and when and how to do it: plans are made, schedules created, and goals accomplished, with the driving force of deadlines. He determinedly works through both financial and technical obstacles. He epitomizes a masculine approach to life—straightforward and practical, pragmatic and utilitarian.

Steve has a tendency toward high blood pressure. When he catches himself spinning out, he gets a massage or spends time with a girlfriend. He loves to go on a vacation that includes a physical activity like skiing or kayaking. Briefly, he sought a therapy that was quick and efficient: transactional analysis. When a friend of his died of a heart attack, it was a wake-up call: Steve is now aware that with his full-speed-ahead lifestyle, he could end up like that as well.

Speech, the Emotional/ Expressive Mode

Steve speaks quickly and moves from point to point. He has mastered the jargon of his trade. His e-mails to colleagues are succinct and to the point. With clients, he has the capacity to explain what his company can offer in an accessible way. With work colleagues and girlfriends, he can be impatient. He freezes when more intimate or emotional topics are brought up. Then he gets defensive and curt, interpreting any communication as an attack. His wife could not engage with him in a way that felt meaningful to her, so, after many years of confronting Steve about his lack of time for her and her interests, she asked for a divorce.

Steve can become overly speedy in trying to achieve the end goal. Then his energy is like a steamroller: he charges ahead and leaves others in the dust. He can be competitive, manipulative, controlling, and dominating. At such times, he can clash with those around him, and these confrontations tend to escalate over time. He has an intelligent paranoia: no one can pull the wool over Steve's eyes. If he sees a contract is too biased toward the other party, he will not sign it.

Because of his need to control, Steve can be insensitive to the welfare of others, who become mere objects to be manipulated to get the job done. Because he has trouble trusting others, he associates with people who have proved to be dependable and competent. Jealousy arises when Steve doesn't get what he wants around control and power, and he becomes more competitive.

MIND, THE MENTAL MODE

In his work life, Steve exhibits tremendous enthusiasm and exertion and is full of positive energy. In the position of power, he can command an overview and be in control. He finds making things happen to benefit others exhilarating and inspiring. He exudes confidence, is at ease with his own abilities, and is clear that this is the way he wants to live his life.

Steve is ambitious, has a strong sense of needing to appear competent, and is always prepared. He works long hours on weekends to keep on top of things. He takes initiative and is diligent and well organized. He is constantly strategizing to cover all the bases. He does not want to miss out on anything, because it might threaten his position. Sometimes Steve lacks an expansive perspective, doing just what is in front of him, with his nose to the grindstone. His energy becomes excessively goal oriented and pragmatic, creating tedium.

However, having so much responsibility weighs on Steve and has led to a certain degree of stress. Trying to keep the company afloat, particularly in financially hard times, has created increasing anxiety and fear of failure. He worries about money and continually tries to juggle finances to balance the budget and repay loans. As well, because the company specializes in custom-designed products, based on trial and error, it can make very costly mistakes.

QUALITY

Karma emits a green energy, swift and lively like the wind. Its sanity is all about accomplishing action for the benefit of others. It is associated with air and the sense perception of touch—functional touch to perform an activity. People who exhibit these qualities strongly are military personnel, laborers, newspaper reporters, workaholics, athletes, dancers, and social activists.

In their wisdom, karma people are highly functional: practical, efficient, and effective. They act in timely and appropriate ways in synchronicity with the world. They like things to have purpose, function well, and get results. They love challenge, adventure, and risk taking.

Karma people in their confusion can be restless, speedy, and hyperactive. They are power-hungry and competitive. They fear failure and thus are paranoid and jealous. They are always rushing because a gap is frightening. They can get into a catatonic stillness from feeling incompetent. Overwhelmed by what needs to be done, they procrastinate.

ACTION

Karmas' inherent nature is activity, all-accomplishing action. They can accomplish many things because of their powerful forward-moving energy. At best, they act in the service of others; at worst, they become power-hungry and domineering. Every one of the world's major cities epitomizes this energy at its best and worst.

The karma principle offers fulfillment because the higher view is that all activities are already accomplished. It is the understanding that to act is to spontaneously meet the energy of the moment. When we see what is happening and are poised for action, then we simply go along for the ride.

ANECDOTE

When describing Steve's body, I had my son in mind but then realized Julian has much too much padma to really be a Steve. One day, I became extremely frustrated because I just wanted to get Steve done. My daughter playfully reminded me that of course I was feeling that way: I was in karma energy. In fact, when writing about all the characters, I sensed them as very present in my everyday life.

BOB: BUDDHA PRESENCE
BODY, THE PHYSICAL MODE

Bob is thirty-something. He has a rounded face, bushy eyebrows, blue-gray eyes, a somewhat flat nose, and a small mouth. His short brown hair is often tousled. His eyes rest gently on whatever they see. He seldom smiles, but when he does, there is a cheery glint in his eyes. His teeth are slightly crooked. He holds his five-and-a-half-foot body straight but with a slight droop in the shoulders. His body is fleshy, with hardly any muscle tone. His very few clothes are in gray, tan, and dull green. Often he wears the same clothes several days in a row.

Bob lived with his parents until a few years ago but now lives alone in a small, perpetually untidy apartment. His furniture is basic, and he owns one piece of art: a minimalist painting reproduction that a friend gave him. He has a very simple life: working in a publishing house where he has been since just out of high school, eating at home while watching TV, and going for walks. He does not know how to cook and thus eats simple things: packaged cereal for any meal, canned soup, or a tuna fish sandwich. Sometimes he forgets to eat.

Not much happens in Bob's world, and that's how he likes it: small and safe. On the one hand, he seems plain and ordinary; on the other hand, there is a sense of profundity to the way he is, like an old soul. To those who know him, Bob seems imbued with a contemplative presence. With no place to "go" and nothing to "do," he can just "be." Because he does not have much agenda in his life, he does not become preoccupied with petty concerns.

Speech, the Emotional/Expressive Mode

Bob speaks slowly, often looking away rather than directly at the person in front of him. He has a sense of humility. In his very routine and repetitive work of handling orders and boxing up books, he is absorbed in a steady on-the-job way and does very well. He has never ventured out to find another job, as he likes the security of the predictable and unchanging.

He is easily overwhelmed by people or activity around him and defends himself by shutting down and withdrawing. His biggest fears are intrusion and the unknown. People who know Bob are familiar with his physical mannerisms—a slight frown, stroking his jaw, a sharp in-breath—when he has had too much. To keep life simple, he ignores and neglects many things around him. It is not unusual for his checks to bounce; his sink has dripped for a year. Habitually he plays blind, deaf, and dumb. He tends to isolate himself, be introverted, and stay self-contained. He can be stubborn, deadly honest, very serious, and have no sense of humor.

Generally Bob wants to be left alone and often shows indifference to those who reach out to him. Several women have fallen in love with him because he is so spacious, accommodating, and easygoing. He provides plenty of blank canvas on which to project! However, they have had varying degrees of success in drawing him out. He is not very expressive, nor does he have much desire to communicate. His friends tend to have either vajra or padma energy, as those qualities can sometimes hook him. He likes un-eventful relationships because he likes things simple: a walk in the park or a movie.

Mind, the Mental Mode

Bob normally has a sense of wholesomeness and basic goodness, a fundamental peace that says, "All is well." Though Bob can be open and accommodating, he also can become solidified. He can be forgetful, absorbed in his own world, and closed into himself. He dulls his sense perceptions to minimize contact with the environment.

Even when life feels OK, Bob experiences a pervasive anxiety about losing ground or falling apart. He knows deeply that ultimately there is nothing to hold on to, so in a mostly subconscious way, he worries about survival, continually attempting to secure himself. Too much activity overwhelms him; too little invites the anxiety of emptiness.

Quality

The wisdom of buddha energy is a sense of all-pervasive space—vast, boundless, and wakeful. As the most fundamental energy, buddha provides the space for all the other energies to manifest. It is completely alive and awake without purpose or direction—an awareness that has no bias. It has a sense of being at fundamental peace. It is existence itself. It accommodates nothing and everything, emptiness and fullness. It radiates a white energy, all-pervasive and peaceful. It is associated with space and no particular sense perception.

Of all the energies, buddha manifests the most sane and the most neurotic tendencies. Their sane aspect has a quiet presence and sense of humility. They are receptive, accommodating, easygoing, and flexible. They are content with just being. They are not ambitious and are content with not knowing. They are always just there. When such people manifest the neurotic aspect, in contrast, they can be dull, lazy, neglectful, and stubborn. Ignoring, avoiding, and denying become the way to keep from experiencing uncertainty and change, the way to create a safe, familiar world.

They will stick to whatever task is set before them with tunnel vision. They can be humorless and insensitive.

Action

Because buddha neurosis exists in a self-contained system, resisting change or any input from the outside, it is the hardest of all the five energies to penetrate. It picks the path of least resistance, does what is simplest. Buddha people tend to either muddle through or become complacent. Because they are numb both to their own pain and to the pain of the world, they feel little motivation for change.

When buddha people become active, they take on the quality of one of the other types. Buddhas with vajra energy have a spacious clarity, which is not as sharp as vajra alone. They are stable and have a broad view. Ratna can add an earthy richness and enjoyment to the basic energy of buddha. Padma adds immediacy, intimacy, and friendliness. Buddha mixed with karma is powerful and direct.

Anecdote

I lived for eight years in Nova Scotia, Canada, where the pace of life is much slower. "No problem" is a common response to everything. A friend of mine wants to put up a billboard on the highway coming into Halifax from the airport: "Warning: Entering Low-Phenomena Area."

3

Experience Speaks Louder than Words

Fᴿᴏᴍ ᴍᴏᴍᴇɴᴛ ᴛᴏ ᴍᴏᴍᴇɴᴛ, our experience is composed of bodily sensations, feelings, thoughts, and perceptions. We string these myriad and constantly shifting elements together to create what we call "I" and "my experience" and "the world." Our sense perceptions are an intermediary between our inner consciousness and the outer world and thus a vehicle for direct experience. Because they are nonconceptual, they enable us to experience the energetic dimension directly. Our senses—which make up our psychophysical barometer—are key to an experiential understanding of the Five Wisdoms. They open us to many dimensions of reality through five fields of experience. Creativity is a natural expression that arises from that fullness and manifests in a colorful display.

> The importance of taking seriously first-person experience . . . [is] that there is an irreducible core to the quality of experience. . . . The founder of phenomenology, Edmund Husserl, was an uncanny and gifted individual. His capacity to actually suspend his preconceptions and examine the structuring, the layering and the genesis of his own experience was uncanny—he was like a Mozart of experience.
>
> —Fʀᴀɴᴄɪsᴄᴏ Vᴀʀᴇʟᴀ, Buddhist practitioner and cognitive scientist

SENSE PERCEPTIONS

We are sense organisms or psychosense organisms. Sense perceptions include our sense organs or faculties (eyes, ears, nose, tongue, skin) as well as sense objects (a tree, a song, the scent of a rose, a bite of chocolate, objects of touch). What is between the faculties and objects we call sense fields: experiences of seeing, hearing, smelling, tasting, touching. They allow an immediate relationship to our environment and physical body: the down-to-earth aspect of experience. So sensing with an open, unbiased mind is fundamental to us. It is the ground of art and health.

We can register a sense perception directly with no concepts about who, what, why, how. We open and connect, not grabbing but receiving. Sense perceptions are not conceptual, psychological, or emotional. They invite us to be open in the moment, fully present, bringing us to the profound experience of seeing things as they are. Direct experience is the true teacher of reality; we can trust it. It does not need the mediation of any philosophy, psychology, or religion. Living life fully means being here without editing.

We have five senses and mind, an all-encompassing sense. Each perception has a unique intelligence, a particular wakefulness, and a different level of experiential intensity. For instance, sight dominates our waking hours, though we might not be so aware of touch. When we see how differently each sense perception interacts with the world, we discover we have five psychophysical intelligences, or fields of awareness, as follows:

There is *no particular sense perception* for buddha. The buddha field of awareness is unconditionally open and so imbues all sense perceptions with space.

Seeing brings us into the vajra field of awareness. There is an interest in shape, contour, structure, design, order, and surface texture. Sight, like vajra, tends to stay at some distance from an object in an observing rather than joining way.

Smelling, tasting, and sensual touch bring us into the ratna field of awareness. These senses are very visceral and experienced deep within the body. Our skin, the touch receptor, is our largest sense faculty.

Hearing or a sense of resonance brings us into the padma field of awareness. Here there is a sense not just of hearing with the ears but of hearing with the whole body, picking up the vibrations of speech, sound, and music. It is intuiting the nuances of energy dynamics and emotional tone.

What I call *functional touch* (to distinguish it from the sensual touch of ratna) brings us into the karma field of awareness. It is a touch that engages muscles in order to do something, connecting to an object to go into action.

Coming to an understanding of the fields of awareness involves not only what we observe but ourselves as the observer. Who is it that observes? How do we observe? What is the nature of our state of mind and body as the observing person? Are we seeing clearly, or are we distorting reality based on an aggressive bias, a speedy agenda, or being blinded by passion?

Becoming sensate means we widen our palate of permissible energies: we embrace ourselves as a psychophysical being. Although our preferred sense perceptions give us a distinct sense of who we are, we might find there is a sense perception or two that we tend to ignore. When we allow ourselves experiences with all of them, we gain greater access to the full range of the wisdom energies, thereby changing how we experience ourselves and interact with our world.

It is through our senses that we receive information of our internal environment (ourselves) and external environment (others and the world). We have the choice of being receptive and accepting and absorbing the information or rejecting, inhibiting and blocking it out. When we absorb the stimuli, we bond to that aspect of our environment; when we block out the information, we defend ourselves from that aspect. Learning is the process by which we vary our response to the same or similar stimuli, depending upon the appropriateness of the immediate situation.

By increasing the efficiency and integration of our sensory systems, we increase our range of choices in the interaction with ourselves and others and thereby widen our learning potential.

—Bonnie Bainbridge Cohen, developer of Body-Mind Centering

HOW WE BLOCK OUR SENSE PERCEPTIONS

When it comes to our sense perceptions, we are usually on automatic; we take them for granted. We never experience the energetic depth of the moment because our concepts take over, then our projections, and finally a superimposed version of reality. Our incessant preoccupations make us close down in familiar ways. Caught up in thoughts and emotions, we hardly really, truly sense anything. Sensing is a more subtle experience, so we often miss it.

The primary reason we block our sense perceptions is fear, our most basic obstacle. Because we have an omnipresent anxiety about our existence, we are preoccupied with self-preservation. Sometimes we feel threatened, other times overwhelmed. Whether caught up in discursive mind, lost in concepts, or emotionally reactive, we become numb to sensation. In general, we don't experience; we conceptualize. We name things, sticking to a series of clichés, influenced by expectations and set modes of relating to the world. It is as if we lived in a tunnel burrowing through our life. Our antennae, our sense perceptions, are retracted. We cloud direct experience and thus have a dull, distorted view of the world. We cannot relate to ourselves or the world in a genuine way.

In our urbanized life, our sensory experience has been marginalized: we live and work in very controlled environments. We fear the natural environment: it is too cold or too warm or too windy or too sunny or not sunny enough. To avoid all these discomforts, we pamper ourselves: getting the temperature, the humidity, and so forth just right. We are also overly fascinated with perception. We create endless entertainment that bombards our senses and are willing to take in the most horrific things. We become numb to the vividness of life in a more natural way.

When our anxiety subsides, our sense perceptions become workable. They are no longer distorted by discursiveness, concepts, and emotions. We can then become simple: attentive without bias, judgment, or concept. So it is a sense of fearlessness and confidence, trusting both ourselves and our environment, that allows us to see our world. We can be gentle and open, simply appreciating the nature of things as they are.

EXPERIMENT WITH HOW YOU CLOSE OFF FROM AND OPEN TO YOUR WORLD

Track your experience as you do the following:

1. Get into discursive thought and thoughts leading to emotions.
2. Abruptly drop those thoughts and directly experience: see, hear, touch.
3. Go back and forth a few times so you have the qualitative experience of both.

OUR SENSATIONAL WORLD

We can be receptive to our world rather than trying to control or manipulate it. This kind of opening feels profoundly good. The senses become a vehicle to open as we touch into our experience in a simple, ordinary way. We have an inherent ability to live in an enlivened relationship to our world, vivid and immediate. We have a standing-still quality from which we naturally expand. It is our most primal state. It is like a gift.

Sense perceptions ground and nurture us: they can bring us into a sense of well-being. The environment feels nourishing because we let it touch us. We find that both our thoughts and our emotional fixations can dissolve when we open to sensing the world rather than reacting to it. We feel spacious; we are not bound up with our ideas and feelings. We can relate to our world without its demanding anything of us. Being grounded in sense perceptions allows us to be gentle, so our existence becomes joyful.

Nature has been dissected by scientists, praised by poets, and is also a teacher of wisdom. When we attune ourselves to it, we are inspired by its magic. Sensing deeply the bountiful garden in which we find ourselves, we could feel the connection between the rich soil and plants growing out of it, Mother Earth nourishing all. Watch a mother robin fly back and forth gathering food for her young until one day they are ready to fly. How does the mother robin know where to find the worms? How does a baby robin know how to fly the very instant it leaves its nest or a colt know how to clamber to its feet and walk soon after it is born? Do you know that bees make more honey when they sense a long winter ahead? Wow!

Most important, understanding sense perceptions is key to understanding reality: we can perceive the world without language, spontaneously. When we see how the world hangs together, we also can see the possibilities of choosing and rejecting. We have discriminating intelligence, not emotional bias. Then we really can dance with the energies. We can see that the energy of the world is constantly moving and in communication with us, each moment. We have an inherent ability to live in an enlivened relationship to our world, fresh, vivid, and immediate. It brings joy and a natural warmth.

During a stay in New York City, I visited major exhibits of Leonardo da Vinci and Albert Einstein. Seeing them in quick succession, I was struck by one thing: the simplicity of what inspired their work. These two geniuses, an artist and a scientist, were observers of reality. Leonardo was able to sketch the perfect horse, create the magic of the *Mona Lisa*, and design the first two-hull boat. Einstein made a major scientific breakthrough with his relativity theory. They seemed to have an open space of mind where such truths could reveal themselves, showing us the great wisdom in keenly observing the world, seeing things as they are.

THE PRACTICE OF OPENING TO SENSE PERCEPTIONS

Sense perceptions involve a natural process: our psychophysical being interacts with the environment. The first flash of perception is pure energy, neither good nor bad. However, our habitual thoughts and reactions intervene, and the whole movie begins. So the first thing is to be able to drop those preoccupations, suspend our interpretation. We can learn to be attentive without bias: not accepting or rejecting; not editing. The foundation for being able to do this is a sense of being, of presence. We commit to the present moment and allow ourselves to occur. The less active we are, the more receptive we are.

PRACTICE PERCEIVING THINGS IN THEIR OWN NATURE AND FULLY TAKING THEM IN

• By practicing how to look, we discover how to see.

• By practicing how to listen, we discover how to hear.

• By noting how we touch, we discover how to feel.

When we are fully present, we are more receptive and thus experience more. There is a tangible experience of the boundary of self dissolving and a sense of mingling with sights, sounds, smells, tastes. When we see a color, we see it with our whole being. When we listen, we hear deeply with our body. When we smell and taste, we savor it in our nostrils and mouth and then our body. When we touch, we truly feel. When we perform a function, we engage with the power in our body.

A THREE-STEP PROCESS FOR EXPERIENCING SENSE PERCEPTIONS (FROM CHÖGYAM TRUNGPA)

First work with sight; then choose any sense perception.

1. Experience a sense of being.
   - Establish a sense of being in the moment.
   - Take in a deep breath and let it go.
   - Cut through the clouds of distraction and preoccupation.
2. Experience a sense of connecting.
   - Quickly project outward and connect to an object of sight.
   - The quality of abruptness further cuts thoughts and creates open ground.
   - Simply look at the object.
   - Be open and inquisitive.
   - This could have a delightful, exuberant quality.
3. Experience a sense of merging, linking.
   - Establish communication between yourself and the object.

- Feel the oscillation, the back-and-forth play.
- Linger and draw the object toward you.
- Have a sense of joining your being with it.

Our sense perceptions also merge and layer. When we fully open to a specific perception, the other sense perceptions come along. When we look at something, we also could smell, hear, and touch it: we can see, smell, hear, and touch with our eyes. When we hear something, we could have an image of it in our mind's eye. When we taste a strawberry, we can see and smell it. Have you ever danced a strawberry?

EXPERIENCE HOW EACH
SENSE PERCEPTION AND
CORRESPONDING WISDOM IS
LAYERED IN AN OBJECT
(FROM CHÖGYAM TRUNGPA)

Choose an object and sit in front of it.
- *Buddha:* No sense perception.
  - Sense the amorphous quality of the space of your object.
  - There is no real definition.
- *Vajra:* Look, then see.
  - Pay attention to its shape, form, design, surface texture.
  - See its overall structure as well as details.
- *Padma:* Listen, then hear in the sense of picking up the vibration.
  - Sense how it communicates, radiates.
  - Sense what it is saying.

- *Ratna:* Smell and taste, then savor; touch, then fully feel.
  - Sense the volume, weight, substance.
  - Sense that you are merging, you are of the same substance.
- *Karma:* Touch, then connect.
  - Pick up the object; become one with it.
  - The object becomes functional.

Bringing more awareness of sense perceptions into our lives provides a shift that helps cut through our habitual patterns and gives us a sense of well-being. Our aim is to cultivate an awake quality of pure, direct perception: to hear sounds, taste food, feel touch. Living life fully means being here. Perceptions become part of our existence, so we feel greater relaxation and gentleness in relation to the environment.

Vacations are often an opportunity to open our sense perceptions, so they could indeed lead to heightened enjoyment—unless we are on a tour trying to cram everything into a few days.

Although my son, Julian Nadel, doesn't take to meditation practice, merely being in our family has given him an understanding of Buddhism by osmosis. Here Julian recounts a meeting that I arranged for both of us with Khenpo Tsültrim Gyamtso Rinpoche.

He is that happy guru thing, the place where calm meets delight. And shows us how. He's very funny. And, ya know, deep. The teaching he gave me happened on a cold fall day in a small apartment he was staying in, near the Panhandle in San Francisco. Khenpo Rinpoche read me immediately and with one wave of his hand and first comment dispelled an argument Mom and I had been in for over a decade: "Julian . . . I know you don't want to sit meditation. . . . You don't want to sit, sit on a cushion." Mom and I looked at each other ("Wow, he's good"). "That's not your way, that's not your practice. . . . But I want to give you a practice. . . . May I give you a practice?" Of course, I bobbed my head. . . . "I want you . . . I want you to . . . just feel. Just notice. But completely. I want you to let yourself pause fully—it doesn't need to be long, that doesn't matter, how much time doesn't matter, it can be no time whatsoever, just a moment—to pause in a sensation, to feel your hand on the brass of the door handle with your whole, whole self. . . . And then let go. . . . And then the next time and whenever, whatever, a sound, a sight, a ripple. . . . And not on a schedule, but whenever, whenever. . . . Whenever you practice, that is your practice." Bless that guy. Got me out of cushion duty. I don't do the long sits. But I appreciate the practice of single-pointed sensation.

ORDINARY MAGIC

The world speaks to us constantly. It makes sense to us, experiential sense. We understand things in a direct, immediate, and personal way. It is a down-to-earth experience: very ordinary, very colorful, and very precise. Becoming sensate connects us to the elemental quality of life. Even pain can be experienced very directly without bias. When we relate to the actuality of things as they are, we invite magic, ordinary magic. We could call such direct connections mini–enlightenment experiences.

On a recent flight, I experienced some ordinary magic. I was served sparkling water. With a lot of time to do nothing, I became completely absorbed watching the bubbles rise, sometimes join with another one, and pop on the surface. I entered a whole world of air and water. It was magical.

Becoming sensate empowers us to discover the world of the Five Wisdoms. We join with the energetic essence of the world and establish ourselves in total communication. We can see the depth and magic of connecting in the moment to all experience, all the time, in whatever we are doing. We can interact with the world with creativity and wisdom. Great spiritual teachers have infinite energy because they are plugged into the energy of the world.

During a training session, Anick described opening to her senses when she went for a walk. She said she had lost herself: she did not know where "she" was. Since we generally think of ourselves as our thoughts and emotions, we can very well feel "lost" if they fall away. Rather than experiencing a sense of loss, we can experience a nonegoic self, fully attuned to our surroundings.

We could have the experience that our sense perceptions become intensified or intoxicated. This happens when our sense of self and our sense perceptions come together: conceptual mind collapses, and sense perceptions open to a dazzling luminosity. There is no duality, no ownership, no watcher. Our experience is centerless. Everything is luminous in the sense that everything seems to emit light. What we experience as light is the radiation of energy. Then our heart opens: there is no barrier between ourselves and our world, no resistance. When open, all our sense perceptions connect to the heart. They activate the heart. Magical!

My annual solitary retreat is the best time of my year. I now understand that it is because it is such an elemental experience. It is a time to invite magic. I feel sensational and my heart is wide open. It is what I try to bring back to share with others.

A PRACTICE FOR INVITING MAGIC

Add fourth and fifth steps to the "Three-Step Process for Experiencing Sense Perceptions" exercise presented above:

1. Experience a sense of being.
2. Experience a sense of connecting.
3. Experience a sense of merging, linking.
4. Draw in the energy of your object of perception.
   - Feel the energy infuse your body.
   - Feel the richness and power of embodying energy.
5. Let the energy into your heart.

We fall in love with the world when we experience its fullness, power, and magic. The limitless fields of sense perceptions are cosmic, beyond thought. They communicate with the depth and fullness of the world: extraordinary smell, sound, color, taste. We experience a sense of vastness as a natural expression of wisdom. It sparks our sanity, so in turn we experience our world as sacred. Auspicious coincidences arise spontaneously: we find that we are at the right place at the right time in tune with the energy of our world. Our sense of being is able to ride the present situation.

> If the doors of perception were cleansed, everything would appear to man as it is, infinite.
>
> —WILLIAM BLAKE

ELEMENTAL ENERGY

We have looked at the Five Wisdoms in terms of personality, our psychological manifestation, and our sense perceptions, our bridge to the world. However, our most primal aspect is that we are made of the four elements: earth, water, fire, and air—as well as space, the basic accommodation of them. Each element also corresponds to one of the wisdom energies. Primal being is not about *who* we are, which is more psychological, but *what* we are, which is more physical, elemental. The elements are more primal because our bodily experience precedes our psychological development.

The elements are continually working within us at a subtle level. They have a natural process and function: water washes away, and fire burns to purify; earth stabilizes, and air or wind provides movement. It is not hard to have an experiential sense of the elements. When things are going well, the elements are in balance, functioning naturally, and we have a sense of well-being. However, due to our habitual patterns, the elements can become unbalanced by overuse or neglect. If they become increasingly unbalanced, we experience mental and physical symptoms. We feel more and more anxious and vulnerable and become more and more self-referential. At that point, we use intensified emotions as a defense. This is the relationship between the physical elements and our psychology, our emotions.

Though the phenomenal world is obvious to all, rarely do we take in its elemental nature. When we do, a whole dimension of reality opens up to us. Being in a natural setting—better yet, living in one—nourishes us. We can enter into an energetic exchange with the essence of our surroundings: the earthiness of earth, the waterness of water, the fireness of fire. Isn't it comforting to sit around a campfire with others? When a downpour comes along, my daughter rushes outside to dance in the rain. When there is a full moon, she climbs a tree and howls at it. The pure joy of fully meeting an element is energizing.

Although we have heard a lot about emotional intelligence, we could stand to pay more attention to elemental intelligence. We can bring the elements into our body energetically by just being and focusing on each one. When we feel spacious and relaxed, we allow the elements to function naturally within us. Then we feel fulfilled, balanced, and in energetic harmony.

We can also pay attention to how we relate to the elements on a day-to-day basis using our common sense. When we are hungry, we bring in the nourishing, sustaining energy of earth by eating. When we are thirsty, dehydrated, parched, drinking water gives us a sense of life energy, pure and fluid. When our energy is stirred up, windy and groundless, we need to come back to earth. When we are feeling sad and lonely, we need to rekindle the fire that has gone out. If we are lethargic, we need wind to move us into action.

EMBODYING THE ELEMENTS (IN COLLABORATION WITH SYDNEY LEIJENHORST)

SPACE / BUDDHA
- Stand in stillness.
- Completely drop the impulse to move; have no agenda.
- Fill every cell of your body with space, expanding from inside and out.
- Feel nourished by space.
- Become all-accommodating spaciousness.

WATER / VAJRA
- Stand in stillness.
- Bend to scoop up (imaginary) water with your hands and pour it over you.
- Experience yourself as an immense river of life energy.
- Become self-existing clarity: fluid and pure.

EARTH / RATNA
- Stand in stillness.
- Make a slow, grounded, earthy movement.
- Feel the affinity between your body and nature's body.
- Experience yourself as deeply grounded and nourished.
- Become self-existing equanimity.

FIRE / PADMA
- Stand in stillness with your eyes closed.
- Touch into your communication centers: throat, heart, and genitals.

- Feel the fire of life, the warmth and vitality, within you.
- Become self-existing passion.

AIR OR WIND / KARMA

- Allow your breath to flow easily, experiencing a sense of well-being.
- Run with a sense of spacious mind.
- Experience action without speediness.
- Feel fully alive, potent.
- Become self-existing activity, activity as already accomplished.

SIX MOVEMENT ELEMENTS

Though, as a lifelong dancer, I have a bias, it is also true that in many cultures, people sing and dance as a way to partake in their social and cultural life and fully celebrate this human existence.

I evolved the six elements of movement during my dance career, and they became part of a pedagogy for both composition and improvisational work. They are the fundamental components of movement and can be recognized in any dance form. They correspond to the energies, as below.

THE SIX ELEMENTS OF MOVEMENT AND THEIR CORRESPONDING WISDOM ENERGY

Buddha has no movement element. It accommodates all the others.

1. Bodily shape: vajra
2. Spatial design: vajra
3. Kinesthetic awareness: ratna
4. Energetic dynamics: padma
5. Rhythm / time: karma
6. Kinetics: karma

FIVE WISDOMS MUSIC

Music is a very powerful and penetrating conveyor of energy. Because it can change one's mood in seconds, I have used it as a way to bring people into the five qualities. However, it is rare to find music in just one energy. Like everything else, music is best when it combines multiple energies. It takes a certain amount of musical sophistication to capture the subtleties of the different energies. Hence, most popular music does not. The music selections presented below were made in working with Bill Douglas, Jan van Bolhuis, and others. As each energy is associated with a time of day, I sometimes like to enhance the energy of that time with music. I particularly notice that in the evening padma energy is the one I want.

EXPLORING THE ENERGIES OF THE FIVE WISDOMS

In keeping with our theme that experience speaks louder than words, we can create experiential situations that evoke and heighten the energies. This is an opportunity for neither impulsively acting out nor suppressing. Expression makes the energies more exposed and thus more vivid. When we experience the energies, creative expression arises spontaneously in a nonconceptual way.

The following are some of the limitless ways to explore the energies. Choose from these possibilities and work or play with them, either on your own or in a group. (A group will need a facilitator.) Allow one to two hours for exploring each energy, except for buddha, which is best "explored" by doing nothing.

EXPLORING BUDDHA ENERGY

Buddha energy wants to do as little as possible.

- Sit, stand still, or lie down.
  - Listen to music, with your eyes open or closed.
  - Write a haiku, a three three-line poem, as an expression of the moment. Use heaven, earth, and human principles:
- Heaven is the dominant statement.
- Earth is a complementary or subdominant statement.
- A human can be statement that both connects and contrasts.
  Traditional Example:

In ancient pond
Frog jumps in
Splash

Japanese Microsoft error message:
Three things are certain:
Death, taxes and lost data.
Guess which has occurred.

- Take a just-being break.
  - Take a short break from work. Sit quietly for three to five minutes, paying attention to your breathing.

BUDDHA MUSIC (WITH ELEMENTS OF OTHER ENERGIES)

Listen to Buddha music anytime to come back to just being.

Brian Eno: "Music for Airports"; Steve Reich: "Music for Eighteen Musicians"; Tan Dun: "Marco Polo"; György Ligeti: "Lux Aeterna"; Charles Ives: "The Unanswered Question"; Béla Bartók: "Music for Strings, Percussion, and Celesta," 3rd movement; Louis Andriessen: "Time"; Edgard Varèse: "A Deep Black Sleep"; Wolfgang Rihm: "Time Chant"; Alfred Schnittke: "In Memoriam," 5th movement.

EXPLORING VAJRA ENERGY

- Do some aimless wandering: walk slowly, preferably outside, with no agenda. Notice shapes, positioning, surface textures, contours, colors, light.
- Change your focus. Switch between a focused or one-pointed awareness to a wide, panoramic awareness.
- Close your eyes and quickly open them, turn your head slightly and repeat. When you look, really see.
- Make a three-object arrangement, being extremely precise as to the placement of the objects. Use heaven, earth, and human principles. Example: Place a large object such as a jewelry box in the upper left corner of your space, a blank sheet of paper or a table. Place a complementary object such as a scarf somewhat close to it. Place a smaller object such a piece of jewelry farther away, perhaps in the lower right corner. In this example there is a theme but it is not necessary.

- Write a haiku, a three three-line poem, as an expression of the moment.

VAJRA MOVEMENT ELEMENTS: BODY SHAPES AND SPATIAL DESIGN

Body Shapes

- Shape shift with music. The focus here is on the shapes your body makes. Be abstract and formalist rather than expressive. Pay attention to negative and positive space, asymmetry and symmetry, angles and curves, small and large shifts, slow and fast transitions.
- Shape-shift or "sculpt" with a partner. Hold each other at the wrists, shift your weight using each other as a counterbalance. Move with awareness of the design or shape you are making.
- Formalist/expressionist interplay. Make an expressive gesture or shape. Then drain the expression out of the body to come to an abstract form.
- Do fast movements and freeze, arresting the action in a shape. Keep the focus on the shape, not the expression.

Body Shapes with a Group

- Create three-person sculptures using heaven, earth, and human principles.
  Example: The first person could stand using a gesture reaching to the sky. The second could take a lower, grounded shape. The third person could be farther away and be reaching toward them.
- Create a kinetic still-life: animate the sculpture by using a repeated movement.
- Create changing tableaus and pictures. Move quickly into and out of tableaus. Have a sense of swarming into and dispersing out of them.
- In a trio, move within an ever-shifting tableau.

Spatial Design with a Group

- Move in spatial patterns on the floor.
  Example: Create a grid and move only in straight lines making sharp turns at the corners. Alternately, move in circles, curves, and figure eights.
- Bring the space you are in alive by moving and taking postures in relationship to it. Highlight aspects of it such as a tree or bench outside in a park or the architectural details inside. Sense the environmental texture: substance, weight, and feel.
- Transform an environment: Place objects in a space, and then play with their relationship to one another.

VAJRA MUSIC

Listen to vajra music in the morning:

Gagaku, Japanese court music; Stravinsky: "L'Histoire du Soldat," "Rite of Spring," and "Symphony Three Movements," 2nd movement; Messaein: "Quartet for the End of Time"; Mozart: "Piano Concerto in G Major"; Chopin: "Grande Polonaise"; Paco de Lucia: "Flamenco"; Boulez: "Marteau sans Maître"; Bach: "Gigue," from "English Suite No. 2"; Maurice Ravel: "Jeux d'eaux" and "Piano Concerto in G," 3rd movement; Sofia Gubaildulina: "String Quartet No. 2"

EXPLORING RATNA ENERGY

- Do aimless wandering while touching things.
- With music playing, color together in a communal way, perhaps creating a mural.

- With a partner, give each other a massage.
- Take a blindfolded walk with a partner. Have your partner lead you. Experience the world without your sense of sight.
- Do an enriching/amassing walk inside or outside. Collect and gather natural objets such as a large branch or anything that has a sense of richness such as a vase or a scarf. Create an environment with these objects and have a communal celebration. At the end, offer the objects to one another.
- Enjoy eating, slowly. Smell and feel the food in your mouth and savor the flavor. Notice how your bodily sensations change.

RATNA MOVEMENT ELEMENT: KINESTHETIC AWARENESS

- Kinesthetics is awareness of bodily sensations, at rest or in motion.
- Lie down, eyes closed, and become aware of your bodily sensations. Pay attention to: weight, tone (tension vs. relaxation), temperature (hot vs. cold), tingling. Awaken your body by sending awareness to different parts of it.
- Lie down and begin to move very slowly with kinesthetic awareness. Experience the sensation of being massaged from the inside as well as the floor massaging you. Move based on the inner dance of sensation, the subtle inner impulses. Listen and then express it through movement. After a while, slowly come up to standing and continue moving from the inside out.
- Play with weight. Lie down on your back. Feel the weight of the your body on the ground, noticing the heavier and lighter parts. The upper parts of your body have an

affinity to air, air-body. The lower parts have an affinity to the earth, earth-body. Feel yourself to be a bag of sand, and let the sand sink to the bottom. Roll from your back to your side, to your front, to your other side, and to your back again. Do this by shifting your weight, shifting sand, using a minimum of muscle. Next, do a free free-form roll moving progressively up to standing. Do movements with affinity to air and affinity to earth.
- Move with varying dynamics, then hold still and feel the kinesthetic sensation.
- Move like certain tastes and smells. (How do you move a strawberry, a steak?)
- With a partner, lean into each other. Move together, keeping the contact (like contact improvisation, if you know it). Let the felt sense of the contact be the primary reference point.

RATNA MUSIC

Listen to ratna music in the midafternoon.

Tibetan Buddhist Chanting; Mahler: "Fourth Rückert Song" and "Second Symphony"; Brahms: "First Symphony"; Wagner: "Die Meistersinger"; Richard Strauss: "Also sprach Zarathustra," 1 and 4, "A Hero's Life," "The Hero"; Luciano Berio: "Sinfonia," 3rd movement; Sofia Gubaidulina: "Offertorium 1 and 2."

EXPLORING PADMA ENERGY

- Do aimless wandering with a partner, in silence. Relate to each other by feeling the energetic resonance between you. Hold hands, if you like.
- Sit with your eyes closed and listen to a variety of different sounds. Listen without concepts

and judgements. Listen to a constant sound like a stream and intermittent sounds like birdcalls. Notice thoughts and shifts in feelings. Hear the sounds with your body; have a felt sense of where they are in your body. Notice which sounds you prefer.

- With a partner, color together as music is played.
- Make up a personal sound language, and have a dialogue with a partner. What meaning is conveyed, even without words?
- In a trio, each choose one word or phrase. Walk around the space and semiaudibly say the word or phrase. Say the same phrase as if in love, or angry, and so forth. Notice other people's words or phrases and say them. Join with others saying the same word or phrase.
- Make a facial expression and then embody it. Do this several times to get the feel of it. Transition from one expression to another by turning or stepping forward.
- With a group, sitting in a circle, make a vocal orchestra. Work with various types of sounds: resonant, elongated vowels and articulated consonants. Listening to others, create a sound poem together.
- Discover a personal melody and sing it to yourself. Share your melody with another.
- Have a padma party: always be aware of one other person (as if you are in love). Be sensitive to when the other person is near and when he or she is far away (out of the room). What are your feelings? Have one intimate conversation sometime during the party. Note when you feel joined with others and when you feel separate.

PADMA MOVEMENT ELEMENT: DYNAMICS

- Play with types of dynamics, the expressive qualities of movement:
  - Free flowing, lyrical versus bound, resistant.
  - Sway with an airy feeling, rock with an earthy feeling.
  - Staccato, caught, or arrested movement.
  - Contraction and release.
  - Twitching, throwing, flicking, flinging.
  - Shaking and reverberating.
  - Suspension and falling.
- Chose one movement quality and repeat it for a time. Then come to stillness and close your eyes. See the after afterimages in your mind's eye, like an instant replay of a movie. Feel the currents of energy in your body. Taste the movement.
- Follow the leader. In turn, each person in the group leads a phrase of movement, and everyone follows. Then the leader calls a name and that person becomes the leader.
- Emotion/motion interplay: Pay attention to the energy, quality, and texture of movement. Repeat a movement quality until an emotion comes. Play with dynamic changes of the breath. Add sounds. Do this with a partner and in a group.
- Create a melting pot, working with transformation and exchange. In two groups start at opposite ends of the room. Move toward each other with contrasting movements. When the groups meet, they exchange material and move to the other side.

Padma Music

Listen to padma music in the evening.

Willie and Lobo, Jesse Cook, Fados and other Latin singers and musicians; the blues; tango music; classical Indian music; Claude Debussy: "Prelude to the Afternoon of a Faun"; Burns: "The Winter It Is Past" and "My Love Is Like a Red, Red Rose"; Bach: "Double Violin Concerto"; Alexander Scriabin: "Desire" and "Étude," Op. 2:1; Wagner: "Liebestod," from "Tristan"; Maurice Ravel: "Piano Concerto in G," 2nd movement.

EXPLORING KARMA ENERGY

- Do aimless wandering, noting how things function.
- Color, cut paper, and use Play-Doh with music playing.
- Design a competitive event. Work in teams with another team of judges. It could be a game, a physical task, or the creation of a human "machine." The machine must be functional, efficient, and well designed, perhaps with props. Possible criteria for assessing/judging (five points each) include: team rapport, job efficiency, technical expertise, quantity and quality of the end product, innovativeness, attractiveness, usefulness.
- Eat a quick bag lunch.

KARMA MOVEMENT ELEMENTS: RHYTHM AND KINETICS
Rhythm and Time

- Play with rhythm using different time signatures or meters. Two beats or four beats per measure feels stable, three and six beats are circular, five and seven are syncopated. Clap, stomp, or walk different meters. Improvise movement in a given meter.
- Five-speed walk: In a group, add these speeds one at a time: normal, slow, fast, stop, run. Notice the psychophysical aspects of each speed, spacing, and groupings. React to people using time and speed.
- Do a repeated movement changing its speed.
- Perform a task such as arranging things in a space being attentive to the time it takes to do something. Do it too fast to be done and then imperceptibly slowly.
- Follow the leader. Each person takes turns leading a rhythmic pattern, a ditty. After the group repeats the pattern a few times, the leader calls someone else's name and that person becomes the leader.
- In a circle, establish a simple rhythm (this becomes the base). One to three people come into the center and juxtapose their own rhythm to the base.

Kinetics

- Kinetic logic means that your body is on "automatic," following the natural laws of the universe. Experiment with inertia, momentum, action/reaction.
- Play with the sheer physicality of movement, with no mind control or emotional motivation. Stand, go off balance, and let swings, falls, and rebounds happen naturally. (This kind of kinetic play feels like a drunken dance.)
- Push a partner. Stand behind your partner, with his or her weight leaning on you. Push

your partner forward as his or her feet take small steps. It is like pushing a cart, feeling the other person's weight and maneuvering it.

- Swing a partner. With both hands, hold your partner's right wrist. Swing them, playing with centrifugal force.
- Weight sharing. Move while staying in physical contact with a partner. Focus on the natural kinetic play of the movement.

Karma Music

Listen to karma music any time of day to rouse energy.

Most popular music with a strong beat; Penderecki: "St. Luke Passion"; Carter: "First String Quartet"; Stravinsky: "Rite of Spring"; Ketjak monkey chant; Ali Akbar Khan: "Raga 2"; György Ligeti: "Piano Concerto," 1st movement; Béla Bartók: "Piano Concerto 1," 3rd movement, "Sonata for Two Pianos and Percussion," 3rd movement; Franz Liszt: "Études d'exécution transcendente: Feux-Follets"; Dmitri Shostakovitch: "Symphony 10," 2nd movement; John Adams: "Harmonielehre," 1st movement.

EXPLORING THE ENERGIES IN RELATIONSHIP TO EACH OTHER
FIVE WISDOMS SKITS

Do this exercise in groups of three. Each person creates a line which is either a statement, a question, or an exclamation in an energy style. Interact with one another, using only your line. The general tone for each style would be:

– Buddha: Monotone.

– Vajra: Bring clarity to the situation.
– Ratna: Become fuller and more expansive.
– Padma: Modulate the dynamics of expression each time.
– Karma: Each line must accomplish something.

Postcards

Spread a large collection of picture postcards out on the floor. Everyone takes a postcard that attracts him or her. Then each person finds a partner and tells him or her why they chose that postcard. Pay attention to the words that are used and the associations they bring up. What energies are present? Discuss what you realized about yourselves.

Sculptures

Make a three- to five-energy human sculpture, adding one person at a time. Intensify by using repeated gestures to make the energies vivid.

Actors and Observers

Divide into two groups, actors and observers. The actors decide which energy they want to portray. Actors make gestures, movements, sounds, and words in their energy quality. Observers look at the body language and sounds, taking note of their energetic responses and noticing the effect of different energies.

Observers describe what they see: which energies are present. Possibilities in what you see:

- vajra: holding back, silent, in their head
- ratna: satisfied, laughing, eating
- padma: talking, buzzing, grouping

- karma: active, physical, speedy
- buddha: coming late

Observers state if the energy is closed or open, based on their reactions:
- positive reaction: open, wanting to align
- negative reaction: closed, wanting to withdraw
- neutral: indifferent

A Scavenger Hunt

Divide into teams. Look for objects that represent the five wisdom qualities in your indoor and outdoor surroundings. Have an exhibition of what you have found.

The Qualities Game

This was one of my teacher Chögyam Trungpa's favorite games. One person, who will be the questioner, leaves the room. The group picks a well-known public figure.

The questioner returns to the room and asks questions such as these: If this person were a car, what kind of car would he or she be? If this person were a flower, what kind of flower would he or she be?

Members of the group respond to the questions, and a scribe writes down the answers.

The questioner tries to guess who it is by considering the qualities. From time to time, the scribe can read the answers listed thus far. The questioner can ask three direct questions. For example, "Is this person male or female?" The game ends when the questioner guesses the person.

The energies always invite both a sense of depth and a sense of play. Let's move on to see how infinitely varied our experience of them can be.

4

Our Energetic Constellations

On our journey with the wisdoms, first we get a sense of the flavor of each wisdom and how distinctive they are. We begin to see not only the predictability of certain energy patterns but also where and when they are more fluid, changeable. The energies can be more fully understood by seeing their dynamic interrelatedness. They are all facets of a larger whole: interconnected, layered, merged, and reacting to one another. In people, they are constantly shifting due to changing life situations, time of life, and circumstance. It is like looking at a prism or kaleidoscope. This awareness allows us to relate wholeheartedly to our mix of colors. It is startling to realize that, as everyone is unique, there are as many combinations of energies as people in the world. We have the potentiality for all five and are our own unique mixture as well.

ENERGY PATTERNS

Some energy patterns in us are more dominant and others more background; some we learn as an enhancement or embellishment of who we are; others are constantly shifting as we adapt to life. Some energies we use as a mask to hide our insecurity about ourselves or as a pretense to respond to what we perceive as a demand. When we wear a mask, we become incongruent, are full of conflicting emotions, and create confusion. We may be able to assimilate a complementary energy, an energy we admire in a friend or partner.

OUR ENERGETIC MIX

- Our one or two dominant energies are both stuck and shining.
- An enhancement energy is one we learn in order to express ourselves at our best.
- A mask energy is a pretense, one we hide behind when insecure about ourselves.
  - The enhancement (shining) and mask (stuck) could be the same energy, depending on circumstances.
- A complementary energy is one we are attracted to and admire in others.

We all have our own style and our own particular nature. We can't avoid it. The enlightened expression of yourself is in accord with your inherent nature.

—CHÖGYAM TRUNGPA, *Pure Perception*

We cannot circumvent our inherent nature. It is what it is: we are born with it. It is our hardwiring. Perhaps we have sensed this and identify with one or more of the energies because they feel most familiar. They feel primal, deeply ingrained, as naked as the day we were born. We have always known ourselves to be that way. Our inherent nature is like a home base, the window through which we experience the world. It is not necessarily the most comfortable, however, as it is an expression of our confusion as well. It can also reflect what we care most about: relationship (red), being respected (green), having material comfort (yellow). Our style stays with us as it moves into its wisdom. Our long-standing, ingrained habitual tendencies start to see the light of day: we see the sanity within the neurosis.

Enhancement energy is, by definition, an expression of our sanity. It is an energy with which we have learned to express ourselves: a skill, the way we dress ourselves up, a tool. Perhaps we have admired it in others, seen it in our family or culture, and appreciate how useful it is. We feel comfortable in it and might be more likely to take it on in a given situation. Others might think it is our inherent nature because they see it first in us. To fully manifest it, we could emphasize and develop it. We could make it into a style, a way to relate to the world. It could change as our life situation changes.

We put on a mask when we feel discomfort with ourselves. We could be afraid to show our true self, not confident in our basic energy. We feel a particular energy is expected of us so we fake it. For instance, if we are working for an architect or lawyer, we might put on the blue energy but feel uncomfortable doing so. This incongruence leads to mental stress and/or physical illness. Interestingly, the same energy could be either an enhancement or a mask: we could be either sane or confused with it, depending on the situation. It is also possible not to have a mask. What you see is what you get.

BECOMING FAMILIAR WITH OUR ENERGIES

To more fully see who we are, we attend to the present moment; we observe what is happening. We collect data about ourselves, familiarize ourselves with ourselves: what we think, feel, say, and do. Over time we recognize our style by paying close attention to our tendencies, from day to day, moment to moment, in different situations. By paying attention to the minute particulars of our psychophysical process, the extremely subtle shifts of mind and body that happen moment to moment, we see the weave and warp of our personality. We look at how our life circumstances shape us and how we identify with who we are.

We can watch how we are in different life situations: when we are relaxed and have no external pressures or when we are in a crisis. When we get upset, do we go to the phone, call one friend after another, and tell our story? Or do we sit down and analyze the whole thing: write it out and become extremely clear about it? Or do we withdraw into a hole and not talk to anybody? These are deeply, deeply ingrained habitual patterns.

It is only through direct experience that we see how the wisdom energies manifest. We could intellectualize our relationship to the wisdoms, but we would miss the point. Using an experiential approach, the felt sense of energy, is actually more efficacious. Then we can bring in our understanding. Rather than being told who we are, we embark on a journey of discovery. Through our thoughts and emotions, we experience the energy of our inner being; through our sense perceptions, as we explored in chapter 3, we experience the energies of the outer world. All of these energies—inner and outer—are very accessible and immediate to us at any time. They are an experience of a subtle level of being and communicating with our world.

Becoming aware of who we are comes from the rub between our understanding and our experience. Insight arises, but we don't jump to conclusions, elaborate, analyze, or fit our insight into a system. We just remain open and let our insight be. There are no formulas, just possibilities. In this way, we allow our innate intelligence to be unencumbered. At the same time, we see how our personal data corresponds to the energies. We begin to see which energies are most pervasive, the ones with which we are most familiar and personally identify. By recognizing our energetic makeup, we learn to appreciate our natural traits and those of others.

HOW DO YOU ENVISION YOURSELF?

- What motivates you, gets you out of bed in the morning?
- What are you like in different situations?
- Do your emotions block you or serve you?
- Do you fixate on certain ideas, or are you more flexible?

- Can you balance your energies with all aspects of yourself engaged?
- Can you be fully who you are on the job?
- Can you bring your full attention to whatever you are doing?

By paying more attention to ourselves, being more self-reflective, we discover that we are all multidimensional. Defining ourselves in terms of one or two dominant energies could solidify our sense of who we are. It could make us more armored within our ego and give us all sorts of excuses for neurotic behavior. By fully embracing our style—the good, the bad, and the ugly of all we are—we find that we encompass more energies in our being. If we box ourselves into one or two, we miss the play of the totality, the full spectrum. When open to all that we are, rather than seeing ourselves as static, we could see ourselves as like a weather map, constantly moving.

We can continue to fine-tune our psychophysical barometer and pick up on the energetic climate of anyone or any situation. When we work with energetic reality, we can creatively apply our understanding anywhere, anytime, no matter what we are doing. We can work in any situation to improve self-awareness, communication, and creative expression. We see that everyone has his or her capacities, aptitudes, and preferences. Everyone engages the world in a unique way.

Here are some shortcuts to recognizing the dominant energies. Simply put, we can ask ourselves what we like. Do we like to know? to enrich? to feel? to do? or to just be? Perhaps there

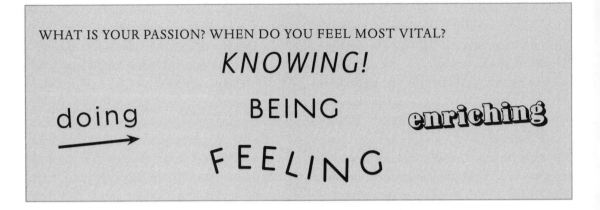

WHAT IS YOUR PASSION? WHEN DO YOU FEEL MOST VITAL?

KNOWING!

doing →   BEING   enriching

FEELING

is a combination. If we say yes to all, on the one hand, "Great; I know my mix," and on the other hand, maybe we need to dig deeper. We could also see if we are primarily concerned with being right or not, adequate or not, loved or not, competent or not, or simply don't care enough about anything. As well, a key to understanding our dominant energy is to ask, How do I desire the world? Hot? cool? many-colored? rich or sparse? exciting or calm? Are we intolerant of confusion, and do we insist on clarity in every situation? Are we always looking for someone to take care of us? Do we want no restrictions put on our energy and just want to go, go, go?

SHORTCUTS TO RECOGNIZING YOUR DOMINANT ENERGIES

• Do you like to know, to enrich, to feel, to do, or just to be?
• Do you have a favorite combination?
• Is your primary concern being right? adequate? loved? competent? indifferent?
• How do you desire your world? Exciting

and hot? calm and cool? colorful and rich? sparse and simple?
• What feels threatening: confusion? not feeling cared for? being held back when you want to act?

Our personality inherently has many facets. With some parts of ourselves, we have a lot of confidence and tend to shine. With other parts, we feel stuck and perpetually fall on our face. With still other parts, we may habitually hide. As well, when we spend every day locked into hours and hours of one kind of energy, we become energetically unbalanced. Living our day with just one quality of energy can be exhausting. We need our daily diet of five energies.

We all have moments when we feel synchronized with ourselves and our world. We experience a quality of openness, relaxation, and inner strength. At these times, our concepts drop away and we ride the energy of the moment. If we feel the sharpness and directness of vajra as we encounter our daughter's wild defiance, we can just let it be. If we find ourselves filled with the wind of karmic accomplishment, we can let it get us down to business. Suddenly flirtatious, we can let the padma energy bubble and spark. Reveling in earthy richness, we can enjoy the ratna feast without gluttony. Simple and calm, we can let buddha reign. These are times when we shine and are the best of who we are. At other times we can't get out of our own way. We solidify and fixate rather than ride the energy. We feel awkward at best or stuck in strong emotions at worst.

When our neurosis starts to fall away and we embody more of the wisdom colors, we can drop these categories: the distinctions of dominant, enhancement, mask, and so forth, no longer apply. Our mask becomes unnecessary. We can be who we are unreservedly. We can assimilate a complementary energy and thus dissolve the duality between self and other. We can become what we admire. We can use our qualities as skillful action in the world.

UNDERSTANDING YOUR ENERGETIC MAKEUP

Refer to the "How We Shine" and "How We Get Stuck" illustrations.

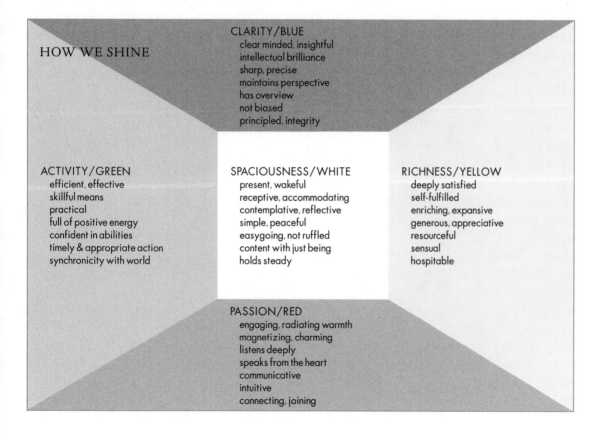

HOW WE SHINE

CLARITY/BLUE
clear minded, insightful
intellectual brilliance
sharp, precise
maintains perspective
has overview
not biased
principled, integrity

ACTIVITY/GREEN
efficient, effective
skillful means
practical
full of positive energy
confident in abilities
timely & appropriate action
synchronicity with world

SPACIOUSNESS/WHITE
present, wakeful
receptive, accommodating
contemplative, reflective
simple, peaceful
easygoing, not ruffled
content with just being
holds steady

RICHNESS/YELLOW
deeply satisfied
self-fulfilled
enriching, expansive
generous, appreciative
resourceful
sensual
hospitable

PASSION/RED
engaging, radiating warmth
magnetizing, charming
listens deeply
speaks from the heart
communicative
intuitive
connecting, joining

- See how many of the seven shining and stuck qualities you have in each energy.
  - Give yourself a number from 1 to 7 for each energy, depending on how many shining qualities and how many stuck qualities you have.
- What did you learn about yourself?

With others:
- Have several people who you know fairly well tell you how they see you.
  - They can assign you a number from 1 to

7 for the shining and stuck qualities of each energy.
- What did you learn about yourself?

COMING INTO BALANCE

As we work with the energies, we gain an understanding of who we are, how we view the world, how we interact with others, the environments we tend to inhabit, and what we enjoy and struggle with in our lives. We begin to see that we have all five energies in some

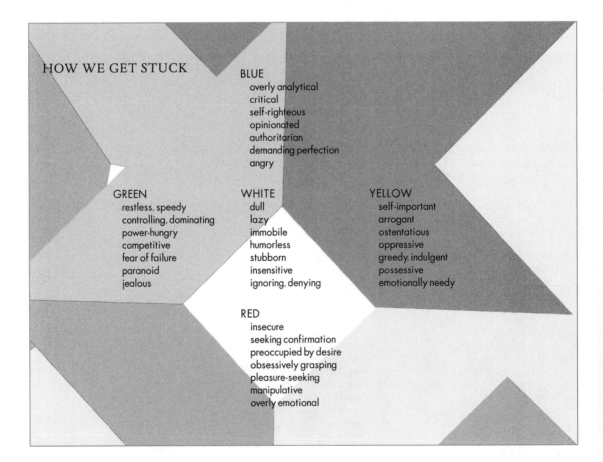

HOW WE GET STUCK

BLUE
overly analytical
critical
self-righteous
opinionated
authoritarian
demanding perfection
angry

GREEN
restless, speedy
controlling, dominating
power-hungry
competitive
fear of failure
paranoid
jealous

WHITE
dull
lazy
immobile
humorless
stubborn
insensitive
ignoring, denying

YELLOW
self-important
arrogant
ostentatious
oppressive
greedy, indulgent
possessive
emotionally needy

RED
insecure
seeking confirmation
preoccupied by desire
obsessively grasping
pleasure-seeking
manipulative
overly emotional

combination and discover our unique mix. As qualities or aspects of being fully human, the energies bring out the best of who we are with a sense of personal integration and wholeness. Knowing the particulars of each energy is like knowing the alphabet, but our unique mix is putting words and sentences together.

Without trying to box ourselves in or find a quick answer, we simply allow ourselves to contemplate our mix of colors. Remember that we are not trying to change or fix ourselves but to see ourselves in a new way. This is how we begin to have all the energies available to us. Becoming aware of all the colors, open to all the aspects of our own being, we can move freely from one energy to another. Becoming highly attuned to the energy needed in the moment, we can change gears. We can function impartially and relate to the total situation rather than latching onto one narrow perspective. We can ride the moment with wisdom activity. Ultimately, we can manifest whatever wisdom is needed in the moment.

We can cultivate an authentic presence, rest in basic being, think clearly and insightfully, be resourceful and generous, be personally engaged and speak from our heart, and accomplish our job efficiently. At different times in different circumstances, one or more of these qualities is needed. Each of our energies has the ability to serve us.

THE DYNAMIC PLAY OF THE WISDOMS

Once we have more understanding of energetic dynamics, we see that the energies play off one another in infinite ways. We can discover the amazing natural intelligence in how they manifest in the world. Here are some examples.

The core wisdom qualities of spaciousness, clarity, and warmth are the essence of buddha, vajra, and padma, respectively. Hence, the three primary intensified emotions of ignorance/denial, aggression, and passion correspond to them. Interestingly, these three came first historically. The fundamental truth that we can be both open and closed, clear and opinionated, and warm and cold seems pretty basic to human nature.

When vajra and padma become exaggerated, in either their neurosis or sanity, they move into karma and ratna qualities. Vajra and padma are more tentative; they allow more space for others. Ratna and karma are the strongest in their expression, very definite. Intensified vajra becomes karma: vajra is sharp and direct, especially with concepts; karma would like to execute that, make things efficient, organized, and secure. Vajra anger can lead to karma jealousy. Intensified padma becomes ratna: padma is seduction, and ratna indulges in that. Padma passion can lead to ratna greed.

The energies can also be seen as an expression of masculine and feminine qualities. Vajra and karma are the masculine energies associated with insistence on being right, competitiveness, and power. Padma and ratna are the feminine energies associated with engaging emotionally, attracting others, and creating enjoyable situations. Buddha is neutral: it is not gender specific. It is important to note that these gender classifications are energetic designations, not descriptions of women and men. We all have both feminine and masculine qualities.

Buddha is the foundation energy; it accommodates the others. It has an affinity to the energetic state we experience in meditation but amplifies it. When the wisdom of buddha permeates the other four, their wisdom arises. However, any energy overly intensified becomes dulled-out buddha. There is nowhere else to go: we zone out. So buddha energy is the fulcrum: experiencing its wisdom liberates the others; engulfed in its stupor, we experience the neurosis of the others.

If we overuse one color in our palette, it not only depletes that color, but the others get out of balance. For instance, if we go on overdrive with karma, vajra's clarity and ratna's nurturing qualities will be ignored and padma's fire will go out. In fact, we will most likely end up in buddha, but a neurotic buddha in which we fall asleep instead of a wisdom buddha in which we wake up. After our hard day at work, we try to meditate and all we experience is fatigue. We do not experience the awake quality of wisdom; we dull out. Instead, if we choose to practice meditation throughout the day, even for brief periods, we will find that the awake quality of buddha permeates everything we do. As buddha is the fulcrum, it is the energy to which we have to pay the most attention. Unfortunately, this is hard to do because it is so invisible, in the background.

As brilliant as we may be in one sphere, we may not be very evolved in another. For example, we could be highly developed intellectually but a babe in the woods when it comes to human interactions. We may prefer to work with complex material on our computer rather than engage with a coworker, particularly one of the opposite sex. In finding a partner, we might resort to a primal instinct: men go for a beautiful woman, and women desire the alpha male. How common is that? This human instinct—the most powerful man coupling with the most vital, youthful woman—is the epitome of the very powerful padma energy: padma wants the best. Although there is nothing inherently wrong with this, unfortunately, at midlife, men's power increases while women's physical beauty decreases. So if padma energy is our main motivator and dominates engagement with the other sex, it creates a middle-aged female population of left-behinds. A healthy relationship will include all the energies.

People with very similar energy patterns can manifest quite differently, depending on the situation. Our energetic patterns always interface with our life circumstance. Jason has lots of money and is constantly out on the town indulging in the pleasures of life with his many friends; Jack has little money but is very appreciative of his warm family ties and sharing a potluck meal with his community. This is padma/ratna expressed in quite different ways.

Combinations of energy also make a big difference. For instance, if James combines formidable intellect (blue) with a very personable manner (red), he could be a great teacher. If Liz has a lot of accomplishing energy (green) combined with a very personable manner (red), she would be out and about, perhaps becoming a great salesperson in marketing or real estate.

The relationship of buddha and karma is particularly interesting: the spaciousness of buddha and the windy quality of karma play off each other. Buddha energy ignores, but when it wakes up, it will speed on automatic with tunnel vision. It then looks like karma. Karma energy goes until it drops. Then it looks like buddha. The way these differ is that the inertia of karma is active resistance and procrastination, whereas the stillness of buddha is like being enveloped in a thick fog. In a more sane manifestation, karma energy knows when to go and when to stop. It is very intelligent about timing to make things efficient. Buddha energy can wait and wait and then press one button at the right time because it has found the perfect moment to act.

The dynamic between padma and karma is very prevalent in our society. The fire of padma can be a small flame, but together with the wind of karma, it will soon flare up into a bonfire of activity driven by passion. This can accomplish amazing things at work, but burnout could be just around the corner. Have you seen people who combine these energies when they are in love? They burn themselves out. Another way these two relate is that karma wind can suffocate padma fire. For instance, in our karma-driven society, it is very common for women to be sexually unfulfilled. Women's sexual energy is more associated with padma: they want meaningful connections from the heart. Male sexuality is more associated with karma, a sense of power. Does this sound familiar?

The dynamics between vajra and padma are also classic: in their neurosis, vajra is absolutely, rigidly clear, and padma is totally confused and desperate to be loved, confirmed. If two people strongly manifest these qualities, they could be very attracted to each other, but can they ever really communicate? Here is another one: karma wants to be respected; ratna wants to be needed. Do they meet each other's needs/desires? Jane, an interesting but rather low-profile person, and Richard, a big player in the world, parted ways, which greatly devastated Jane, at first. Then her career took off. She realized she could never have done this while still married to Richard. Why? Because she respected him more than she respected herself. This dynamic could have been workable with coworkers, but not in a marriage.

When completely stuck, rather than embracing our neurosis, we would all like to go to another energy. We would love to have a pill that we could pop as a quick antidote. Commonly we do this. For instance, if stuck in green, we get a quick "fix" of red energy; when stuck in red, we might go to green. However, habitually switching to another energy as an escape from dealing with the particular flavor of our stuck energy is not effective in the long run. We need to face our challenges. However, a conscious choice to go to another energy is a way to bring us into balance.

In looking at how the different styles fit in our society, we see which ones are rewarded and which ones are denigrated. What becomes obvious is how much karma energy has taken over. Our lives are so complex that this energy is an absolute necessity in order to survive. In the upper echelons, vajra wins the day. These are people who have worked their way to the top: they feel they know how things are and what to do and therefore have a right to tell others. So to a large extent karma and vajra run the show for us. It is thus inevitable that many feel ratna's low self-esteem, inadequate and unworthy, when surrounded by vajra's authoritarianism and karma's get-ahead mentality. Padma's energy is very much desired, but it comes out in desperate ways, like the lunchtime quickie.

A helpful tip: when in doubt, go to buddha. Hold still. Don't try to figure it out. Do nothing. From buddha, at the center of the mandala, we can go in any direction. Wait for clarity to arise. We might find that what we need is the grounding, nourishing qualities of ratna, or perhaps the melting softness of padma's heart.

SLOGANS, AS QUICK REMINDERS, CAN BRING US BACK TO THE WISDOM OF EACH ENERGY

- When in doubt, go to buddha.
- Practice unbiased perception.
- Appreciate the richness of the situation.
- Trust in your heart to compassionately intuit.
- Let your actions be humble offerings.

DISCOVERING YOUR MIX OF COLORS, YOUR ENERGETIC CONSTELLATION

This is a facilitated group exploration to see who you are: how you shine and get stuck.

- Set up a mandala on the floor.
  - Review the qualities of each energy in your mind. (Refer to the "How We Shine" and "How We Get Stuck" illustrations.)

- The facilitator guides group members through the following:
  1. Go to what you think is your inherent or dominant energy.
     - If you think you have two dominant energies, choose one.
     - Sit in a circle of not more than four people.
     - Take turns answering the question "Why did you choose this energy?"
     - Speak from experience, not concept.
     - If you are very confused, the facilitator could ask you, "Do you like to know, enrich, feel, act, or just be?"
     - When the groups are finished, the facilitator asks, "Did you make the right choice?" Those who did not can try another energy on the next round.
  2. Go to what you think is your enhancement, a sane manifestation.
     - You could also go to your second dominant and speak from there.
     - Do the same as you did in the first round.
  3. Go to what you think is your mask, your confused manifestation.
     - You could also go to your enhancement and speak from there.
     - Take turns answering the question "Why did you choose this energy?"
  4. Sitting in a circle with the whole group, the facilitator then asks, "Do you have more clarity?" and "Are you more confused?"
     - Although clarity is good, confusion keeps you questioning. It allows you to go deeper.

POSSIBLE FURTHER QUESTIONS AT A LATER TIME

1. Who do you know that has an energy that's complementary to your own? What is your relationship to this person?
2. What is the energy of your workplace, and how does it correspond to yours?
3. Which energy is missing in your life?
4. Which energy or energies do you need to make you feel more fulfilled?

YOUR ENERGETIC CONSTELLATION (ANOTHER VERSION)

Do this in a group with a facilitator. Everyone should have five colored index cards, one for each energy.

- The facilitator describes the essential characteristic of each energy, closed/open.
- Going through each of the energies in turn, the facilitator asks, "In what life situations, do you experience the _____ energy?"
- Note your responses on the card of the appropriate color, then place the cards in front of you.
- In small groups, share thoughts and feelings that have arisen.
  - Say which energy or energies seem dominant, an enhancement, and a mask.

MANDALAPLAY

This game can be played with a group of ten to forty people.

- Everyone chooses an energy and forms a team with others in the same energy. Try to have the teams somewhat evenly split.
- All five teams decide on a life situation, such as you won the lottery, you are experiencing your first kiss, you are dying, you are taking a vacation.
- Spend some time making up a skit to illustrate how your energy manifests through this situation.
- The teams will take turns enacting their skits.
- The teams that are watching note which qualities are being displayed.
- Scoring (see below):
  - There are a total of twenty qualities split among the four teams watching.
  - Each team names the qualities being displayed and gives a point for each. The total is that team's score for the game.
- The game ends when all the teams have done their skit. The team with the highest score wins.

BUDDHA SCORING

- For the vajra team:
  1. clarity,
  2. anger,
  3. abstraction,
  4. coolness and aloofness,
  5. sharpness
- For the ratna team:
  1. possessiveness,
  2. oppressiveness,
  3. expansiveness,
  4. richness,
  5. appreciation
- For the padma team:

1. discrimination, no bias,
2. concern with self-image,
3. desire,
4. compassion,
5. concern with relationship
- For the karma team:
  1. all-accomplishing action,
  2. cutting through,
  3. paranoia/insecurity,
  4. confidence in own abilities,
  5. efficiency

VAJRA SCORING

- For the buddha team:
  1. spaciousness,
  2. just being,
  3. ignoring, denial,
  4. learning by repetition,
  5. blissfulness
- For the ratna team:
  1. enriching,
  2. craving,
  3. fertility, potentiality,
  4. concern with self-worth,
  5. greed/hunger
- For the padma team:
  1. magnetizing, charm,
  2. radiating warmth, engaging,
  3. imagery/metaphors,
  4. emotional/excitable/dramatic,
  5. concern with communicating
- For the karma team:
  1. competitive/fear of failure,
  2. timely and appropriate action,
  3. activity/doing,
  4. project-oriented,
  5. stillness in motion

RATNA SCORING

- For the buddha team:
  1. absorbed,
  2. plodding,
  3. receptive,
  4. stubborn,
  5. accommodating
- For the vajra team:
  1. pacifying,
  2. visual perception,
  3. opinionated,
  4. withdrawn,
  5. visionary
- For the padma team:
  1. appreciation of beauty,
  2. bittersweet,
  3. sentimental/romantic,
  4. seduction,
  5. superficial/facade
- For the karma team:
  1. destroying,
  2. envy/jealousy,
  3. ambition,
  4. connecting/contacting,
  5. pragmatic

PADMA SCORING

- For the buddha team:
  1. flexible,
  2. nonaction,
  3. dull,
  4. stuck,
  5. inquisitive
- For the vajra team
  1. precision/detailed,
  2. intellectual/conceptual,

3. philosophical,

4. principled,

5. crisp

- For the ratna team:

  1. poverty-stricken,

  2. consuming,

  3. abundance,

  4. generosity,

  5. resourcefulness

- For the karma team:

  1. destroying,

  2. envy/jealousy,

  3. ambition,

  4. connecting/contacting,

  5. pragmatic

KARMA SCORING

- For the buddha team:

  1. stupidity,

  2. simplicity,

  3. inertia,

  4. everything OK,

5. sense of wonder

- For the vajra team:

  1. guilt/should,

  2. objective,

  3. boundaries,

  4. sparkling,

  5. analytical

- For the ratna team:

  1. equanimity, well-being,

  2. pride,

  3. smelling and tasting,

  4. amassing/collecting,

  5. concern with substantiality

- For the padma team:

  1. picky and fussy,

  2. unrequited love/broken heart,

  3. concern with intimacy,

  4. ambivalence/push and pull,

  5. seeking confirmation

The basic message here is that if we enjoy our mix of colors, they will dawn as wisdoms!

5

The Brilliance of the Five Wisdoms

THE PROGRESSION in our understanding of the Five Wisdoms goes like this: first it is all about me, then it is all about us, and finally it is all about all. At this point, it is like leaping into space: our perspective becomes transpersonal, non-self-referential, and vast. The Five Wisdoms view offers a perspective of self-existing wisdom, not appropriated by any godhead or religion.

ALL ABOUT ME, ALL ABOUT US, ALL ABOUT ALL

When the wisdom energies are brought to a personal level in an immediate and direct way, we can see ourselves more clearly. We are fascinated. We all so want to know who we are: our personal mix of colors and how we manifest. We might say, "Got it: I must be green," or we could become totally confused and want someone else to tell us who/what we are. So, to begin, it is "all about me." But why would we want to put ourselves in a box labeled "green" or "red" or "blue"? Then we take the perspective that we are a mix of colors. Our sense of "me" just got bigger.

Going further, we see it is all about us: the energetic dynamics in our relationships and in those with whom we identify (nationality, religion, profession). Seeing the way we engage with different people in different areas of our lives yields enormous insight into our patterns of behavior, emotions, and relationships. We find we feel more aligned and identified with some people and less so with others. At some point, we discover everyone's uniqueness: there are as many combinations as there are people in the world. As an esoteric Buddhist text says, "As many as there are sands in ten Ganges Rivers." We have just arrived in a very big, very colorful world!

Finally, we get to the point of seeing the interconnectedness of everyone and everything, the constantly moving, unceasing, dynamic, primal energy of the totality. This is a knowing that is transpersonal.

TRANSPERSONAL KNOWING

Ultimately the energies allow a transpersonal perspective. That contemporary scientists now see energy as the basis of everything is gratifying. Recognizing that the world is constantly in flux and impermanent corroborates the

Buddhist view. Science has finally caught up with the Buddha!

Interestingly, all Buddhist traditions acknowledge that the things of this world do not truly exist, an understanding that arises from the profound experience of emptiness (which some traditions call the divine). A Buddhist practitioner exists in the confused concrete world but acknowledges the absolute reality of emptiness. The goal is to renounce the relative world in order to experience the higher state of absolute reality. You get one or the other, your choice.

The special contribution of the Vajrayana or Tantric Buddhism of Tibet is to see appearance and emptiness as inseparable. A Vajrayana Buddhist lives fully in the relative world of appearance—embracing sensory perception, embodied experience, and the vicissitudes of life—yet acknowledges its ephemeral nature. Its allegiance to the energetic dimension is fundamental. In this dimension, all that is confused is also all that is intelligent; the two are inseparable. This allows us to completely embrace the relative world and simultaneously see its connection to ultimate reality: not one, not two. Living with sensitivity to energy creates a sense of sacred world—right here, right now. These Tantric teachings are the underpinnings of the Five Wisdoms. As well, the Five Wisdoms are an illumination of Tantra. If we understand one, we will understand the other.

Shambhala Buddhism, sourced in both Tantric Buddhism and the warrior tradition of Tibet, is based on an understanding of primordial, unconditioned energy: the ground and activating force of all that exists. Only a vast,

open state of mind—beyond the constricting mind of hope and fear—can experience this. So the practice is to raise our confidence, raise what is called windhorse. When we connect to a sense of basic goodness and unconditional confidence within ourselves, we experience this positive life force called drala, or wisdom energy. Whereas we understand the Five Wisdoms as the inseparability of wisdom and confusion, we understand drala as either present in places and situations or absent, a diminished power.

Embracing this view of existence with the confidence of windhorse allows us to connect to basic goodness in ourselves and our world. Though difficult to describe, windhorse can be experienced as a quality of wakeful sanity. It can be pointed to, recognized, and cultivated. It is close to us, and we can touch into it all the time. It has tremendous power, vital and energizing. It allows us to view the totality as an energetic process without the need to centralize on ourselves. This enables us to relate with life straightforwardly and directly. We train ourselves to cultivate an authentic presence capable of experiencing the magic of primordial energy. Our lives are felt fully and thoroughly so we appreciate that we are genuine, true human beings. We feel joy, we feel sadness—fully. Things feel real, ring true.

Quakers also have some understanding of this. They speak of the light within and the light in the world. One morning I attended a Quaker meeting with my parents during which time my father, aged ninety-one, spoke of the presence of god as even closer than ourselves. Over lunch, I asked him what he meant by *god*.

He said, "It is the fact of goodness even closer than ourselves." I could hardly believe he was saying this, so akin was it to my understanding of basic goodness. By using the word *fact*, he was talking about direct experience. By using the word *goodness*, he was pointing to something very omnipresent and accessible to all. By saying it is "even closer than ourselves," he was pointing to its being more primal than the self. I was very touched: he spoke to our common humanity beyond any religious designation.

On the one hand, basic goodness is very ordinary. It is so simple that we often miss it. We don't appreciate what is in front of us. On the other hand, it is magical: the experience of it is inspirational, beyond concept. We learn to align with the genuine experience of wisdom: simple, direct, and sane. It is not theoretical, conceptual, or idealized. We can have confidence enough to open our heart, feeling raw, tender, or perhaps sad in a sweet/sad way. Then we touch the depths of our being; there is a sense of perpetual warmth toward ourselves and others. Basic goodness is basic because it is primal; it is good because it is true. We can have a certain authentic pride that basic sanity exists in our state of being. Then our characteristics become our wisdoms.

As mentioned, wisdom is characterized by three basic qualities: openness, clarity, and warmth (buddha, vajra, and padma). Openness, or nondual awareness, is the fundamental way in which each of the energies becomes wisdom. Taking anything personally creates duality and thus inevitably elicits the neurotic aspect of the energies. An open perspective sees things as they are: empty of fixation but full of clarity. This self-existing awareness is more basic than the colorful display of the Five Wisdoms: it is wisdom beyond them yet also their source. When the inherent human qualities of openness, clarity, and warmth infuse each of the energies, they radiate as five types of wisdom, intelligence, or brilliant sanity.

As the Five Wisdoms perspective comes from a contemplative tradition that understands energy, it is beyond most ideas of wisdom. The wisdom energies provide an unparalleled opportunity to transform all that we see as negative or confusing into what is positive and wise. As the events of the world take their shifts and turns, holding our deepest values can be our guide, a rudder to keep us on course. From the perspective of the Five Wisdoms, the ability to do this lies in discovering the wisdom at the heart of confusion, a wisdom that responds to the energy of the moment with openness, clarity, and warmth.

In coming to understand energetic awareness, the analogy of light and refractions of light is often used. There is a sense of luminosity and radiation. Traditionally, a diamond or crystal is used as a metaphor for this: a colorless, sparkling brilliance that includes the full range of colors. Just as the color of light radiates, so do energetic qualities. We can also use the analogy of a rainbow. Like a rainbow, which we can see but not grasp, we know energy to be there, yet it is also not there to grasp. Things are simultaneously both there and not there: apparent but empty. Has everyone seen a rainbow? Yes. Has anyone ever touched one? Not likely. So it is there and not there.

When things radiate their essence, we want

to engage with them; they are magnetizing. We listen to a beautiful piece of music, smell a flower, sit and watch the clouds go by. However, we can only "catch" their radiance, their vitality, when we open to them. When we relate to the world in this way, we both feel its vibrancy and note that nothing stays the same; everything is inherently in flux, impermanent, ephemeral, and illusory.

> Since everything is an apparition, perfect in being what it is,
> Having nothing to do with good or bad, acceptance or rejection,
> One may well burst out in laughter.
>
> —LONGCHENPA, a major Buddhist teacher in the fourteenth century

---

ENERGETIC WISDOM

- Energy is the basic vitality of our existence.
- We can experience energetic wisdom as a positive life force.
- When we tune in to self-existing energy, we are empowered by it.
- We ride the energy of the moment, and our qualities become our wisdoms.

OPEN AND CLOSED ENERGY

We are affected by the energy around us whether we are aware of it or not. When we are unaware, energy has the upper hand and we feel tossed around by life's circumstances. When we are aware of the play of energy, we can ride it. With awareness, we can gauge our atmospheric condition in a given situation, sensing the energy of the moment, whether "open" or "closed." We can begin to see that habitual patterns of closing take us out of the moment. We literally lose track of where we are.

Energy in the environment is fundamentally neutral: it is what it is. It can seem tremendously inviting, seductive. OK, maybe so, but not to everyone. To some, it seems malevolent. Ultimately, it is just energy doing its thing. What happens happens. Energy is not personal; it is self-existing. Energy is neutral; it is our attitude toward it that determines whether we are open (sane) or closed (confused). When we are open to our own energy, we experience ourselves as spacious, warm, and clear. When we are closed to our energy, we feel confused and stuck. Being open or closed determines how we view ourselves and consequently the world: we can experience energy as inspirational or threatening.

The wonder of our world's diversity never ceases to amaze me. We are all uniquely ourselves, yet we are one in the basic goodness of our humanity. This is brought home again and again in my travels. No matter what our circumstances, we can touch our inner wisdom. I am reminded of Etty Hillesum, who, as she walked the barbed-wire fence of a concentration camp by moonlight, reflected on how wonderful the world is. So this is possible: it has been done before and will be done again. We can light the torch of wisdom to illuminate the darkness of suffering and confusion we see around us. After all, it takes only one match to bring light into a dark room. We can rouse a wholehearted intention to work with ourselves and others to create a better world. Even two

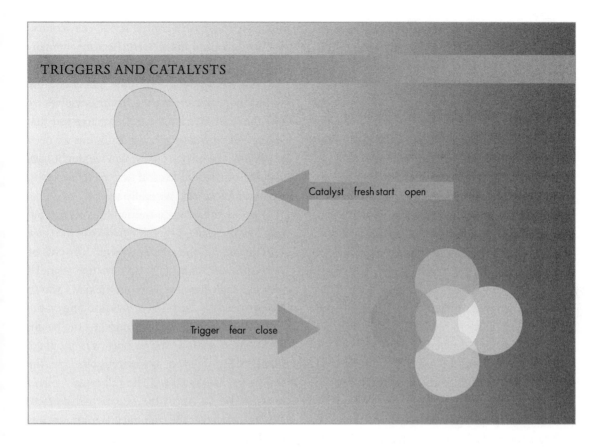

TRIGGERS AND CATALYSTS

Catalyst   fresh start   open

Trigger   fear   close

of my tango teachers agree. Their slogan is, "Creating a better world, one tango at a time."

Life is constantly challenging us to open to the situation, to embrace the fullness of the moment, or shrink from it, go into self-protective armoring. In any given moment, we could say yes or no. The *no* is the inertia of our confusion; the *yes* is the innate confidence of our wisdom. We do this all the time. We wake up or go to sleep. We discover that our confusion and our sanity exist in a common matrix of energy. When we expose those parts of ourselves that we like the least, we gently, lovingly, embrace them. Being aware of energetic

dynamics creates the possibility of aligning with our sanity and choosing to say, "Yes!"

TRIGGERS AND CATALYSTS

It is helpful to get more specific about what situational energy closes us and what opens us. I call these situational energies triggers and catalysts. Triggers are sensed threats: when afraid, we close down to protect ourselves. Catalysts are inspiration: we open up and are receptive. When we freeze and withdraw from the world, we feel stuck, dense, and claustrophobic. When we are open and welcoming, we experience the play of energies as full of possibility. We ride the edge between confusion and sanity: anything we do can be done with either a neurotic twist or a wisdom twist. Sometimes we invite the energy and join with it; sometimes we resist it. When open, we experience five qualities of intrinsic sanity. When constricted, we are most likely self-referencing. We can be open or closed, fluid or frozen, intelligent or confused. Simply put, we react to triggers; we respond to catalysts.

Let's look at an analogy: the energy that a battery generates is a function of its positive and negative poles. Our energetic poles are similarly constantly at play: one moment we are crying, the next laughing. When we laugh and cry at the same time, we are fully energized! We need both to be full. Our wisdom is our brilliance, skill, genius, how we shine, the best of who we are. Our neurosis is our "shadow," parts of ourselves we like the least, our stuck places. It is crucial that we recognize and own these states. That is where the juice is. Usually we flip-flop between extremes of feeling good or bad about ourselves and never find any real bridge or connection between these two states. The power of the Five Wisdom energies teachings is that they show us how we can find our wisdom within the very darkness of our confusion: then we are energized, not polarized.

At the most intense times, our emotions arise as a vivid display of energy. "Feeling" emotion is both psychological and physical, so it affects us psychophysically: we become mentally constricted and have bodily tension. At times when we experience intense emotion, our wisdom is also very close at hand. Fully embracing the emotions that bind us can liberate us. If we are aware of our habitual patterns and our default emotions, we have a choice; if not, they control us. We get out of balance and become mentally or physically sick. The whole process of coming into our wisdom could be quite messy because we first need to expose the parts of ourselves we like the least. We might feel embarrassed that we have such dark places inside us, but we need to get into the nitty-gritty, which we might have avoided our whole lives. If we try to bypass it, we never know who we really are.

One day there was a tremendous storm. Sitting quietly inside, I was able to take in the powerful energy of the elements: wind, torrents of rain, thunder, lightning. Isn't nature grand! I was so delighting in it. Later in the day, I was to travel to Amsterdam. There was flooding on the roads. Could the car get through? At the height of vacation season, the airport was mobbed. Planes were delayed. I was rebooked. In the shuffle my bag got lost. The full catastrophe. I resisted the situation the storm had created. When I arrived at the training program, my lost bag became a topic of conversation, and other stories poured out: it was a bonding experience. My situation created some amusing encounters: "Does anyone have some underwear I could borrow?" Over the course of this experience, I watched my mind flip-flop dozens of times: open, closed, open, closed (damn it) . . . open.

OUTER CIRCUMSTANCES CAN EXACERBATE OUR CONFUSION AS WELL AS PROMOTE OUR SANITY

What are you doing to arrange your life so it promotes your sanity?

So how can we stay open to the energy within and around us? We need to catch ourselves being ourselves—catch ourselves in the act. We can learn so much from our energetic comeback: are we overly reactive or appropriately responsive? When we have direct experience that, in a given moment, we teeter on the edge between our neurosis and our sanity, this is a big step: my bag is lost forever, and I will never again see the ring my mother gave me; relax, it's only a ring. We see how our habitual patterns close us when we fixate, solidify, and believe things to be true. We see how we can open in the moment and glimpse the true nature of reality: life is full and life is empty. No big deal. When we can catch ourselves in that very moment, our response can come down to simply making a choice: "Why, yes, I think I would prefer to be open. It really does feel so much better. What a brilliant idea. Thank you."

REWRITING OUR HISTORY:
CAN YOU TURN A TRIGGER
INTO A CATALYST?

- Recall a situation that triggered you.
- Now reconsider that situation in terms of how it could have inspired you, how it could have been a catalyst.

What we come back to again and again is that fundamentally our sanity is intrinsic: we are good, sane, intelligent people. We have a soft spot and can relate to the world in a gentle way. When we experience a sense of well-being, we know this. The problem is, we keep forgetting.

We can train ourselves to have access to our goodness in the moment, whatever occurs. The basic point here is that it is our attitude, our state of mind, that determines whether we are open or closed. This is good news because we can actually do something about it. We can let the storm be the storm and enjoy it or not. What we are trying to eliminate is not our style itself but rather the frozen, dysfunctional version of it.

It is not that we filter every minute of our day through the perspective of the five colors. However, some situations become clear and workable only when we connect to their energetic dynamic. Eventually we become more sophisticated about the whole process. We become connoisseurs of our confusion and relax into our wisdom. We celebrate our strengths and see our weaknesses as work points, or growth areas. The ease we begin to feel in our basic being creates a sense of potentiality: we are more able to encompass the totality.

As all the energies become more accessible and are included, we become capable of switching gears. If a situation needs this, it's easy to do this; if it needs that, we can do that. We don't have just one energy regardless of the situation. When we reach this point, the energies have become skillful means, tools. We are ready to meet the world, no matter what the circumstances. If we resist, confusion and struggle arise. Responding proficiently to the demands of a situation with all our energies is a very sophisticated approach—one that we can cultivate over time.

THE PRACTICE OF THE FIVE WISDOMS
By far the most exceptional thing about these teachings is that we can directly experience

the energy of the Five Wisdoms. Chögyam Trungpa Rinpoche devised the practice of using five different postures in colored rooms—reminiscent of forms of Tantric yoga—to work with the energy of our body and evoke specific psychophysical qualities. In traditional Buddhist practices these same energetic qualities are personified as wisdom deities. Historically the Five Wisdoms, or five Buddha families, come from early Vajrayana or Tantric Buddhist teachings in India around A.D. 400–500. Later these teachings took root and flourished within Tibetan Buddhism.

Presented without the trappings of traditional Buddhist teachings, the postures are unique to Chögyam Trungpa. In keeping with his genius for making esoteric practices immediate and accessible, he introduced the postures to the West, allowing us to have a direct and vivid experience of the energetic qualities of our body, speech, and mind. Because the postures heighten or intensify energy, they are considered a Vajrayana practice. They penetrate and illuminate our dark corners with a laser beam. Stirring up buried emotions, confusion, and irritation, posture practice holds up a magnifying glass to each nuance of our being. The practice challenges habitual patterns that might have been locked in our body for years and intensifies whatever stuck patterns are present. By heightening the pattern of energy and surrounding it with loving-kindness, we can transmute it into brilliant sanity. This is the power of the practice.

While working with people in the use of these postures, I have observed a number of things. People may have done Vajrayana practice for a long time but in a cerebral way. Others may have done talk therapy but remain stuck. Working with the power of embodied energy, people are opened in an immediate and direct way. Everyone is a beginner when it comes to doing the postures. As a training participant in his sixties said, "It got me to a place I had never been before, painful yet liberating."

It has never ceased to amaze me that people—not everyone every time but often enough—with no prior knowledge of the qualities can do a posture for twenty to thirty minutes and give a textbook description of their experience of both the wisdom and neurotic qualities. How can this be? The answer requires an understanding of embodied wisdom and the practices that work with the energy channels and centers in our body (which are beyond the scope of this book). Observing people's reactions to the postures over a period of thirty-some years has given me a lot of trust in them. For me, these reactions constitute proof of their authenticity.

Our realization and actions are of one mind. We see how our innate qualities become our unique brand of wisdom. We can use our qualities as skillful action in the world. When our neurosis falls away, then there are just wisdoms, wisdom activity. *Be who you are* is the core teaching of the five wisdom energies.

THE FIVE WISDOMS AS A PRACTICE AND A PATH TO BECOME THE BEST OF WHO YOU ARE

Do this with a partner.
- Tell your partner who you are in a very spontaneous, free way.
- Do this for about five minutes.

- In particular, take note of where you are stuck and where you shine.
- Then switch roles.

As an alternative, do this on your own by writing it down.

Working with the five energies is a path of insight, not a conceptual overlay or a system to use by rote. The more we make a project out of the five energies, the less genuine our connection to them will be. Working with the five energies is an expansion of our awareness and a spontaneous way of interacting with the world.

When we bring the energies into our everyday lives, it is as if our world is illuminated by the play of the energies. We see both how people shine and how they get stuck. We become sensitive to environments where our energy is constricted and those where we feel completely at ease. We don't have to take things so personally because we see it all as just a play of energy. This is much easier said than done, but at least holding that view is a good start.

The Five Wisdoms are like the family jewels. They are the ornaments that make us shine. As we know, jewels are derived from rocks, so our practice is to polish them again and again to bring out their different facets.

Part Two

● ● ● ● ●

The Five Wisdoms Applied

6

A Quiet Presence

I<small>T WAS NOT UNTIL</small> halfway through a conference on sustainability—where we were doing the Five Wisdoms practice—that I realized what my role is. My contribution is working with people to help them become sustainable. What do the Five Wisdoms have to do with sustainability issues? Everything! Cultivating sustainable well-being in people is pivotal in how we can be players, rather than victims, in the world. It is at the core of every human effort. More and more people are realizing that the best is within us and we can access that goodness through contemplative practices.

> The simple realization that people are our only real asset illustrates the core of what will probably determine which countries and which organizations will thrive in the 21st century.
>
> —P<small>ETER</small> S<small>ENGE</small>, author of *The Fifth Discipline* and founding chairperson of the Society for Organizational Learning at MIT

This part of the book is about applying our understanding of the Five Wisdoms in the world. However, we must first establish home base. We can use "home" as a metaphor for coming into our basic being and for feeling the warm hearth of home. Coming home—to ourselves, to our basic being, to a quiet presence—is perhaps the most effective thing we can do to find happiness and a sense of inner peace and strength. Why? Because all qualities that are ultimately fulfilling are within us. Let's look at how we can be of benefit from home base.

> The leaders of this global revolution will be people of quiet presence, the calm ones at the center of great corporate and global enterprise.
>
> —J<small>OHN</small> J. G<small>ARDINER</small>, professor of educational leadership at Seattle University

> If you reach deeply into yourself, you are reaching into the very essence of mankind . . . the generating depth of consciousness that is common to all mankind. The individual's ability to be sensitive to that becomes the key to the change of mankind.
>
> —D<small>AVID</small> B<small>OHM</small>, quantum physicist

As mentioned, buddha energy is the one that is most absent in our Western culture. It can be accessed through meditation, a time-proven way to come home to a sense of basic being. The practice of meditation is the foundation of the path for working with ourselves. It is the keystone that locks everything together. It is our primary tool for working with ourselves and integral to working with the energies. Meditation allows us to take a break in our daily life, not with a sense of flop but with sense of awake, alert. How good is that?

Our state of being is the real source of our ability to change the world.

—John J. Gardiner, professor of educational leadership at Seattle University

MEDITATION MAKES NEWS

An article on meditation in the August 2004 issue of *BusinessWeek* had this to say: "Stress does amp up performance to a certain level but sustained too long, it erodes productivity. Some businesses are now providing meditation instruction and a quiet room to practice." The article added, "Health insurers are starting to realize that meditation, like preventative health and exercise programs, may help them control costs."

This is no surprise to researchers at the University of Massachusetts and the Mind/Body Medical Institute at Harvard University. For many years now, they "have sought to document how meditation enhances the qualities companies need in their human capital: sharpened intuition, steely concentration, and plummeting stress levels" (*BusinessWeek* Online, August 30, 2004). In an article Richard Davidson, a professor of psychology and psychiatry at the University of Wisconsin at Madison, says, "Buddhism has directed its energy inward to train the mind to understand the mental state of happiness, to identify and defuse sources of negative emotion, and to cultivate emotional states like compassion to improve personal and societal well-being." The Dalai Lama, preeminent Tibetan world leader and winner of the Nobel Peace Prize, is supporting the work of neuroscientists as they attempt to understand how meditation works.

Mainstream society's increasing interest in Buddhism, Buddhists, and meditation is an interesting development in our contemporary world fraught with disharmony. As my son says, "Buddhism has cachet." In particular, the meeting of science and Buddhism creates some intriguing possibilities. Like science, Buddhism is based on experience and investigation, not on dogma. The Buddha himself said not to take anything to be true unless we have found that truth within ourselves. We have empirical proof from many meditators; now science can test and prove the benefits of meditation. Though anyone who has meditated for any amount of time needs no scientific proof of its benefits, this juxtaposition of the best of the East and the West strengthens the case for meditation. East and West are working together. This is good news!

Mindfulness is contemplation, meditation—and it is not only for Buddhists. Most spiritual traditions, including Christianity, Hinduism, Judaism, and Islam, have profound contemplative practices. The Buddhist approach to mindfulness, however, is often seen as a valuable tool for people of all faiths (or no faith) because it doesn't require a belief system. Therefore, it's possible to engage in Buddhist-style mindfulness without having to give up a belief in Allah or science or skepticism or any other form of belief.

—Andrea Miller, "The Mindful Society,"
Shambhala Sun

Current research finds that the neural characteristics of the brain change in the meditative state. Powerful mind-monitoring technologies enable scientists to scan a mind in the midst of meditation as well as to "detect enduring changes in brain activity months after a prolonged course of meditation." (Stephen S. Hall, *New York Times,* September 14, 2003) revealing fascinating insights about the plasticity of mind and meditation's ability to alter it." They have discovered that meditation changes the brain's biochemistry. In particular, the left prefrontal cortex, associated with positive emotion, becomes enlarged and more active.

When study participants are tracked over time, researchers find "enduring changes in brain activity months after a prolonged course of meditation." They also find that meditation causes physiological changes not only in the brain but in the immune system as well. Changes in neural physiology allow people to experience more equanimity and be more detached from emotional reactions, and hence respond more appropriately. Reducing stress, defusing negative emotion, and improving our immune system are what we now understand we can expect from meditating. In short, the power of meditation can be harnessed to promote not only emotional but also physical well-being. Science has been the truth sayer, but in seeming contradiction to spiritual values. Now science itself points to a fundamentally different understanding of the world and our place in it. Finally science is catching up with the Buddha. This is indeed newsworthy.

I prefer to meditate, I have come to view my meditating as serving. Somehow the quiet and peace of anyone's meditation communicates and enriches the culture. I feel the fruits of other people's meditation.

—Robert K. Greenleaf

Leaders today are faced with global economies, time measured in internet seconds, and a future that is increasingly interdependent—challenges that require leaders to use all of their capabilities, including the innate abilities of mindfulness. Yet, we are not usually taught to cultivate the brain's ability to be present, to be focused, to be less reactive, to listen deeply. . . . To date, employees at all levels—including more than eighty vice presidents and directors—have participated in mindfulness programs ranging from a half-day to seven weeks. . . . General Mills' human resources department does not offer or announce these programs. Instead, participants have been so moved by the impact of mindfulness training on their work that news of the programs has spread completely by word of mouth. One key factor contributing to the programs' success is that they are secular.

—Janice Marturano,
vice president of General Mills

FINDING OUR WAY

Within us is an energy potential as real as radium or uranium, a potent source that can literally "turn us on." We might already know some ways of coming back to a sense of being in order to recharge. When we settle into just being with ourselves, for even a few moments, we find our potency. When we synchronize or align ourselves through centering exercises, such as focused breathing or meditation, we touch into our natural resource, our vital energy. If we do not have time to do that on a regular basis, we find ourselves running out of gas through the day, the weeks, the months, the years. Having a daily practice discipline that benefits mind and body seems essential.

A daily discipline, a practice, takes a great deal of investment if we are to reap its rewards. It involves being so committed to what we are doing that outer activities don't steal our mind away. We see this kind of commitment in those who take up sports or an art form. We are awed by the prowess of such individuals and find them inspiring. Martha Graham, a woman of grand style who was a major contributor to the development of modern dance over seven decades, knew the discipline it takes to attain excellence.

> Practice means to perform, over and over again in the face of all obstacles, some act of vision, of faith, of desire. Practice is a means of inviting the perfection desired. I believe that we learn by practice. Whether it means to learn to dance by practicing dancing or to learn to live by practicing living, the principles are the same. In each, it is the performance of a dedicated precise set of acts, physical or intellectual, from which comes shape of achievement, a sense of one's being, a satisfaction of spirit.
> —Martha Graham

I feel fortunate to have learned the rewards of discipline early in life, as a dancer. To perfect a turn, a jump, or a movement ending up on someone's shoulder, we have to do it many, many times. It takes strong motivation and diligence. Once we get it, it is effortless and we do it with ease. Nevertheless, coming to the practice and study of Buddhism at the height of my dancing career was not easy. It uprooted most of my concepts about life, dancing, and art. Though as a professional dancer and the director of my company, I showed confidence, capability, and creativity, inside I knew things were not quite right. I was driven by elation and despair. As many of us did in the 1960s, I was seeking a spiritual path, though I was hardly aware of it at the time.

To my dismay, when I first started sitting, I found it to be the hardest thing I had ever tried to do. Like others, I often felt it was a complete waste of time. Chögyam Trungpa's retort has been, "Please waste time." The hardest injunction for many of us to follow is "Don't just do something, sit there." As I was naturally active, outgoing, and creative, the sheer act of sitting still confounded me. The very idea of taking an hour out of my day to just sit seemed inconceivable. The one thing that made sense to me, as a dancer, is that I understood discipline. I realized that talking and reading about it would only go so far. I had to do it. So I sat. At that point, I felt I had danced my way into stillness. When meditation started to take a hold on my being, I discovered how stillness informs dance.

TAKE THIS MOMENT NOW
Just be. Be spacious, breathing stillness. Be a quiet presence.

The juxtaposition of our distress and the possibility of relief from it is a primary motivation to put us on the path of practice. As practice becomes part of our life, it is helpful to have an understanding of our psychology and how meditation will affect it. From a Buddhist perspective, the particular predicament we find ourselves in as human beings is that we are not only propelled by desire but also believe that what we desire truly exists. In fact, the more we desire something, someone, the more "real" he/she/it seems. "I want that because I can't live without it." If we do not get what we want, we complain vociferously, feeling wronged and unworthy. Whatever we are attached to, that is what binds us. It is our downfall. Like Winnie-the-Pooh, who gets stuck in the hole because he so desires the honey inside, we become similarly trapped by our desires. In short, we are victims of our own mind.

We tend to trust complexity: complicated answers, complicated logic. Meditation is a way of simplifying the logical mind, which attempts to fixate, hold on to, grasp, and take things to be definite and solid. However, the thought of doing one thing repeatedly, as Martha Graham suggests, is unattractive. The thought of doing nothing for a period of time is even less desirable. So although the basic practice of simplifying our active mind into just breathing might be the best thing for us, it is hard to commit to. Its very simplicity is disarming.

As helpful as meditation is, we might face numerous obstacles. For many the taming effect of sitting still and setting aside thoughts is not attractive. It is an outrage to the creative mind, to the industrious person. Resistance can be a major obstacle. As well, it can perpetuate a black and white, good and bad, worldview. Our radar as to what is right and wrong becomes heightened: we long for an open state of mind and beat ourselves up when we feel constricted. We feel we are being good when we practice and being bad when we don't. We experience a heightened self-consciousness. We can't act because we are afraid of exposing our neurosis, so we shut down. I call this contemplative constipation.

There are two basic ways we resist: we either cling to certain states or want to eliminate everything. When we fixate on something and build it up, we feel we could finally figure it all out: win the game. We are propelled by our triple-espresso "I'm feeling good" state of mind. We want to continually find ways to rouse and hold on to what we most desire. This is an addictive mentality. On the other hand, we could want to eliminate, pacify, calm down, become increasingly secluded, and withdraw from life. We want to get rid of the difficult stuff so we can be truly spiritual. This is like trying to push back the ocean waves or hold off the avalanche.

The way these states manifest in meditation is that we either get lost in thought or rigidly resist each thought that arises. These are ways of being lazy: we are not attentive enough to what we are doing. We are gone, gone, gone from the present moment. So we lose our inspiration. When we hold our intention, keep it in our heart, then we can use the powerful instrument of meditation practice—being attentive moment to moment—to work with ourselves.

UNDERSTANDING OUR MIND

Buddhist teachings on karma are very helpful in unraveling the conundrum of human existence.

Karma is a self-existing universal law, the study of cause and result: our thoughts, feelings, and actions and their consequent effects. Whatever we put out, negative or positive, will have a corresponding result. Our life situations come about through a complex mix of causes and conditions. We not only participate in creating these situations, but once enmeshed in them, we react to them. We marry the person we think we love only to find he or she is not exactly the perfect being we thought and end up feeling trapped. How common is that?

Being carried away by the dramas of our life causes so much of our suffering. We sabotage our sanity. We think we can avoid psychological pain and unwanted experiences. So it is hard to catch ourselves being ourselves. In the midst of a situation, we tend to decide what to do based on impulse rather than good sense: we react rather than respond. We dig ourselves deeper into our hole. If we are aware of our habitual patterns, we have a choice; if not, we are slaves to them. By becoming aware of our habitual patterns, we become sensitized to what is wholesome and unwholesome in our life. The decision-making process can be a way to discriminate between what is or is not most beneficial.

The good news is that awareness is more powerful than karma, so it is the tool that allows us to progress along the path and work through our karma. Quite simply, if we pay attention to our thoughts and feelings and can act in ways that are in line with our understanding of cause and result, we have taken the first step in being on the path. We need not use complex methods; the most important thing is awareness. It is always on the mark. Our only real safety zone is to be able to meet with awareness whatever arises.

FOLLOWING A PATH

Buddhists talk about their practice as "being on the path." We arrive on the path because we have a vague idea that something is not quite right. We have tried to maintain the fiction that we are not suffering, that we are OK, but it is not working. We are somewhat embarrassed about the pain, chaos, and confusion we find ourselves in. Because we fear exposing ourselves, we try to hide behind coping mechanisms. We might feel that our pain is our little secret, but in fact, we all have it, so it's very public. Getting on the path involves committing to exposing what is there. As well, we might begin to taste another way of being, which in turn makes us more curious about what this path has to offer.

We could see our whole life in terms of a journey of awareness. As important as it is to open to the mysteries of our inner world, we can get too caught up in ourselves. It is equally helpful to commit to an authentic discipline. A balance between open, creative self-exploration and discipline works best. As Merce Cunningham, preeminent modern dance choreographer, once said, "Too much discipline dulls the mind; too much creativity makes the body flabby" (or the mind mushy). As Chögyam Trungpa said many times, "Not too tight; not too loose."

Time and again I notice how slippery the mind is. We create endless justifications for our thoughts and actions that sabotage our best interests. We are lazy—too lazy to wake up. We forget, alienate ourselves from what feels good. We feel insecure about ourselves and thus shrink from the best of ourselves. We would rather keep up a good facade, go with the flow, snuggle into a comfort zone. Desiring comfort is human and not a problem; when it is a substitute for awakening, we might be missing something more fulfilling. Yet taking on a daily practice seems somewhat antithetical to what feels natural. It is not so surprising, then, that the child going to school for the first time, when asked by his mother how it was, says, "It was fine, but I have to go back tomorrow." Most of us get so caught up in the mundane tasks of life that we feel we have no time for anything else. But is this really the case? Writer H. Jackson Brown commented, "Don't say you don't have enough time. You have exactly the same number of hours per day that were given to Helen Keller, Pasteur, Michelangelo, Mother Teresa, Leonardo da Vinci, Thomas Jefferson, and Albert Einstein." And then there is Barack Obama.

TAKING OUR SEAT: MINDFUL AWARENESS

Meditation is based on a very sophisticated understanding of mind. Synchronizing body, speech, and mind is the act of being fully present. Being in the present moment stabilizes the mind and realigns us into energetic balance. When we are attentive to the present moment, we are not jumping from one distraction to another, nor are we engrossed in our thoughts and emotions. Instead, we are attentive to what we are doing in the moment in which we are doing it. Training the mind to settle is unparalleled as a pacifying and stress-reducing technique. Acknowledging, but not indulging, our thoughts and coming back to basic being is the most skillful thing to do. A stabilized mind is a sustainable mind.

It is a way of looking at what is, not indulging in spiritual transcendence. Understanding the skillful means of meditation also provides an understanding of any discipline and can be applied to any activity. When we synchronize our body posture, our breathing, and our mind by staying in the moment, we feel at our best. This is fundamentally true whether playing the violin or doing the dishes. There is a reciprocal relationship between body, breath, and mind; when we focus on one, the others come along. We develop conscious mind, conscious breathing, and conscious body.

An organization that incorporates mindfulness enjoys psychological, spiritual, and emotional well-being. Mindfulness creates acuity of presence, acuity of decision making, and acuity of collaboration.

—Amy Fox, executive coach and vipassana meditator

In the practice of meditation, the way to be daring, the way to leap, is to disown your thoughts, to step beyond your hope and fear, the ups and downs of your thinking process. You can just be, just let yourself be, without holding on to the constant reference points that mind manufactures. You do not have to get rid of your thoughts. They are a natural process; they are fine; let them be as well.

—Chögyam Trungpa

The precision of mindfulness expands to awareness. As the mind settles and becomes more focused, it naturally expands. This kind of awareness has no object. Whatever arises in our surroundings is part of the atmosphere. Not only do we become more aware of what is around us, but we also recognize the insubstantiality of our experience. Rather than one-pointed attentiveness, there is a lighter touch.

In meditation, our grand attempts to cover up our pain begin to unravel. The simplicity of the technique exposes us completely. It's like walking onstage, under the spotlight, naked. Working with the breath brings us closer to our body and emotions. A heightened awareness allows us to contact the deepest parts of ourselves, making it impossible to escape from ourselves. We are right there looking at ourselves moment after moment. We become aware of our restless body, erratic breath patterns, and overly active mind. The discipline is a crystal clear mirror.

Two things become obvious. On the one hand, emotional upheavals seem more exaggerated, more flagrant. It is not that they actually are but that we are much more aware of them as our neurosis comes to the surface. On the other hand, we could experience a taming quality in our being. The technique allows both space for things to arise and a way to work efficiently with whatever arises. Sitting meditation acts like a lightning rod. It grounds overly volatile energy in the simplicity of just being here. There is no need to hang on to anything. Nothing is that important. We can just let go. Through continued practice, the dropping away of the busyness allows us to experience a simple sense of being and cultivate a

dispassionate awareness of our endless dramas. Awareness and life become one.

MINDFULNESS IN ACTION

Try this: for a week brush your teeth with mindful awareness. Bring one-pointed attention to this task. The result might be not only whiter teeth but a sparkling mind.

Jane had a pattern of getting speeding tickets when driving home from visiting her family. She would often be in emotional turmoil and put her foot on the gas. Then one day she practiced simply paying attention to (being mindful of) the speedometer. This allowed her to relax. No speeding ticket.

Attentiveness develops precision; awareness develops panoramic vision. Settling the mind by attending to the present moment brings relaxation. Relaxation creates the space in which to see clearly what is happening in the moment. We begin to have direct experience without the reference point of the self. No one needs to watch and keep track.

Awareness gives us the freedom to receive the total environment and interact with it attentively. It allows us to develop appreciation for where we are. Most people report that after a session of sitting quietly, they find the world to be much more vivid and alive. When we are open in this way, we aren't thrown off by circumstances, because we are more stable. Within the stillness of mind, the activity of mind can be seen more clearly. When we fully open in this moment, the next situation arises out of it naturally. We gain trust in the moment. In letting things be, we allow them to unfold in their own way.

The relationship between the precision of mindfulness and the spontaneity of awareness became very vivid for me when the focus of my creativity shifted from choreography to improvisational work. Rather than hone and polish a product created in the past, it seemed more natural to let things arise in the moment of performance. I value and appreciate both. What intrigues me is the difference in mind-set from which each arises: one from precision, the other from open awareness.

Awareness is "going with the flow." When I bring my mind to stillness and hold my seat, whatever happens, I will not get upset. Alternatively, if I become speedy and caught up in the circumstances of a situation, flying all over the place, I react negatively to the slightest inconvenience. Speed is the glue of habits, so cutting speed and distraction helps create room for something fresh. Awareness allows us to see things clearly and position ourselves wisely in relationship to them. We become more aware of our mistakes and so learn from them. We discover ever-greater confidence and humility. We can move into the way of conscious living.

I had touched the timeless awareness . . . a place of peace and power, harmony and joy, a place of unconditional love. I had also touched my dharma of truth directly, knowing then that my life mission was to bring people together to help to heal themselves and, thereby, the planet.

—JOHN J. GARDINER

WARM HEART AT HOME

When we come home, come to stillness, our heart opens. We give our heart enough space to feel itself. Rather than perpetually acting on our desires, we stay with our heart and feel its fullness. We are more available to others because we have less anxiety about ourselves. We allow our heart warmth to embrace ourselves and others. By having fully experienced the poignancy of our own life journey, we are more open to others. The more we have tasted our own stuck places, the more we are able to meet others in their stuck places. The more intimate we become with self and other, the more universal is our understanding of self and other; we transcend the particulars of people to touch the universal truths of humanity.

We can also find a warm heart in the most surprising situations: Union Station, Washington, D.C., Memorial Day. The place is mobbed. I am just back from Amsterdam, had a two-hour delay at the Washington airport, and am trying to get a train ticket to Philadelphia. I am tired, hungry, impatient, and definitely going into a "poor me" mode. The woman at the ticket counter, while helping me, has one person after another get her attention. To a slightly disabled young woman: "Don't worry. I have not forgotten you. I will let you know." To another in great agitation, she explains where a policeman can be found to report a stolen wallet. Then another and another. To everyone, she is gracious and caring. Am I still impatient? Somehow not. I begin to see her not as someone just issuing tickets but as a whole person.

As I leave, I say, "You are kind to many people. I see that." She lights up and we have a moment of heart-to-heart connection. I leave not only clutching a ticket but feeling nourished.

You also never know where you are going to meet the Buddha. Trying to make a quick connection between my flight and a train in Frankfurt, Germany, I bypassed the long line at the ticket counter and just boarded the train. Sitting on the train, I anxiously pondered what I would do when the conductor came through to check tickets. Should I make a quick dash to the rest room and avoid the situation? Suddenly there he was. Not speaking German, I did a brief, apologetic pantomime: "No time, no ticket." He beamed and I got the gist: "No problem." I relaxed and, glancing at his name badge, saw it read "Herr Bouda."

Mindful awareness practice is the most fundamental discipline to honestly face whatever is happening with us without judgment but with a warm heart. We come back to ground zero and open to whatever arises. We learn that we can just stay with it: whatever is happening is happening. We can ride it out. When we become convinced that our situation is unworkable, we close down. When we are willing to stay with what is awkward or painful, we come alive.

IT'S TIME TO MEDITATE

Training ourselves to come home, to settle into just being with ourselves, for even a few moments, is not that hard. The sustained and focused attention that meditation requires can seem overly demanding at first but can become the very thing we seek in order to find rest. We can set aside some time each day, even ten minutes, to practice fully being present and aware. The more often, or longer, we can do this, the more settled and calmer we will feel. Quiet presence is an act of renewal. Making time early in the day for just being changes the quality of the day and affirms what is primary for us.

MEDITATION INSTRUCTION

Though it is best to find someone to instruct you and then connect to a community of like-minded people, the following overview will give you a sense of meditation.

- Sit on a cushion on the floor with your legs crossed or in a chair with the soles of your feet on the floor, in an upright posture.
  - Let your arms rest on your thighs.
  - Keep your eyes open and let your gaze be relaxed, about four feet in front of you.
- First, just take note of how you are: tired? speedy? emotional? Acknowledge how you are without judgment.
- Decide how long you want to meditate, but do it for at least ten minutes.
- Arouse strong motivation: "I am sitting here with the sole intention of stabilizing my mind."
- Take note of your posture from time to time throughout the session. (Holding a strong but relaxed upright posture naturally harmonizes your energy.)
- Put your primary focus on your breathing.
  - Breathing is the object of your meditation, your reference point.
  - Allow your breath to go in and out without trying to change it in any way.

- Bring your body, breath, and mind to quiet and stillness.
  - You are just sitting and breathing.
  - Your mind is just with your sitting and breathing.
- When you become aware of mental activity, acknowledge it by saying "thinking." Then return to your breath and body, an embodied breathing.
- Sit like a rock, a rock that is breathing, alive.

Again and again, we come back to square one, basic being. The technique says, "Sit, just sit. Be here right now." It is intentionally blunt and bold, able to cut through endless mental chatter and dramas because it is so straightforward. Impulses and desires are neutralized as you sit in stillness. The fundamental instruction, as Buddhist nun Pema Chödrön puts it, is, "Stay, stay, stay."

On a regular basis, we need to press the "Refresh" button of our being, so at work or home, I advocate breaks. Not for coffee or gossip or whining but to come back to basic being, return to a sense of peace and quiet in order to recharge. A break could be a brief moment of self-awareness that brings us "back home." We could just sit and breathe deeply. We can do this anytime, anywhere: showering, brushing our teeth, attending a meeting, traveling. These breaks rest the mind so it can work to the best of its ability. They sustain us.

TAKE THIS MOMENT NOW
- Stop what you are doing.
- Tune in to your breathing.
  - Is it relaxed or held?
  - Do some deep, gentle breathing for a few minutes.
- Now return to what you were doing.

Fundamentally, when we talk about coming back home, we are talking about being more present, being authentically present. Now that we have begun to develop our personal awareness skills, we will turn our attention in the following chapters to developing our skills in working with others.

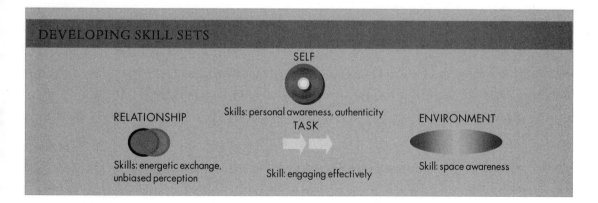

DEVELOPING SKILL SETS

SELF

Skills: personal awareness, authenticity

RELATIONSHIP

TASK

ENVIRONMENT

Skills: energetic exchange, unbiased perception

Skill: engaging effectively

Skill: space awareness

7

Personal Authenticity

AUTHENTIC IS A WORD OF OUR TIMES. It is in reaction to the lack of authenticity in much of our culture: the glitter, the hype, the hard sell, the spam, the get-ahead mentality, taking advantage of others, corruption in high places, no matter on what continent. It is a cry for genuine people having genuine relations. We could continually connect back to our fundamental goodness rather than being alienated from it and starved for it. Authenticity can transform our life!

THE NATURE OF AUTHENTICITY

The word *authentic* has its roots in Greek and Latin, so it has resonated with people in many cultures. Authenticity arises from our inherent sanity, our ground of goodness: it comes from our natural power or strength, our vital energy. It is an expression of the depth and potency of our being. There are times when our mask falls away and we might feel most authentic, as in the major markers of our life: birth, illness, old age, and death. Extreme life-threatening situations such as natural disasters also allow people to open and bond with others in an authentic way.

> CONTEMPLATING AUTHENTICITY
> - What does it mean to be authentic? to have authentic presence?
> - Who do you know that is authentic?
> - What qualities does he or she have?

Authenticity has a sense of power: it is the catalyst for the wisdoms to shine. Our authentic wisdom qualities are what we need in these speedy times. Haste makes waste; when we slow down, our best qualities emerge, a sense of grace and dignity arises. We can begin to feel a mental stability, a capacity to stay with ourselves: strong, present, and focused. Being genuine unmasks who we are—which could leave us on shaky ground but ultimately gives us confidence. Living in a busy, often chaotic world, it is easy to lose our authenticity. However, if we think of those we most admire, they are the ones who seem grounded in deeper values.

Finally, it is the soul that must be preserved, if one is to remain a credible leader. All else might be lost; but when the soul dies, the connection to earth, to peoples, to animals, to rivers, to mountain ranges, purple and majestic, also dies. And your smile, with which we watch you do gracious battle with unjust characterizations, distortions and lies, is that expression of healthy self-worth, spirit and soul, that, kept happy and free and relaxed, can find an answering smile in all of us, lighting our way, and brightening the world.

—writer ALICE WALKER in a letter to
President-elect Barack Obama,
November 5, 2008

In 1990 Vaclav Havel, president of Czechoslovakia, addressed the US Congress in a remarkable speech. . . . "The salvation of this human world lies nowhere else than in the human heart, in the human power to reflect, in human meekness and in human responsibility. Without a global revolution in the sphere of human consciousness . . . the catastrophe toward which this world is headed—be it ecological, social, demographic or a general breakdown of civilization—will be unavoidable."

—PARKER J. PALMER, writer and teacher on education, spirituality, and social change

Authenticity is the willingness to embrace all of ourselves, to hold all of our aspects, even the darkest ones. . . . It asks us to face our internal and external challenges with awareness and compassion. But if we do that, authenticity allows us to transform our demons and our enemies into teachers, and gives us congruence, a sense of harmony that aligns our thoughts, our words, and our emotions.

—FRED KOFMAN, author of *Conscious Business* and co-founder of Axialent

Authenticity is aligned with integrity, discipline, and responsibility. Integrity involves living by our core truths, which come from deep within. Discipline involves steadfastly putting our commitment into action. Responsibility involves taking the initiative to act rather than being reactive or playing the victim. It is being 400 percent accountable for what we think, feel, say, and do. So we have to work with our mental models, beliefs that we hold dear, and our emotions, how we get triggered.

We must become the change we want to see in the world.

—MAHATMA GANDHI

FIVE ASPECTS OF
AUTHENTICITY

1. Genuine, true: humbly present in a simple way
   - Not a lot of neurotic static, emotional baggage
   - Honest, straightforward
2. Congruent: synchronized and in the moment with self and others
   - Having an open mind rather than fixed ideas
   - Free from deception, a hidden agenda, or defensiveness
3. Confident, trusting in oneself: a sense of human dignity
   - Transcending hope and fear
4. Openhearted
   - Kind and generous, accepting others unconditionally
5. Sense of humor

> – Able to see the comic side of situations and have a light touch

We are the only ones who can bring ourselves into personal authenticity. It happens when we commit to working with ourselves, become willing to open to a more wholesome way of being. Being authentic means walking on the edge between our sanity and our confusion, being willing to suspend our egoic self and stay groundless. It is about entertaining the question, not grasping for the answer. It means surrendering to what comes rather than demanding what we want to come. In contrast, *in*authenticity breeds neurosis: we are false, fake, masked. We are incongruent: have a slippery mind and are deceptive, manipulative, and untrustworthy. We often rationalize being dishonest in order to justify our behavior. With an authentic presence, we are wakeful and gentle and have an unconditional positive regard. If we relate to ourselves properly, it will magnetize others. Then we become a catalyst for the rest of the world.

> CONTEMPLATE PERSONAL AUTHENTICITY
>
> - At what times and in what situations have you been authentic?
> - How did the external circumstances contribute to your authenticity?
> - What in you allowed you to be authentic?
> - Which of the five aspects of authenticity were manifesting?

TOOLS FOR CULTIVATING AUTHENTIC PRESENCE
- Centering: good posture, easy breathing, settled mind
- Cultivating mindfulness and awareness, attentiveness in the moment
- Relax: getting in touch with basic being, inherent goodness
- Acknowledging a sense of our human dignity and genuine confidence
- Being kind toward self and others

TUNING IN TO AUTHENTICITY

Do this as a group with a facilitator or on your own as a way to focus your awareness.
- Walk around in a space with discursive talking to yourself.
  - Stop, inward oscillation: cut thoughts, experience basic healthiness.
  - Be aware of being embodied.
- Continue walking around in the space with discursive talking.
  - Stop, outward oscillation: shift your awareness to those around you.
- Continue walking around in the space with discursive talking.
  - Stop: shift your awareness to the environment around you.
- Continue walking and intentionally shift from one consciousnesses to another: inward, others, environment.

Let's take Charles, an exceptional family therapist, as an example. He has a genuine, caring presence and remarkable ability to get his client families talking about their highly sensitive issues. He has great insights into the sources of their constriction. When Charles is at home, however, his family generally does not get this amazing man. They get someone who is depleted: grouchy and snappy. What would it take for Charles to bring his authentic qualities home?

There is no better way to cultivate personal authenticity than to practice meditation: we drop into basic being with good posture, easy breathing, and a settled mind. We let go of fixed mind, are attentive in the moment, and can direct our attention flexibly. We gain the strong back of confidence and the gentleness of a warm heart. We trust ourselves enough to open. As we relax, we can extend kindness toward others. This is powerful training for being in the world. An authentic presence is the embodiment of our inherent wakefulness. There is no greater gift than to be fully present for others, unconditionally. One day I was upset and crying. My daughter Karuna came in, sat with me on the bed, and held my hand. She did not talk, become emotional, or try to fix my problem. She was just there, present. It is what I most needed.

> The authenticity of our words and actions comes from a presence that is developed through the practice of a discipline.
>
> —Chögyam Trungpa

We can look at ourselves as being layered: a public face, perhaps a mask, which is somewhat inscrutable; a rich, juicy layer of emotions; and an inner core, which is unchanging and basically good. When we tap into our essential nature through meditation, we radiate that goodness. Staying in touch with our inherent goodness, we purify our emotions and no longer need a mask. When all our layers—thoughts, feelings, and actions—are synchronized with one another, we are congruent and radiate authenticity. We are integral.

> Authentic is a truth that is not learned but comes from within.
>
> —Mary Whitehouse, founder of dance therapy, which led to authentic movement

Anthony Tudor was my ballet teacher when I was at the Juilliard School. In one very exceptional class, he worked with a small group of us on how to enter a stage. Most of us assumed it involved getting in touch with a feeling. Much to our surprise, he said it was all technique. He told us of how he had had to come onstage just after having learned of his father's death. In retrospect, I see he was calling on his ability as a Zen practitioner to come to a centered place, an authentic presence.

At the age of twenty-one, I danced in Tudor's enchanting choreography "Lilac Garden," about a wedding party. It was quite demanding technically, and I was at the peak of my technical ability. However, my clearest memory was his working with me on how to slowly turn my head to give the gesture a particular meaning. (I had just come upon the bride with her former lover in the garden.) For Tudor, this simple movement was as important to the choreography as its many technical challenges. His insistence on finding the truth of movement was uncompromising.

FIVE ASPECTS OF AUTHENTICITY AND THE FIVE WISDOMS

The five aspects of authenticity, sourced in basic goodness, are fundamental and universal. The Five Wisdoms point to the diversity in people, places, and situations. Whereas, fundamentally we all share the same nature; relatively, we are different. Our basic nature is generic; our wisdom qualities make us distinctive. So being authentically and fully who we are has many subtleties. Like an ever-shifting kaleidoscope, we manifest different energies in different situations. Becoming self-aware means knowing all our colors. Aligning with the best of who we are brings out our authentic wisdom.

HOW DOES THE AUTHENTICITY OF THE FIVE WISDOMS APPEAR IN YOUR LIFE?

- Spacious acceptance of what is
- Insightful clarity
- A sense of abundance and generosity
- Warmth and engagement with others
- Effectiveness in whatever you do

EXPRESS YOUR AUTHENTIC WISDOM THROUGH MOVEMENT

Do a gesture for each quality.
- Make your gestures very big to get the expansive feel of them.
- Make them smaller while maintaining the expansive feel.

OBSTACLES TO AUTHENTICITY

It is not hard to see that our surface layer—our public face—can block our authenticity. Being nice has its time and place but can sometimes be quite false. As well, when emotionally hooked into a situation, we have a defensive routine. Dropping our defensiveness might leave us feeling more vulnerable but with unconditional confidence. It is also true that we may find someone's genuineness (or a situation that is dazzlingly authentic) overwhelming. We could feel a sense of inadequacy in someone's presence and awkward in relating to him or her. Our own insecurity could even make us feel that the other person is not genuine, and we might project all sorts of things onto him or her. Believing in our projections, we could disparage the other person. Such are the convolutions of the neurotic mind.

OBSTACLES TO AUTHENTICITY

- When are you incongruent? When do you wear a mask, pretend?
  - Do you become tense because you want to be accepted, loved, respected?
  - What outer circumstances tend to create this tension of being split?
- Which shadow sides of the energies in you are at play?
  - Buddha's unwillingness to engage
  - Vajra's protective shield of concepts, judgments, and opinions
  - Ratna's arrogance and/or low self-esteem
  - Padma's desire to please, tendency to skim the surface

– Karma's speed, ambition, fixation on a goal
- Do particular situations feel familiar?
  – Is your past coloring the present?
  – What are you getting out of staying stuck?
- What could you change in yourself or the external situation to feel more authentic?

Fear of "other" and self-doubt are the root causes of *in*authenticity, incongruence. We respond with fear when something feels threatening. Then we doubt ourselves and resort to our habitual way of coping. We shut down. Once we have cultivated confidence, we dare to be open and compassionate: it all centers around our ability to manifest genuine confidence.

THE FEAR/DOUBT AND
CONFIDENCE/COMPASSION
EQUATION

Fear of "other" ⟷ self-doubt
PARADIGM SHIFT
Self-confidence ⟷ compassion

TRANSFORMING FEAR AND
COPING

- Contemplate a difficult situation in your life, asking these questions:
  – What kind of fear does it bring up?
  – How do you habitually cope with that fear?
- Recall a situation in which you felt totally confident. How does it feel?
- Reframe the first situation with yourself as totally confident.

– Can you be unconditionally confident?

Moments of authenticity can elude us, especially when we are surrounded by confusion, falsity, and chaos. So we need to be aware of when we have the felt sense of an authentic moment: we can catch a glimpse of authenticity on the spot. Authenticity is a path, a journey, a process. A wakeful moment of authenticity could happen in the blink of an eye or be slowly life-transforming.

OUR AUTHENTIC PATH

There is a gradual shift of allegiance from the content to the process of experience. We feel our life is good and genuine, so we open. When more present, we can be openhearted and invite people in. Each moment, each day, when we drop our preoccupations, we are more available to others. First we empty; then we engage. We find calm and peace, as well as warmth and generosity. When we feel gentleness in ourselves, we are more able to feel compassionate toward others: because positive things are happening in us, they naturally extend outward. Our capacities and intelligence expand, and we are more inclined to engage with the world. We find that others trust us and we trust them. We find that everything in our life becomes more workable. Our tastes change: we find that so many things we do are a waste of time. What we think, feel, say, and do becomes congruent, integral.

We could finally feel that we are using our full human potential, embodying all aspects of ourselves, and having more overlap in the different spheres of our life. We have a sense of wholesomeness and use our full human potential. Our life could have more meaning, greater purpose. We have a spontaneous presence and are able to engage in the fullness of the present moment. We are in synchronicity with ourselves and the world. We see that our personal experience is actually universal and that authenticity can be cultivated in every aspect of our life.

When we touch our "open nature," our emptiness, we exert an enormous attraction to other human beings. . . . And if others are in that same space or entering it, they resonate with us and immediately doors are open to us. It is not strange or mystical, it is part of the natural order.

—FRANCISCO VARELA

PRACTICING AUTHENTIC PRESENCE

Do this as a group with a facilitator to guide you.

- One at a time, walk into the room.
  - Stop and stand in the center.
  - Say one phrase and/or do a gesture.
  - Exit.
- The group asks the person how it felt.
  - They say what they observed without judgment.
- The group could repeat this several times changing what to look for, such as:
  - Quality of presence and ability to connect
  - Mannerisms, habitual nervous coping mechanism, or awkwardness

On this path, we could be drawn to seek communities of like-minded people because it is easier to be authentic if others are. Then we can feel more at ease with ourselves and our surroundings. As well, we can use one another's energy to strengthen ourselves and radiate it out. When we model authenticity, we magnetize others.

ENVISIONING OURSELVES

As leaders, whether leading our life or leading others, we must ask several important questions: What are our dreams? How can we best serve? What is needed? What aspects of ourselves stand in the way of realizing our vision? The bigger our vision, the more we need to face our dark side. Envisioning how we want to be in the world keeps us honest about how we lead our lives. We must also have a sense of really loving that vision, a vision of ourselves at our best. Fulfilling the vision could be arduous; it could take a long time, so we need to commit to whatever it takes. It boils down to this: do we have enough passion? When coaching people, one of my first questions is, "What is your passion?" It gives me a sense of both who the person is and what he or she might do in life. When we have passion for what we do, we have sustainable performance.

Julian's father and I had different ideas about what Julian should do after college. Ernie wanted Julian to go to graduate school to study law or some such established profession. I kept saying, "Julian, pay attention to your passions. What turns you on?" Since Julian was a people person, I knew it had to be something to do with people. So he created a database company,

Beezwax Datatools, in which his role involves relating to the people: internally with forty five database designers and externally with the clients.

Regardless of whether we have the privilege of doing what we want to do in the world, we must keep our passion and our commitment alive. Periodically reenvisioning ourselves makes our life a lively journey. Most of us wait until a so-called midlife crisis to make an about-face with our lives. But we could stay in love with life and make a commitment to it every day.

Since I was eight years old, dancing has been important to feeling my juices. I started in ballet, followed by modern dance, my own version of movement theater, then contemplative dance. I have created hundreds of choreographed pieces and given many improvisational performances. Then interest in others' process—creative or growthful—took precedence over my own. So I developed trainings in working with others. This culminated in the emphasis on the Five Wisdoms, which encompass everything. At each turning, there has been a sense of breaking through constriction to reach another way of expressing my passion. Becoming single, I took up tango. I joke that, living on the edge of mainstream society as I do, I have never made much money, which gives me great freedom to move from one thing to the next. Nothing to lose! At various times, my husband and son have said, "Why don't you just get a real job?" I simply cannot. I have been stubborn about sticking to my passions, which in turn allows me to give the world my best.

When we have a sense of being an authentic human being, full of heart, we feel complete.

From that place, we can cultivate our intention or purpose in life. We could have a deeper purpose than getting through the day. Then we need to act; otherwise, there is no momentum. We must have patience and courage in not giving up on what we intend. Appreciating ourselves gives us energy and confidence to redirect our life. How would the world change if we learned, individually and collectively, to access our deepest capacity to sense and shape our future? Gandhi was an outstanding example of this: the British did not know what to do with him, so he defeated an empire.

CREATING A CASE FOR CHANGE

Coming from a connection to our passion, we can create a case for change, an intention to make the most of our life. If we feel that we have much to give, we are like a shining star expressing its radiance. However, if our motivation is coming from a place of feeling inadequate, it is misguided. We could feel unworthy and inadequate in many ways: not enough intellect, resources, love, power, and so forth. How could we possibly succeed if our motivation comes from a place of poverty? It is a setup for failure: we ground our actions in a black hole we want to fill. Do you see how the former has an expanded view and the latter is self-referencing? It all comes back to the basic split: when we are self-referencing, we feel unworthy; when we look at the big picture, we shine. Who would we follow: someone who fills the hole or someone who shines? What do we need to do to feel worthy? The only answer lies within: we need to align with our authentic wisdom qualities.

CONTEMPLATE YOUR INTENTION

Answer the following questions, in writing if you wish.

- What is the best of you that you can offer the world?
- What do you see is needed in the world?
- Can you be the best of who you are and serve the world at the same time?

CATALYSTS OF CHANGE FOR SELF, RELATIONSHIP, TASK, AND ENVIRONMENT

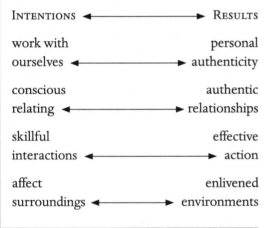

INTENTIONS	RESULTS
work with ourselves	personal authenticity
conscious relating	authentic relationships
skillful interactions	effective action
affect surroundings	enlivened environments

Making a case for change could be challenging but well worth the effort. The Buddha couldn't figure out what it was all about. He decided to sit under a bodhi tree until it became clear. He sat there until he saw how we perpetuate our own suffering and how we could be liberated from it. He made a case for change. Fundamentally, the change must happen from within. Can we take 400 percent responsibility for our lives?

THE CHANGE MODEL

This model works with the gap between where we are and where we would like to be. Both cognitive and experiential learning takes place in the gap. We can learn how to fulfill our vision. The four aspects of self, relationship, task, and environment allow us to think about all aspects of our life. This process involves reflecting, exploring, experimenting, and testing our vision.

Answer the following questions, either with a partner asking the questions or by writing down the answers on your own.

WHAT DOES YOUR LIFE LOOK LIKE TODAY?

1. Self
   - Which energies bring out the best in you?
   - What is your most familiar emotional tone during the day?
   - Do you get stressed? What triggers it?
   - What coping strategies do you use?
   - Do one or two gestures that capture all this.
2. Relationship
   - Which energies do you predominantly use in relating to others?
   - Do you feel a lack of attunement with your family members and work colleagues?
   - Are you in conflict with any of them?
   - Do one or two gestures that capture all this.
3. Work/job/task
   - Which of the energies is most needed at work and at home?

- Is it a good match for your energetic style?
- Do you feel efficient in what you are trying to accomplish?
- Do one or two gestures that capture all this.

4. Environment
   - What are the dominant energies in your home and work environment?
   - What disturbs you in your environment?
   - What inspires you about the environment?
   - Do one or two gestures that capture all this.

How would you like your life to look tomorrow?

- What are your most compelling desires in terms of self, relationship, task, and environment?
- Envision your life as you would like it to be. Take one situation from your past and replay it based on what you realize now.

How would you make those changes happen?

- What do you need to learn to bring about change?
- What realistic timelines are you willing to commit to?
- What aspects of yourself stand in the way of realizing your vision?
- What lessons have you learned from the past?

We might find change very difficult. But if it was to "save our life"—a life worth living—would we do it? Our current situation has to be enough out of sync with who we feel we are to face letting go of it and dealing with the fear that that triggers. Our motivation needs to be greater than the resistance that naturally arises from loss. As well, our vision for the future must be compelling. Living our deepest values in an impassioned way is indeed a life beyond compare.

My personal experience with the change model has been very profound at several junctures in my life. After an almost thirty-year career in dance, I became a therapist. To my dismay, I found I was at the bottom of my new profession. My good friend Susan Skjei said, "Define a new profession; then you'll be at the top." This did not happen overnight. It wasn't until years later that the Five Wisdoms Institute and Five Wisdoms @ Work training came into being.

> There is, deep down within all of us, an instinct. It's a kind of drum major instinct—a desire to be first. . . . We all want to be important, to surpass others, to achieve distinction, to lead the parade. . . . Don't give it up. . . . Keep feeling the need for being first. But I want you to be first in love. I want you to be first in moral excellence. I want you to be first in generosity. That's what I want you to do. . . . I want you to say that I tried to love and serve humanity . . . say that I was a drum major for justice; say that I was a drum major for peace; I was a drum major for righteousness. . . . I just want to leave a committed life behind.
>
> —Martin Luther King Jr.

There are further understandings that can contribute to making ourselves better able to participate in modern life. In particular, we can look at current ideas on learning and leadership, which apply to any walk of life, any life situation.

LEARNING

In today's changing world, if we are not learners, we cannot manage our life. Life's tasks, once simple, are increasingly complex. We need an immense amount of know-how to get through our day—from how to work our digital stove to setting a clock's alarm to using the ATM machine. With every bought item, from a hairbrush to a computer, there are endless things to learn how to do. We must be learners.

Our workplace may have undergone much technological advancement, from a new phone system to upgraded computers and programs. Those who can learn have stayed on the job and advanced; those who can't now live on unemployment insurance or scrape by with dead-end jobs. They didn't make the grade. People who have grown up in this technological, materialistic world have a better chance, as technology is second nature to them.

We all have preferences regarding what we want to learn and how we learn. We can also resist learning, particularly in certain areas. We may be delighted to harness our intellectual capacities but have no patience with anything practical. We may be great at the practical but won't go near emotional processing. We could fear displaying our ignorance: we want to appear competent or feel we already know or don't need to know. Sometimes there is a big

gap between what we need to know and our learning curve. The most important step in dealing with our learning gaps is to acknowledge their existence.

> In times of change, learners will inherit the Earth, while knowers will be perfectly equipped to live in a world that no longer exists.
>
> —ERIC HOFFER, author of *The True Believer*

Peter Senge says that we are in a "knowledge-based economy," that knowledge and learning are the key competitive advantage. Interestingly, this now puts the focus more on people, understanding them and bringing out their best. Senge also comments that during the industrial age, people were just one type of resource, indistinguishable from other resources. A knowledge era will require more sophistication. Learning is the currency of our future.

> In the future, understanding the diversity of human functioning will play a central role in the success and sustainability of both organizations and societies.
>
> —PETER SENGE

Clearly, learning needs to be something that becomes a healthy practice, a necessary ingredient in our life. We must stay perpetually on our learning edge, poised to learn what is needed in the moment or over a period of time. A healthy approach could be: we live; therefore, we learn.

Creating a culture in our workplaces that supports these views can be particularly powerful. In our organizations, how are we going to ventilate the sense of oppression with some fresh air? How can we begin to shift the bottom line from the budget to people's well-being? What changes might we need to make in the physical environment?

LEARNING HOW TO LEARN

The question is, what do we need to learn? Yes, of course we must learn the tools of our trade. But, as we have seen, we must also learn about the tool that is ourselves. Without paying more attention to how we are, we can never synchronize effectively with our world. So we need to start with ourselves. What we think are our mental models. How do we envision ourselves? others? the world? What we feel is our emotions. Do they get in the way, or do we harness them to serve us, giving us an intuitive understanding of people, places, and situations?

The traditional view of learning is that first we gain a theoretical understanding and then we translate it into practice. The learning paradigm has shifted. New leaders see the traditional approach as ineffective, as it does not yield practical competence or encourage creativity. It places too much emphasis on the "knower" downloading knowledge to the "learner." The new approach, which focuses on the relevance of the information to the learner's life, can increase our capacity to accomplish the desired results. Knowledge is then defined as the capacity for effective action. Although this is certainly a far cry from the liberal arts understanding of learning as a means to enrich one's life, it is an extremely useful definition of the learning needed in our fast-paced world.

For any learning to take place, we must first admit that there is a gap or creative tension between what we know and do not know. Then we rouse our aspiration to take a learning plunge. It can be scary and challenging: being on the edge of what we know and do not know can be difficult to articulate, murky and vague, more felt than seen. The fear could make us retreat into rigidity and habitual patterns. If we can acknowledge our fear and step over it, we surrender into a state of "I don't know"; we find ourselves beginners. The learning edge can be a source of insight, creativity, and intuition; it can be exhilarating.

FROM BEGINNER TO EXPERT TO MASTER

In their book *Mind over Machine,* Hubert and Stuart Dreyfus propose that there are five stages of learning, which can be paraphrased as follows:

1. *Novice or beginner:* The learner lets the teacher or coach take the lead in a learning environment.
2. *Advanced beginner:* The learner is introduced to real-life situations and relies on the coach to provide supervision and instruction.
3. *Competent learner:* The learner's sense of involvement and responsibility increases as he or she sees a situation as a set of sequential steps toward a certain goal.
4. *Proficient learner:* The learner combines analytical thinking and intuition for almost automatic execution of a task and can anticipate a situation.

5. *Expert:* An expert generally knows what to do, and his or her solutions defy explanation, as they are not logical and rational but based on what seems to work best in the moment.

The master has reached a stage of such expertness that he can now change the container of performance itself, manipulating it, developing new standards, even changing the paradigms of the task. . . . Unlike experts, the true master sees his domain with beginner's eyes, allowing him or her to approach the work with freshness and openness to possibilities that may elude the expert.

—PETER SENGE

We know the masters or geniuses of our world: Charles Darwin, Albert Einstein, Leonardo da Vinci, Mahatma Gandhi, Johann Sebastian Bach, and many more. They attained such a level of understanding and expertise that they actually redefined and altered the evolution of their domain. These people did not rely on what they knew; they were open to learn.

LEADERSHIP

Our world needs good leaders. We become leaders in our own right when we take the initiative to respond appropriately rather than reactively to events. Anyone who is proactive in his or her life is a leader. In the Shambhala community, we talk about leaders as warriors, warriors who build an enlightened society.

Whereas in the old model of leadership, leaders are task-oriented and completely in charge, everyone has the potential to act as a leader, even though he or she may not be the officially designated leader. There is a sense of identity at a deeper level, not "I am" but "I have a role." Taking responsibility without being given it has a very different feel. We could learn to shine, but without solidifying into becoming territorial. So it is a question of how to see, handle, and positively manipulate power.

People in both authentic leadership, as espoused at Naropa University and Authentic Leadership in Action (ALIA), and in servant leadership, at the Greenleaf Center for Servant Leadership, talk about service above self. In contrast to autocratic leadership, the new leader facilitates the process of involving others: everyone develops a shared vision and has some say in how the vision is implemented. A good leader takes his or her seat and gives everyone else their own seat. It is not about being the best at everything, a superhero, but about galvanizing everyone involved and drawing out their gifts. We cultivate others rather than trying to do the whole job ourselves. New leaders need a new kind of training. In turn, trainers need to facilitate learning instead of expounding on a topic or demonstrating a skill. As well, they must work effectively with differing learning styles.

If our primary motivation is helping others, we open to a greater world. We become a leader not to gain power but to empower others. We help others to see their possibilities, create environments where they can shine and where community is valued. A dynamic and responsive community based on a continual sense of exchange among all its members keeps things constantly fresh and in flux.

The main point is that whether we call ourselves authentic leaders or warriors, when we discover and align with our wisdom, we originate our own power: we become powerful. It is not about exercising power over others but rather tuning in to the immense power of goodness in people and the world. This power is very magnetizing. It begins in small ways and expands into leading others.

Leading from Within

What has emerged in current leadership circles is the lack of attention that has been paid to the self—termed the "blind spot"—and the realization that knowing ourselves is crucial for navigating our world. To work with this, Senge has brought "personal mastery" to the fore, and Otto Scharmer, author of *Theory U* and *Presence*, uses "presencing" as a basic component of leadership training. The new leadership models give us a sense of fresh air. People are discovering that the prime distinguishing feature of effective leaders is that they know themselves well: they are capable of self-reflection and have greater personal awareness. This enables them to be more present, open in mind and body and heart, listening unconditionally. There is a sense of invitation, not manipulation. In old age Robert Greenleaf came to accept that he would "best serve by being. . . . That leadership of being, that quiet presence, that living in the present moment is greatly needed in our rapidly changing world."

To bring self-awareness into action, our ability to continually oscillate between self and other—whether people, environment, or task—is paramount. When we go out in the world, we must take ourselves with us. Our overriding tendency is to lose everything we have cultivated in meditation practice when confronted with "other." For instance, e-mailing and surfing the Web may get such a tenacious hold on us that we forget to eat and sleep. As well, we are too focused on what others think of us and expect from us. Our external referencing trumps our sense of being. Although opening to the outside is good, listening to ourselves is equally important.

> A journalist asked Mother Teresa what she asked god when she spoke to him. She said, "I don't ask; I listen." "Well, what does he say?" "He is listening too."

As meditation practice deepens, we stay more grounded. The practice acts like a deep rudder, stabilizing us as we steer ourselves through the ocean of phenomena. Being grounded in our authenticity is key. We remember the five aspects of authenticity: being genuine, congruent, confident, openhearted, and having a sense of humor. Having confidence and joy in our own richness is the essence of generosity, so we are resourceful in dealing with whatever arises. The bottom line here is that we must first align with our sanity if we are to be of service to others.

We need to bring along all our colors. Having a public face at work and another self at home—splitting ourselves in two—creates tremendous tension in us. If we have done some deep work with our mix of colors, we realize that we can be present with all of them. We need not express them, but we can be aware of them, read events correctly, and discriminate which energies are called for in a particular situation. Being relentlessly padma, or any energy, wherever we go is simply not skillful. We can learn to modulate our energies for every occasion.

In this day and age, probably what we struggle with the most is speed, neurotic karma energy: "Let's get it done as fast as possible." This mentality dominates our waking hours. Fundamentally we distrust ourselves, others, and the situation. We feel we must accomplish more and more. There is no sense of joy. This struggle has overtones of being spilt off from reality: we don't trust the natural order.

> Instead of hard at work, let's try heart at work.

The conscious intention of nondoing, which requires a lot of trust, allows previously inaccessible information to come to us; we have a greater sense of what is required in a given situation. We need not come up with all the answers; we can wait for them to come to us. The inner stillness also merges with outward activity. The result is effortless action: we know what to do and spontaneously meet the situation. When we discriminate between impulse and spontaneity, and have a keen sense of timing, we synchronize with our world and our actions are appropriate. This is the best of karma energy.

In the past, taking action was considered the hard part; now the important issue of personal and interpersonal human dynamics—of cultivating good relationships—is increasingly acknowledged as the hard part, since it is what enhances effectiveness in everything we do.

> Times of uncertainty and tumultuous change have stretched traditional leadership and managerial models beyond capacity. A new kind of leader is needed—one who can see situations from multiple perspectives, foster a culture of trust and collaboration and respond creatively and effectively to change.
>
> —SUSAN SKJEI, director of Authentic Leadership at Naropa University and founder of Sane Systems

COLLABORATIVE LEARNING DISCIPLINES AND CONTEMPLATIVE PRACTICES

In recent years, many organizations and communities have begun to work with new models of leadership, communication, and planning. Disciplines such as systems thinking, dialogue, scenario planning, and new approaches to mediation and conflict resolution are being increasingly embraced as essential tools to thrive in a rapidly changing, increasingly interdependent world. Underlying these new disciplines are principles held in common with many contemplative traditions:

- There is no certainty; we need to be willing to let go of fixed ideas and assumptions to let new insights and approaches evolve
- Events always have subtle and unexpected influences; we live inside of interconnected systems

- All individuals have, in most cases largely untapped, resources of intelligence, creativity, and decency

We view the collaborative learning disciplines sharing these assumptions as essentially group contemplative disciplines. We believe that they can be significantly enriched by going deeper into the contemplative aspect.

—Authentic Leadership in Action
Web site

Core practices that revolve around sensing and actualizing opportunities
- Observing: seeing reality with fresh eyes
- Sensing: tuning in to emerging patterns that inform future possibilities
- Presencing: accessing one's inner sources of creativity and will
- Envisioning: crystallizing vision and intent
- Executing: acting in an instant to capitalize on new opportunities

—Otto Scharmer

The new leadership has a lot to do with understanding and appreciating complexity, seeing every situation as part of a bigger whole. Generally, creativity and change come from smaller, more independent organizations rather than larger ones, which need to be more conventional. How larger companies can develop the ability to work in smaller "communities" within their organization is a key question. In the rush to be bigger and better, we forget the power of the small, which brings out the human element.

A qualification for leadership is that one can tolerate a sustained wide span of awareness so that he better "sees it as it is."

—Robert K. Greenleaf

8

Authentic Relationships

When we understand energy, we understand the dynamics of relationships. Our energetic qualities have as much potential to divide or join us as religious, cultural, and sociopolitical differences. They are as significant as age, race, culture, and gender but more subtle. They are our hardwiring. What keeps us from having more successful relationships is our deeply ingrained tendency to defend ourselves. Our concepts and feelings that we believe to be "true" see "other" as a problem. These uncomfortable but familiar defensive routines create tension in all our relationships. Because we conspire to create closed, rather than open, relationships, it is very hard to break out of them. Societal norms that keep us locked into stereotypical roles exacerbate this. Caught up in our differences, we create a dualistic world, a barrier between ourselves and others.

The future of our planet . . . depends on increasing the level of authentic relationship among human beings . . . redefining relationship as a living reality, instead of the coming together of two selves. The context of relationship offers new hope for responding to the "primary motivation for all humans . . . a desire for connection." Service to others may be the driving mechanism to bring on the global transformation on a personal level. The day of the servant/leader may be upon us. Connection with one's core and with that of others is the key. Our self is not separate but a field within larger fields. Service to others offers the mechanism to move our attention outside of ourselves.

—Charlene Spretnak, author of *The Resurgence of the Real: Body, Nature, and Place in a Hypermodern World*

Whether they involve a difficult family life, perennial conflicts at work, or a position of leadership, relationships can be the most difficult thing we deal with. They may seem intractable, and we are often stumped as to how to proceed. Most of us take our relationships for granted. We assume that our colleague James, our neighbor Molly, or our student Brian is going to meet our expectations of how a colleague, neighbor, or student should think and act. We are surprised to find this is not necessarily so. Misunderstandings lead to conflicts, which lead to a frozen atmosphere. Communication comes to a standstill.

It quite astounds me that though we interact with people daily, there is little guidance on how to foster genuine relationships and communicate meaningfully.

Sharing what we think and feel is difficult and thus rare. But how rare does it have to be? We all know people we find irritating, those we are more attracted to, and those who arouse fear. Yet that is only the surface layer. To go deeper, we need to spend some time revealing ourselves to one another. Whether in our more intimate sphere or work relationships or on a global scale across cultures and religions, we need to discover how best to relate and communicate. This is our challenge. Otherwise, we create layer on layer of *in*authenticity.

People are our business.

—Chögyam Trungpa

COPING MECHANISMS WE USE TO KEEP US "SAFE"

- If we maintain a facade of rationality we can avoid difficult thoughts and feelings.
- If others are always to blame, then we can always be right.
- If we wear an inscrutable mask, then we can avoid difficult emotions.
- If we tightly control our world, life becomes more predictable.
- If we don't take responsibility for our misdeeds, we reinforce how we see things.

Because working on our relationships is just too threatening, we don't make it a priority. Coping mechanisms protect us from what we most fear: failure, embarrassment, and losing control, to name a few. Revealing our vulnerability and stuck places to another is very scary. The more we have invested in perpetuating our particular version of ourselves, the scarier it is. So we accept having superficial relationships. To turn this around, we could commit to having conscious relationships. They can be a vehicle for essential change, bring out the best qualities in each of us, and enhance communication. This is a creative and dynamic way of working with others.

My son Julian was having trouble with a work colleague. I said, "If you regard working out your differences as a distraction, the problem will never resolve itself. If you make it a priority, then things will improve." Later he called this "the most important business advice you ever gave me."

Business is about relationships—it's a very difficult thing to remember.

—Cynthia Kneen, author of *Awake Mind, Open Heart* and management consultant

KEY POINTS FOR SUCCESSFUL RELATIONSHIPS

- Motivation: make them a priority.
- Generosity of spirit: offer the best of ourselves.
- Discipline: bring working with ourselves into working with others.
- Patience: remember that it takes time.
- Persistence: stick with it.
- Understanding: always hold big mind, full of wisdom and compassion.

Although we may have had some training in working with others, our ability to help others is not so much based on learned theories, techniques, and systems. Having a tool bag may reduce anxiety, but anxiety can be a necessary learning ground. Set ideas destroy creativity and insight and obscure what is really helpful. So it is more important to be trained in trusting our heart and innate intelligence. Great teachers, healers, and leaders achieve dazzling results not because they are following a book but because of their authentic presence and intuitive powers.

SKILLS FOR CULTIVATING AUTHENTIC RELATIONSHIPS

Cultivating genuine relationships requires that we develop skills to deepen our understanding of the interpersonal process: the four aspects of authentic relationships.

THE FOUR ASPECTS OF AUTHENTIC RELATIONSHIPS

1. Authentic presence, which includes managing our emotions and thoughts, is open and receptive and lets go of seeing only our own side.
2. Energetic exchange opens the door to intuition, the felt sense of another.
3. Unbiased perception allows us to see the other person, see things his or her way.
4. Effective action involves spontaneously knowing what to say or do.

The inseparability of these four aspects, deepened by experience, is very powerful: when we

are present, we experience another more intuitively, see him or her more clearly, which increases the possibility of open communication and engagement. Then we can be more effective. Within each situation, we can be aware of these four aspects, as well as the interplay of the five qualities and the five modes. In these ways, we are fine-tuning our psychophysical barometer. The four aspects hold the essence of the contemplative approach to working with others.

AWARENESS IN AUTHENTIC RELATIONSHIPS

- Four aspects of working with others to skillfully engage interpersonally
- Five qualities or styles to see the intelligence and constriction in ourselves, others, and our interactions
- Five modes, BSMQA (body, speech, mind, quality, and action), to encompass all aspects of a person—the physical, emotional/expressive, mental, quality/essence, and action

---

The Five Wisdoms enhance each of the four aspects: when we embody all five, we are present with the fullness of our being, which allows us to tune in to other people's particular mix of colors. Then we can see both how they shine and how they get stuck and know what action to take with them.

BRINGING THE FIVE QUALITIES INTO A CONVERSATION

Have a conversation with a partner on a topic of mutual interest. Then take turns answering these questions:

- Do you have a sense of the five qualities being present in you?
- Are you relating to a whole person?
  - Or are you just "picking his or her brains"?
  - Or just trying to get something done?
  - Or just aroused without connection?
  - Or something else?
- In what relationships have you felt these tendencies?

AUTHENTIC PRESENCE IN RELATIONSHIP

Establishing a good relationship with another starts with establishing a good relationship with ourselves. We need to like who we are and not try to be somebody else. Besides, as the saying goes, everyone else is taken! If we have a lot of padma and karma energy, we tend to compare ourselves to others and forget the key point: being the best of who *we* are. When we like who we are, we are more open.

> Making contact with an embodied presence communicates the essence of living things.
>
> —RICHARD HECKLER, author of *Crossings* and Director of the Hakomi Institute of San Francisco

Once personal authenticity is cultivated, we radiate an authentic presence: we hold the space with a sense of nowness, wakeful and gentle. Authenticity has a sense of big mind. It shows a willingness to make a genuine connection with a sense of unconditional positive regard. We are not thrown off by the unpredictable; we open to whatever arises. This is the language of the heart. Genuine connection with another is sharing our being, the best of who we are, and helping to bring that out in the other. Because it is a shared experience of well-being, we benefit mutually and quite delightfully, as in a good, warm hug.

When genuinely present, we transmit sanity just by being. We drop our agenda again and again and create a fundamental shift from self-referencing to compassionate space. If we are spacious, it suggests that the other can be, too. This is our trusty friend the buddha energy, mixed with the warm connecting energy of padma. Being in the moment with someone, whatever he or she brings to us, allows the other to have his or her experience just as it is. Then we can actually feel the situation rather than focus on the problem. As our sense of being able to be with a person deepens, we make interpersonal connections that are profoundly felt, no matter what the situation.

Being authentically present is the greatest gift we can give someone. We need not armor ourselves with defensive reactivity and strategize how to get what we want. The more we work with ourselves, the more we open to others; the more we know ourselves, the more we can know others. It is a potent combination of a personal and interpersonal path. Our relationships are not on automatic; rather, we oscillate continually between self and other. We touch people and are more spontaneous. It makes relating a very lively journey.

I found the last car I bought on Craigslist. Meeting with David, the car's owner, I was quite nervous. I found myself spontaneously saying that I had never bought a car without the help of a partner. This is probably the last thing you would say to someone who is about to sell you a used car. This was not a damsel-in-distress ploy (though I know myself capable of that). It was genuinely where I found myself. It worked. We joined. He was extremely helpful in giving me a few tips both during and after the sale.

Habitually, we panic when confronted by an uncomfortable or unfamiliar situation and grasp onto whatever might fix it. This takes us away from the moment. Instead, we can go deeper into ourselves. When we are willing to stay with what is awkward, we come alive. We cut through whatever roles, credentials, or professionalism we might have. We transcend one-up relationships. We just stay in the moment. With a spacious mind, we are more intuitive and creative: we spontaneously know how to be and what to do. In this way, our own work with ourselves becomes a powerful tool for working with others. As we try to help someone, our suggestion might not be heard; it could be the wrong time for him or her to hear it. Then again, the other person might come up with something completely appropriate. The other's intelligence is in play too.

The inspiration and openness of compassion invite larger-scale thinking, a freer and more expansive way of relating. They allow us to relate with people more fully because we no longer regard people as a drain on our energy. We feel their pain and respond with compassion. In so doing, we acknowledge our wealth and richness and are recharged. Compassion without intelligence, in contrast, is a spurious gesture.

Our heart is big but our mind is small, like giving money to a drunk. We can also be so emotionally enmeshed with another that we do not relate to him or her skillfully, like spoiling our child. Genuine compassion has a dignity that does not let it get mushy.

Compassion is the ultimate attitude of wealth: an anti-poverty attitude, a war on want.

—CHÖGYAM TRUNGPA

There are many examples of intimacy, caring, friendship, sharing humanity. Our relationships are not static; they are constantly in process. They are based on intrinsic goodness, mutual inspiration, and trust. The key is cultivating compassion, the foundation of contemplative approaches to authentic relationships both personally and as a leader, teacher, coach, or therapist. President Barack Obama had the insight to nominate a Supreme Court justice in whom he saw not only professional excellence but also a sense of compassion and an ability to empathize with "the lives of ordinary people."

Interrelatedness has been experientially grasped in myriad cultural contexts and variously expressed as the core perception of the wisdom traditions. Yet the forces of modernity continually deny and degrade it. Human society needs grounding in the unitive dimension of our existence.

—CHARLENE SPRETNAK

I did my contemplative psychotherapy internship at Friendship House, a therapeutic community with five resident clients and interlocking teams of thirty-five people. One afternoon there was an incident with two clients, whom we'll call Tim and Martha. I heard a ruckus and, heart pounding, bounded up two flights of steps and caught Tim in the act: he stood with a chair raised high, about to crash it over Martha's head. What to do? Nothing. I remained in the doorway, afraid yet powerfully grounded. Tim lowered the chair. I felt vulnerable yet confident, compassionate yet firm, even playful: "Tim, how would you like to come with me? I haven't talked to you in a while." I met the aggression with authentic presence: no big deal, no attack, no blame. Everyone relaxed. Tim and I had a chat. This was a very powerful lesson for me in trusting myself. I discovered that authentic presence brings confidence.

MANAGING OUR EMOTIONS

We want to be authentic without carrying around a lot of emotional baggage, which can sabotage our relationships. Our ratna neediness or our padma manipulation can turn off a prospective partner. The vajra's "needing to be right" and karma's controlling can get very old in a work relationship. Though we all have many fears and insecurities that we try to conceal, our energy communicates them clearly, even if our words don't. So we need to work with our emotions: own them, hold them, but not allow them to take over. It will be painful, as our defensive strategies are covering old wounds.

Emotions are what they are: we feel what we feel. We can honor them as an aspect of our intelligence. Whatever we feel is always true. However, this does not mean that we always express them: ostensibly being honest but actually just venting. Greater awareness gives us greater ability to choose what we say and what we keep to ourselves. In fact, once we are aware of having an emotion, we are already managing it. Then we can simply declare it rather than vent it, with "I" statements: "I am angry [joyful, sad, confused]."

Most of us believe that if we express our anger or passion, we will destroy our relationship. This could be true: we can't just dump our toxic waste on others. Although doing so might provide momentary relief, it actually perpetuates and escalates the situation and puts our relationships on shaky ground. How many relationships have been sabotaged by our anger, desire, or jealousy coming to the fore? Having strong emotions can seem tremendously vital: we could feel as if we were having an energetic breakthrough, gaining a new lease on life. That is why passionate affairs are so irresistible and we actually "enjoy" getting righteously indignant. But emotions can blind us, and our integrity can fly out the window. In an attempt to "speak our truth," we could create a mess and hurt many people. What would that accomplish?

When we are not fully present with our emotions, our relationships lose vitality. Yet we might think that expressing what we feel is too risky, particularly if we intuit that the degree of openness we want is too threatening to another. This is particularly true when those who lead with emotions (padma and ratna) are trying to relate to those who are not as emotionally oriented (buddha, vajra, and karma). Candor could be more damaging than helpful to the relationship and any shared endeavor. We are damned if we do, damned if we don't.

In many situations, it's fine to maintain a veneer of socially acceptable behavior and keep relationships polite and superficial. If the emotion remains repressed over time, however, the energy is not just superficial but frozen. Communication comes to a standstill, and we are left with our projections, which escalate in the absence of a reality check. We become more and more polarized. We dare not deal with the baby elephant in the room. We refrain from talking about it, then refrain from talking about what we're not talking about. Meanwhile, the elephant soon reaches adult maturity and starts trampling everything in sight. In a work situation, our options for dealing with the frozen energy depend very much on the other person and our respective roles. In a personal relationship, we will never have the desired intimacy if we do not find ways to open to each other.

Most of the time, we have another conversation going on underneath what we verbalize. This subtext is important, juicy material. We need to keep those thoughts and feelings alive for us; they nourish us inwardly and are the source of a deep intimacy with ourselves. They are the food for intimate conversations with primary partners and close friends. They are what we talk to therapists about, the material from which we could create art, the basis for diaries, and what surfaces in meditation. If we have no place in which to express our inner life, we wither and die in some way.

The two-layered conversation exercise is used to uncover the conversation beneath the conversation. This method, renamed and modified here, has been used in several professional arenas. It is a way of documenting both what we said and the thoughts and feelings we did not articulate. Tracking our inner commentary gives us a sense of when we are being authentic and vital and when not.

TWO-LAYERED CONVERSATION

Sit facing a partner.

1. Converse about a heated topic for five minutes.
   • Be aware of the inner dialogue of thoughts and emotions.
2. Draw a vertical line down the center of a sheet of paper.
3. In the right-hand column (RHC), write the dialogue that was spoken aloud, including only the words that both of you actually said.
4. In the left-hand column (LHC), write the thoughts and feelings that either of you refrained from expressing.
5. Discuss the same topic with greater candor, bringing more from the LHC into the RHC.
   • Share more of the inner aspect.
   • You need not express everything you

think or feel. Things will emerge at the appropriate time.

We will probably find that our left-hand column mostly contains assessments, judgments, prejudices, or assumptions. We may also find feelings such as fear, anger, sadness, shame, guilt, resentment, alienation, stress, or anxiety. We could also be uncomfortable about revealing feelings of tenderness, compassion, care, sympathy, and love. Most of us find these as difficult to express as negative emotions.

The most insidious emotion is critical, blaming anger. When we feel squeezed, it is our knee-jerk reaction: the other person is at fault. We fail to see that we are the ones having an emotion. A statement like "You make me angry" judges the other, but underneath, the more genuine emotion is that we are hurt, and perhaps angry, too. When we can express our emotion with the use of "I" statements, the other person is not immediately put on the defensive. Simply by letting our emotion be what it is we remain free of blaming. When we use "I" statements, we are being authentic, what we say rings true. "You" statements sound like a fact but are actually an opinion: they purport to describe a person but are actually toxic and blaming. Distinguishing between emotion and judgment becomes all the more confusing because we use the word *feel* to mean both an emotion and an assessment—a subtle but critical distinction.

Blaming others confirms how we see things and allows us to claim innocence. However, we fail to see how we contributed to the situation.

Actually, everyone is guilty—has played some part—and no one is to blame. People create all sorts of difficult situations that they will not own or lack the capacity to amend. So in coaching I always ask, "What part are you playing in this?" By blaming others, we disempower ourselves. If we see ourselves as part of the problem, we empower ourselves to be responsible for the solution.

When stressed, I can get pretty snappy. My rule of thumb for myself is that I must make amends, acknowledge my aggressive behavior, in the next twenty-four hours. I need to do the deep work to own my part in the confrontation. It really works. I feel more aligned with myself and with the target of my aggression. This is not about which of us was "right." If we keep thinking we are right, we can never see it his or her way, never own our part, but just carry around our self-righteousness.

A Buddhist slogan: "Drive all blames into one."

This slogan means: "Take it on." We are not taking on the blame; we are taking on the big mind that says, "I can handle this." When we take it on, there is no longer a battle. We face the situation as it is, right here and now. We do not even bother addressing the issue of who is to blame: that lies in the past. Delving into the history just so we can identify a culprit is a waste of time.

In several work situations, I found that the energy between me and someone else got frozen. I invited each of these people to join me in a process of opening up to each other. We set aside time on a somewhat regular basis and committed to meet until the energy shifted. Doing this the first time was very scary, so I was quite amazed that years of contention between my colleague and me seemed to melt away. Subsequent times it was also hard but proved equally useful. With one person, I found another way of working. Knowing we both had a good deal of karma energy, I predicted that friction between us was inevitable. So there it was. This time there was no verbal processing. I modeled, and saw that the other person modeled, that there was basically no problem: what happened happened; it was a mere blip.

We need to be aware of when, where, and how to work with our emotions, and with whom. Most important, we need to neither repress nor express them; we hold them. Although we might be full of emotions and think we must express them, we choose not to blurt them out; we feel them and contain them. We can feel them fully and just let ourselves be with them. It makes us feel so full and rich and embodied when we can hold our emotions in an intelligent way.

ONE-LINE E-MAILS: SEEING THE NEUROSIS AND WISDOM IN AN EVERYDAY EVENT

Do this in a group, with everyone sitting in a circle.

1. On a piece of paper, write a one-line e-mail with a neutral statement, such as "The sun is shining today," and pass it to the person on your right.
2. Answer the e-mail with completely neurotic reactivity—for example, "I know I said we could work in the garden next time the sun shines, but I'm simply too busy today. Why can't you stop bugging me and leave me alone?"—then pass it to the person on your right.
3. Answer the second e-mail showing the wisdom in the neurosis—for example, "Thanks for being clear about what is going on with you. I'm happy to leave you alone and enjoy the garden without you."
4. Pass the response along one more time and allow everyone to read the e-mail exchange.

Insight: E-mails are not the best tool for emotional processing.

MANAGING OUR THOUGHTS

Our mental models create our personal world. Our deeply held beliefs and assumptions are so hardwired that we are oblivious to having created them. They guide how we think and act and are self-reinforcing. However, they are an incomplete picture; they reflect only our version. The reality we experience is not reality per se: my truth is not your truth. When we forget this, there is a breakdown in communication. How differently do a poet, a gardener, and a scientist see a flower?

In the unconscious process of inference, which happens so quickly we are unaware of it, we form beliefs that become our truths. We make assumptions, give them meaning, become selective about facts, and draw conclusions. We live in our truth and swing into action. If we do not develop an awareness of this process, we become slaves to our recurrent patterns. Bringing them to the surface and willingly opening to others' perspective gives us a shared understanding. This increases our flexibility and capacity to respond to the world.

BECOMING AWARE OF YOUR THOUGHT PROCESS

You can develop a greater awareness of your thought processes by examining the steps in your reasoning.

1. Look at the observable data that anyone can see.
2. Create a story, theory, or interpretation about what is happening.
3. Draw conclusions and formulate your stance on the situation.
4. Make decisions on how to work with the situation.
5. Take action according to the conclusions you have reached.

Others may assess the same situation differently. When we become curious about their reasoning and concerns, we have an "empathy shift." When these differences are examined, we have more common understanding. We can look again, together, at the observable facts, and share our reasoning and assumptions. Self-awareness keeps us honest so our mental model does not prevent us from hearing another's

stance. Being willing to be mistaken provides space for more opening. Working with our thoughts can help us differentiate between inferences that are based on biased perception and awareness that comes from unbiased perception. We can make enormous changes in our understanding by sharing our thinking process.

Just as it takes two to tango, it also takes two to tangle. However, the primary work is always with ourselves: becoming aware of and owning our mixture of thoughts and feelings. The better we understand our mix of colors, the clearer this will be. Always, always, keep asking, "What do I contribute to the situation?" We need to clean up our own act first. It empowers us: we have effected some change. We don't wait impatiently for the other to change. Just consider: if we think, feel, say, and act differently, 50 percent of the problem is resolved!

Authentic relationships permit essential change to take place. We can have genuine experience that is simple, direct, and sane, bringing out wakefulness and well-being. This is a union of spontaneous presence and innate intelligence. Being willing to tackle difficult and confusing situations takes a sense of fearlessness. Committing ourselves to work with others is a big leap. It is a powerful way to integrate personal practices and interpersonal work with others. It can bring great joy. When we truly appreciate others, we see that everyone is not, as the saying goes, "a piece of work" but a work of art.

9

Energetic Exchange

I F THERE IS ANY one thing that could help improve relationships, it is breaking down the barrier between us: student/teacher, client/ therapist, CEO/manager. Our ability to be sensitive to others involves our whole being. To fully experience another, we need two things: energetic resonance and unbiased perception. We must feel and see—heart and mind. Energetic resonance has to come first. Why? Because mind trumps heart: concepts smother feelings. Since seeing is a mental activity, it can quickly turn into judging people and situations as right or wrong. Whereas concepts divide us, energetic exchange joins us. We can be the one to break the barrier: daring to go first is being generous.

Energetic exchange is a natural process of merging or sharing energy with another, an openness with the intention of relating, direct and intuitive, taking into account the full flavor of both people. We tune in to ourselves to resonate with another. There is a constant inward and outward oscillation of awareness. Joining with another in energetic oscillation requires a willingness to suspend our protective shield. It is nondual: not one, not two. Commonly, it is

understood as empathy, the ability to identify with and understand another. However, because we access empathy through energy, we use terms like *resonance, sympathetic vibration,* or *attunement.* My friend Sydney Leijenhorst calls this "intervibing." Our whole being holds the situation in a way that is not conceptual; we listen at a deeper level, in our body. It is more primal: we feel before we talk. We could also think of it as deep listening or the felt sense.

You accept both extremes of your friend's basic makeup as resources for friendship. If you make friends with someone because you only like certain parts of that friend, then it is not complete friendship, but partial friendship. So maitri [unconditional love] is all-encompassing friendship, friendship which relates with the creativity as well as the destructiveness of nature.

—CHÖGYAM TRUNGPA

The psychophysical barometer occurs in all relationships, whether we are aware of it or not. Whatever is in the room colors our mind. We can learn to use ourselves as a highly sensitive instrument to gauge the climate of energetic states in the environment. Moments of intuition (padma feeling) and insight (vajra clarity) arise when our mind and body are both penetrated. We tune in to what is rather than to our version of reality. We see how our projections, interpretations, opinions, and judgments get in the way. However, while exchange is about visiting someone else's world, it is not about living there. If we are confused about what is the other's world and what is ours, we are enmeshed. That is why we also need unbiased perception.

On one level, two (or more) individuals are relating; on another level, nobody is doing anything: whatever is happening is happening. We are just sharing the space of that happening. This is holding big mind, not the self-serving mind of ego. People experience it as genuine. Though opening could make us feel confused and holding fixed opinions could make us feel more secure, it also makes us more closed. Big mind allows whatever arises to remain without answers. We just hold the energy of confusion and sanity simultaneously. Then we are using relating as a mutually healing and empowering tool. This is all we really have to offer others.

Holding both the neurosis and the sanity is the powerful teaching of the Five Wisdoms. We resonate in five colors and have the potential to exchange with others in all of them. We could have an intellectually brilliant conversation and/or a heart/sensual encounter.

GETTING IN TOUCH WITH
YOUR ENERGIES IN RELATIONSHIP
Do this with a partner.
• Each of you pick one of the energies, and
have a conversation in the stuck version of that energy.
• Have an energetic exchange without words, looking at each other's face.
• Have a conversation in the shine version of one of the energies.

TANGO LESSONS: EXCHANGE IN LEADING AND FOLLOWING

Tango is an interesting model to examine the dynamics of relationships, as the "essence" of tango is exchange. Any dance or activity that is about the connection between two people is extremely powerful and tremendously fulfilling (better than sex, some tango aficionados say). Making love, the dance form of contact improvisation, horseback riding, padma energy exploration, and tango all have this in common. Much to the surprise of one of my tango partners, I said, "Dancing with you is like riding a horse!" The synergistic experience of movement, grounded in energetic exchange, is a delightful sensation.

Tango is an embodied symbiotic experience of the masculine and feminine energies. At best, the leader and follower join: leaders with clarity and purpose, followers with connection and surrender. Elementally, leaders are clear, pure water and moving air, and followers are dancing fire and grounding earth.

Where we begin is that the leader leads and the follower responds. As we work with the form further, the particular response of the follower guides the leader's next lead. The role of follower has to be as "strong" as the role of leader. At some point in this reciprocal relationship, both people ride the energy of the moment, the epitome of good collaboration. In the many exercises I have developed around padma energy, this basic principle can be taken into working with a group.

The Five Wisdoms inform tango by giving us five key principles for becoming sensitive to when and how to lead and follow. A tango dance always begins with the partners in a quiet presence (buddha), where they open to connecting with each other (padma). From there the leader initiates the movement (vajra/karma), and the follower responds (padma). The dance then becomes the expression of the joining put into action (padma/karma). If we start right off with karma, we miss the point, the essence, of tango. Ratna enters the picture later, with embellishments, sometimes led and at other times spontaneously coming from either partner. We can then use these same principles to make collaborative partnerships more effective: tango teamwork.

HOW DO YOU FEEL AS A LEADER AND FOLLOWER?

Stand in a circle facing the back of the person in front of you.

- Walk around in the circle. Think of yourself as being the leader.
- Then think of yourself as being the follower.
- What is the felt sense of each?
- Now move in open space, sensing how you lead and follow.

WAYS WE BLOCK EXCHANGE

It is an open secret: we all feel a barrier between ourselves and others. We habitually create a fortress of self-defense: "closed" rather than "open," with many excuses for not opening. We could avoid open exchanges, intensify our differences. When we are not joined with another, we may feel as if we are open but could be mutually colluding to project our version of reality. We can't enter another person's world unless we are somewhat free of our own heaviness. We fail to see how we are coloring the space.

MISCOMMUNICATION IN FIVE COLORS

Do this with a partner.

- Have a conversation around a potentially heated topic, with each of you being firmly fixated in one of the energies.
- Switch colors.
- Converse with one person holding the wisdom, the other the neurosis.
- Share your observations.

We can get stuck in a negative exchange: we find someone difficult because of our feelings toward him or her. The person triggers us, so we become defensive and reactive. The closer we are to the other (primary partner, child or parent, everyday work colleague, and so forth), the stronger our reactivity. This leads to very solid armoring on both sides, and we become polarized. Stuckness like this can be very destructive, especially over a prolonged period. Particularly poignant is when children grow up in a family whose mode of exchange is constantly negative. Such a dynamic is very hard to recover from if we are "infected" with it in our younger years.

BLOCKING EXCHANGE IN
FIVE STYLES

- *Buddha*: spacing out, feeling separate, not involved. ("Leave me alone"; or "I'm tired"; or "Let someone else do it.")
- *Vajra*: intellectual, analytical, judgmental, critical, intolerant, rigid, feeling superior. ("Obviously she's wrong. This is the way we should see it.")
- *Ratna*: intimidated, overwhelmed, inadequate, not good enough, arrogant, needing to be needed. ("I just can't do that"; or "Please let me help.")
- *Padma*: distracted, preoccupied, absorbed in own emotion, depressed, claustrophobic, irritable, unable to discriminate ours from theirs, sense of enmeshment or fusion that precludes the perception of "other." ("He's my friend. I'd do anything for him"; or "I'm so confused.")
- *Karma*: speedy, no time, impatient, bored, certain what is coming next, grasping power, competitive. ("I'm too busy"; or "It needs to be done now.")

We all have ways in which we block exchange, are somehow not present. When we are unable to experience the exchange, our relationships are full of projections (unconscious ascrip-

tions of thoughts or feelings to somebody) and we wander in confusion. We don't know if it is their story or our story. Awareness slowly undermines our avoidance strategies. We see when we get lost or more concerned with our own needs. This returns us to being more present, reengaged, and energized.

TUNING UP YOUR
PSYCHOPHYSICAL BAROMETER

This exercise is adapted from the focusing work of Eugene Gendlin. You can do it on your own or ask someone to facilitate it for you.

1. Think of a person with whom you feel an energetic barrier.
   - What is the felt sense in your body when you recall him or her? Feel the unclear, murky discomfort of it.
2. Deepen the felt sense.
   - The facilitator can repeat what you say, reflecting it back exactly. He or she mirrors, confirms experience, is supportive.
   - What is the quality of the felt sense?
   - What one word, phrase, or image describes it best?
     - Put words to the feelings and then see if the words fit the feelings.
     - Go back and forth between word(s) or image(s) and the felt sense.
     - Have the sensation of matching several times.
   - The felt sense could move to another part of the body.
     - If the felt sense changes, follow it with your attention.

– When you get the perfect match, stay with it.
3. Let your body answer these inquiries.
   - What is it about this person that makes it difficult for you?
   - What is the worst of this feeling?
   - What does the bad feeling need? Wait for the feeling to give you the answer.
4. What would it feel like if it was OK to feel that way?
   - Wait for the feeling to give you the answer.
   - Protect it from critical voices.
5. Experience appreciation.
   - Welcome what came.
   - Recognize it as familiar when it returns later.
   - What energies were at play?
   - Just let it be.

EXPERIENCES WITH EXCHANGE

One of the most delightful experiences I've had with exchange was when I was teaching in a three-year Karuna Training program in Germany. (Karuna, meaning compassion, does not refer to my daughter.) I would facilitate deep interactive group process work with Maria, our translator, at my side. She was completely in sync with me and would translate so spontaneously that there was no interruption to the flow of the process. One day I asked her how she could be so attuned to another. She said she thought it was because she is a twin.

Animals don't talk. They communicate nonverbally. This may be one good reason why we can love our pet dog or cat so unconditionally. Dogs, horses, dolphins, and other animals are now being used therapeutically for their healing ability to love. My daughter Karuna's journey has led her to work with horses. There was a turning point in which she became more interested in communicating with a horse nonverbally than by telling it what to do while riding it. So there was Mom, patiently sitting in the stable's viewing room waiting for her to come into the arena with the horse we had recently leased for her. No Karuna; no horse. I went back to the stall. "What are you doing? Why aren't you riding?" "I'm massaging him." So that was it: we were paying a big hourly fee so she could massage the horse! It took me a while to catch on to the intelligence in this.

Over the years, I have been greatly informed by Karuna's work with horses. She trains, rides, teaches therapeutic riding and an approach she developed to contemplative riding. In all her activities around horses, she is more interested in cultivating a sensitivity to them and relating to them as partners rather than dominating or controlling them. She talks about their personalities the same way most of us talk about people. She guides both people and horses to bring out the best of their potential. Some powerful experiences with horses have led her to work toward a career in equine-facilitated psychotherapy. The sessions are generally done in a round pen with a horse without any tack or devices. The following description illustrates the oscillation of energy between self and other, moment to moment.

Karuna writes, from her thesis in Clinical Psychology:

I enter the round pen. Star flicks an ear toward me, but she continues to make her way around the pen, sniffing the wet ground. I follow the black, solidly built mare. As we go, I bend down, touch the earth, and then bring my fingers to my nostrils. I breathe deeply. In this way, I smell what she smells. I also keep my awareness of the world around me, as she does. I know she does this because her ears are continually flicking to take in new sounds. After a time, she stops, and I approach her. She lets me come into her space and put my hand on her shoulder. We stand like this as the clouds shift across the sky. I am aware of the other horses in the herd watching us from their different pens. I feel supported, whole. I hear a message in my head: "Do not be afraid of your powerful ability to love."

I begin to cry. The sadness of not acknowledging my ability to love as a strength and power runs deep. I clutch my fingers into her mane and lean my forehead on her shoulder as the sobbing overwhelms my body. Star brings her muzzle around to touch my hip. In this way, her neck cradles me. As quickly as it comes, the surge of sadness passes. I feel cleansed. I slide down her body until I am sitting on the ground right at her hooves. It feels almost rebellious. Countless times I have been told never to sit on the ground around a horse. I rebel because I trust her. I even lie back on the wet sand and look at the clouds skipping across the pale blue sky. My knees are up, and Star brings her warm muzzle to rest gently on my knees. We are connected. I have never

known such intimacy. It comes from a deep connection with myself and with my world. From this place, I can truly trust and connect with another.

This session created a deeper kind of learning. My experience with Star has greatly influenced how I have chosen to manifest in the world. This learning experience affected me on a very deep level, reflecting the power of working with horses.

In Five Wisdoms trainings, we create a community whose members are in constant exchange with one another. Everyone is tuned in to the ambience, the tone. There is a generosity to exchange: we say we are willing to be with another and really feel him or her. In a monthlong program, I felt so open that it was as if my body were porous. With this kind of openness, the dynamics among people are seen for what they are: just energy. There is no need to take it personally nor to blame others. It is just things as they are. We find that there is an invitation to be ourselves.

WORKING WITH EXCHANGE

The commitment to working with others in this way can be a big leap. It goes beyond professionalism and beyond the safety of a one-up relationship. It aspires to a willingness to take on confusion and difficult situations. However, it can be immensely rewarding and mutually beneficial. Our work with ourselves becomes the most important tool for working with others. It requires that we know ourselves very well, so we can be a clear channel. We need to rouse motivation to get in touch with our permeable nature, where the distinction between self and other gets blurred in a positive sense. We could put ourselves in another's shoes: identify with the other, resonate with his or her energy, enter his or her world.

Energetic exchange requires tremendous trust in our intrinsic sanity. Our sanity can both absorb the other person's confusion and draw out his or her sanity. Sensing the intensity being avoided and staying with it increases our capacity for energetic resonance.

We work with a sense of touch and go: it creates openness. For some, touch is easier, but without go, it becomes indulgent. We find that when we have resonance and clarity, our heart opens: we have an unconditional love toward ourselves and others and, out of compassion, want to relieve their suffering. It could break our heart.

Particularly with a primary partner, the tension could be too much to handle at a given time. Allowing the relationship more space, more distance, we could see his or her energy as just energy and recognize how it triggers us. We work with where we are stuck, not where the other is; we could realize that perhaps we cause ourselves more pain than anybody else ever does. Moreover, we have a choice: our pain is optional.

When the inner turmoil is heightened, we could establish some ground rules: "Can we agree to work on our issues only at designated times?" "What do you think about having silent mornings?" If there is a lot to be processed, committing to a time each week to do it is invaluable. It helps to forestall bringing up sensitive topics impulsively, which is sure to trigger the other person. Even in the best of relationships, late-night talks when we are tired will not be very effective.

Intractable relationships occur. We could see a sharply polarized relationship as a perfect storm: the coming together of intense energy. When we see the energetic dynamics, there is no need to blame. Things are what they are. However, we can justifiably decline to live our lives in a perfect storm. Ultimately, it might be most skillful to bow out of the relationship.

In working with exchange, we come back to our common humanity, which is basically good. It makes us equal—equal but different. Seeing others as different rather than a problem, we can embrace their diverse energy. This is profoundly transformative. Then we can rejoice in the rich and amazing diversity of humanity. Energetic exchange is an invaluable tool to work with all our relationships.

The following are ways we can work with exchange in a group setting. Note that these experiential exercises primarily work with padma energy.

MOVING WITH ENERGETIC EXCHANGE

Do this as a group and have a facilitator guide it.
• Everyone finds a partner and designates person one and person two
  – stand facing them with your palms together, eyes closed
  – breathe and connect to your partner through your palms
  – breathe in and take in the energy of your partner

- breathe out and send your energy into them
- this does not have to be synchronized with your partner
• When the facilitator says ones that person begins to move and twos follow
  - move the hands going into bigger and bigger arm movements
  - slowly expand the movement so the whole body is moving
• The facilitator will call out ones and twos progressively faster
  - the facilitator then says "no leader"
  - at that point, ride the energy you have created with your partner
• Continue the energetic connection and open your eyes
  - then let go of your hands
  - play with proximity, near and far
  - play with doing contrasting movement to your partner, but stay connected
• Join another couple, then join a quartet, then move with everyone

CIRCLE TALK: PRACTICING EXCHANGE

Do this as a group, standing in a circle.
• Person A makes a statement: a neurotic gesture or movement

- person B (to their right or left) duplicates it and makes a responding gesture
- person C duplicates B's gesture and makes a responding gesture
- go around the circle several times, escalating neurosis
• In the next round add sound or words
• Then break from the circle and move into space
  - everyone follows the same person they did in the circle
  - others in the group can echo (duplicate) the movement/sound at any time
• Repeat the exercise with gestures or movements that express sanity

EXCHANGE ENCOUNTERS

Do this in a group.
• Walk around, being aware of others' psycho-spheres as you pass them
  - briefly stop near someone and have an exchange
  - be aware of entrances and exits, when you are alone and when joined
  - stay with your own energy, feel theirs
• When you stop to exchange with someone, make it longer
  - have a brief movement episode

10

Unbiased Perception

IN THE OPENNESS of authentic presence and energetic exchange, we use unbiased perception as a tool to see someone clearly. We use the empathetic heart of padma and the mirror-like clarity of vajra. We join heart and mind, intuition and insight. Energetically, the eyes are connected to the heart, so an open heart sees compassionately. Compassion is very powerful, but it needs the intelligence of clear seeing, just as intelligence needs the open heart of compassion: they work together. We have a cheerful mind and a tender heart.

USING ENERGETIC EXCHANGE AND UNBIASED PERCEPTION AS TOOLS

An environment of compassion lays the groundwork for accurate communication. We are aware not only of what people say but of their tone of being. Words represent a fraction of people's communication: equally important is their energetic quality. We need to feel their energetic presence and learn their language. We go below what people say to the heart of the matter, drawing the covert out of the overt, the unknown out of the known. We need to read between the lines. Since other people's story line could be a smoke screen, we must listen to what they don't say. We want to see who they are, not who we think they are.

> If you really want to understand us, you must listen carefully to what we cannot say.
>
> —HARVEY GILLMAN, Quaker speaker and writer

We need to see each individual as a full person, not just a set of problems. This is really difficult when his or her neurosis is screaming at us. We tend to label and dismiss the other: "He's a pathological liar"; "She's a control freak." In the healing professions, it's standard to diagnose and cure. Our sense of professionalism and expertise lead us to jump in to fix problems. This is an itch/scratch mentality. Though knowing what is unhealthy and having the means to alleviate it are helpful, this can be a Band-Aid approach, treating the symptom rather than addressing the deep-rooted cause. We just cover up the wound instead of seeing how it fits into a larger picture. Although we need not go into the history of the problem, we acknowledge the history that is energetically present in the moment.

PROJECTIONS AND PERCEPTIONS

It is easy to get caught up in projections, the unconscious ascription of a personal thought or feeling to somebody else; we do it all the time. When we project our version of reality onto someone and relate to him or her in terms of our version, we do not see the other person. For instance, if we are entrenched in karma energy, we see everyone around us as part of our workforce. If we have a lot of padma energy, we would rather just hang out and chat. Tremendous tension is created if someone does not comply with our version. We are in dualistic separation, convincing and solid.

This is particularly challenging if we are close to the other person. In any relationship, there are four people: ourselves, our version of the other person, the other person, and his or her version of us. For instance, if someone is in a state of intensified anger, which could have many layers, we feel threatened and react to him or her with anger or fear. We believe in the other's projection and project back. We create a world of bouncing projections, a hell realm of aggression. We pollute the world.

We could be more ecological. When our perception is unbiased, there is a sense of space around our perception. There is room for natural intelligence to arise, in an ever-shifting pattern. We can see things the other person's way, and because we do, a mutual dance can take place. Unfortunately, the ability to perceive in a truly unbiased way, without the contamination of projections, is quite rare. When it does happen, it can be so fleeting that we hardly notice. It could also be electrifying: insight about another person dawns.

UNBIASED PERCEPTION ESTABLISHES GENUINE RELATIONSHIPS

- We cultivate awareness of both inner and outer energy.
  - The energy can be heavy, intense, as if polluted—claustrophobic with projections of red or green or whatever.
  - Or it can have muted tones, infused with buddha energy—luminous blues and greens, soft yellows and reds.
- When with someone:
  - First we see the other's confusion, where he or she is stuck.
  - Then we sense the quality or style of the other's energy and let it be as it is.
  - Knowing the wisdom version, we can align with it.
- We learn to hold our seat.
  - We relax and allow a gap between listening and responding.
  - We see solidification in ourselves and the other but don't get hooked.
- Moments could come into focus in a heartfelt/mind-penetrating way.
  - Such focus feels very meaningful.
  - We feel completely touched and could get tears in our eyes.
  - It is a sign that we have hit the mark.
  - Those moments have a wakeful quality and resonate over time.
- We hold the quality of wisdom and let it expand into the environment.
  - Aligning with wisdom dissolves negativity.
- When our mind is more spacious, we see things as they are.

– We are more likely to see someone's fleeting, impermanent, transparent quality.

In this chapter we are going to reexamine the five modes. These psychophysical aspects make us more aware of the particularities and characteristics of each energy.

THE FIVE MODES: BODY, SPEECH, MIND, QUALITY, AND ACTION

We have everything we need right here to know ourselves and our world: our body, our speech, and our mind, or physical, emotional, and mental. Once we have a sense of these basic three, we begin to see that each person or

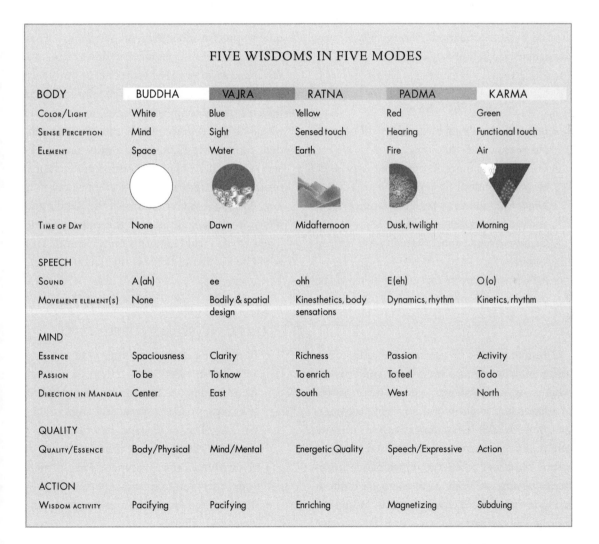

FIVE WISDOMS IN FIVE MODES

BODY	BUDDHA	VAJRA	RATNA	PADMA	KARMA
Color/Light	White	Blue	Yellow	Red	Green
Sense Perception	Mind	Sight	Sensed touch	Hearing	Functional touch
Element	Space	Water	Earth	Fire	Air
Time of Day	None	Dawn	Midafternoon	Dusk, twilight	Morning
SPEECH					
Sound	A (ah)	ee	ohh	E (eh)	O (o)
Movement element(s)	None	Bodily & spatial design	Kinesthetics, body sensations	Dynamics, rhythm	Kinetics, rhythm
MIND					
Essence	Spaciousness	Clarity	Richness	Passion	Activity
Passion	To be	To know	To enrich	To feel	To do
Direction in Mandala	Center	East	South	West	North
QUALITY					
Quality/Essence	Body/Physical	Mind/Mental	Energetic Quality	Speech/Expressive	Action
ACTION					
Wisdom activity	Pacifying	Pacifying	Enriching	Magnetizing	Subduing

situation has a quality, a subtle energetic depth. Going further, we see that an inevitable style of action emerges from that energetic quality. Then, as we saw in chapter 2, we have five modes: body (physical), speech (emotional/expressive), mind (mental), quality/essence, and action (BSMQA). We can begin to see each of the wisdom energies in terms of their BSMQA. As well, each wisdom energy has an affinity to one of the modes. Vajra, for instance, is associated with the mental mode, though it has a way of manifesting in body and speech.

THE FIVE MODES: BSMQA

- *Body*: the outer or physical world of people, places, and situations
- *Speech*: the inner or energetic world of emotions and subtle energy
- *Mind*: the hidden or private world of ideas and mental models
- *Quality*: the dominant quality of expression
- *Action*: the activity that emerges from the quality

The five modes of the five energies, open and closed, encompass everything and thus are what we need in order to understand ourselves in relationship to our world. In seeing the energies from the BSMQA perspective, we cultivate our ability to observe in an unbiased way and attune ourselves to energetic resonance in order to be able to "read" how energy is embodied in people, places, and situations. When we see the energy patterns, we immediately have a sense of how someone or something is shining and how the person or thing is stuck. This gives us a tool to see any style as workable, just as it is. With BSMQA awareness, insight can arise spontaneously in the midst of our oceans of discursive thought. We can have a spontaneous flash about someone, a moment of wakefulness suddenly free from preoccupations. It is a tangible, physical sensation of being synchronized, a feeling of clicking in. It has a sharp quality, precise and intelligent.

We can use observation and description as a discipline in order to see someone, or ourselves, objectively. We need this highly precise and penetrating descriptive process, an extremely revealing laser beam, to counteract our tendency to project. Cultivating a discipline of observation and withholding our preconceptions, projections, interpretations, and expectations is key. We could pay attention to the details and nuances of every aspect of the other's being. Then we can truly enter his or her world. This could be the first time we really see the other.

READING ENERGY AND
KNOWING SOMEONE FULLY

- To fully experience another, we need to both feel and see.
- We experience a resonance, an oscillation of energy, or an energetic exchange.
- We use observation and description as a discipline of unbiased perception.
- We withhold our preconceptions, projections, interpretation, and expectations.
- We break down the barrier between ourselves and others.

- Our heart opens, and our mind becomes clear.

Practicing unbiased perception is difficult, particularly with those closest to us, because we are enmeshed with them. By enmeshment I mean an unconscious collusion in which each of us accepts the other's projections on us. For instance, a conventional marriage has this setup: the husband financially supports his wife, who cooks, cleans, bears his children, and satisfies him sexually. There is an unspoken understanding that they are codependent, each agreeing to be what the other one wants. In this scenario, we become captives of each other's projections: we create a version of reality for two. Any behavior from the other that is not in line with this version is a threat. It becomes impossible to see who the person is beyond our need for our version of him or her. For instance, we could fail to see how someone wants to be loved. When we love someone the way he or she wants to be loved, we are loving the other. If we only love someone in our way, he or she becomes an extension of ourselves and doesn't experience our love. A workaholic husband and father, for example, may feel he is expressing his love by supporting his family, but because he is never around, his family feels unloved.

The following is a list of characteristics, which is rather comprehensive, that can be used to see someone clearly. Some of these characteristics will be more obviously relevant than others, depending on how well you know the other person. Feel free to pass over what does not resonate.

THE THREE MODES: PHYSICAL, ENERGETIC, AND MENTAL

PHYSICAL/BODY

- Age, gender
- Physical appearance (You could start at the head and go down the body.)
  - face: shape of eyes, eyebrows, nose, mouth, teeth
  - body type: shape, size, height, weight, muscle tone
  - coloring: hair, eyes, complexion, skin tone
  - ethnicity
- Physical well-being
  - healthy, ill, or disabled
- Posture, stance, mannerisms
  - frail, stooped or strong, upright
  - how the person holds himself or herself in various situations
  - gestures, facial expressions
- Style of dress, types of clothing, ornamentation
  - attentiveness to appearance: grooming, cleanliness
- Physical activity
  - how the person relates to his or her environment, inhabits space
  - inquisitive and explorative or confined and limited
  - style of walking
  - physical contact with others
  - physical discipline(s)
- How the person spends time, both scheduled and free time
  - profession or job
  - talents, hobbies, recreational activities

- Physical environment, where the person lives and works
  - landscape, culture
  - messy or neat
  - other members of the household
  - car or other means of transportation
- Cooking and eating, diet, medications
- Sleeping habits

ENERGETIC / EMOTIONAL

- Breathing
  - breath as shallow, deep, vigorous, or fragile
- Sense of being
  - aliveness or deadness
  - well-being or fear, anxiety, insecurity
- Energetic quality of speech, conveying (or not conveying) emotion
  - tone, pitch, volume, modulation, inflection, rhythm, articulation, speed
  - verbose, elaborate or economical, simple
  - direct, stick to the point or vague, lose track, incomplete sentences, trail off
  - slang, profanity
  - modulation and phrasing of sentences, pauses
- Style of communication, expression, energetic quality
  - gestures, eye contact, facial expression
  - talks to, through, or beyond someone
  - reciprocity: ability to listen, give others space to talk, allow silence
  - private or open
  - use of metaphor or story
  - congruency between what is said and what is meant
- Language, culture, education
  - vocabulary, grammar

- accent, dialect, diction, pronunciation
- ability to articulate
- words or phrases used frequently
- Emotions
  - dominant emotional tone and what emotions are not felt
  - what happens when emotions are experienced
  - how feelings are expressed: experienced, suppressed, or acted out
  - repertoire of moods and the situations in which they arise
  - experience of confidence or depression, and conditions that elicit these
- Relationships, how the person extends outward, interacts with others, with whom he or she talks
  - friends, intimates, coworkers, authority figures, groups
  - same and opposite gender, children, animals
  - emotional tone in relating
  - level of intimacy
- Relationship to passion or sexuality
  - how passion or engagement with life is managed
- Relationship to money
- Dreams and images

MENTAL / MIND

- Reflected and revealed through physical and energetic modes
- The nature of his or her awareness
  - self-aware, self-knowing, or oblivious to what he or she says and does
  - range in how the person views things, the world as big or small

- what expands or contracts the person's view of the world
  - spirituality, religion, wisdom
- Mental landscape, textures
  - spacious/barren, clear/sharp, resourceful/crowded, lively/obsessive, speedy
  - narrow and focused, vast and clear, confused and chaotic
  - intellectual capacity, knowledgeable or not
- Mental models
  - vision, view, core beliefs
  - scripts, values, attitudes, rules, thoughts, concepts, ideas
  - what the person thinks about passion, power, health, sex, money, job, relationships
  - how the person sees himself or herself in the world, his or her role
  - assumptions made about the world—that it is safe, dangerous
  - interests, motivation
  - optimistic or cynical
  - strategies or coping mechanisms to protect self
- Relationship to mind, mental state (sane and confused)
  - style of thinking, thought process
  - analytical, intuitive, by example, concrete images
  - ability to solve problems, make choices
  - memory
  - imagination, fantasy, dreamscape
  - experience of gaps, doubt, uncertainty, confusion
- Honesty, integrity or irresponsibility, carelessness

- humor, how the person laughs (requires taking a different point of view)
  - how the person relates to surprise, pain
  - what are turn-ons, passions
- Engagement with a mindfulness discipline
  - formal or informal
  - ability to be in the present moment
  - where in life the person is cultivating attention to detail
- Activities that reflect the person's worldview

QUALITY

When the physical, emotional tone or expression, and the mental attributes are clearly seen and felt, we get a sense of the overall energetic quality. We feel the texture, ambience, or tone of people, places, and situations. We have a felt sense, intuition. If we have truly dropped our projections and judgments, the experience is very open and awake. This is not about clever labeling or diagnosing but an experience of reality that is very deep, a truth beyond concept. It is at this level that the energies are fully seen.

ACTION

Action, how we interact with the world, arises out of the coming together of BSMQ. If we are stuck in our neurosis, our actions arise out of the projections we make onto a person or situation. These projections are then exacerbated by emotional reactivity to this false reality. We find that all our thoughts, feelings, and actions reflect an intensified reality rather than a down-to-earth reality. If we are in tune with our wisdom, our actions are based on reading the situation clearly.

We can meet the situation without hesitation and act spontaneously in accord with what is needed. What we do could happen effortlessly.

QUICK FIVE-MODES EXERCISE TO RECOGNIZE SOMEONE'S STYLE

Do this with a partner or group.

- The presenter describes someone.
  - Body: physical appearance, places the person inhabits, behavior patterns, activities
  - Speech: emotional tone, style of communication, relationships
  - Mind: mental models, views the person has of himself or herself, others, and the world
- The listener or listeners exchange energy with the presenter and the person presented.
- At the end of the presentation:
  - See the described person's energetic mix without judgment.
  - See his or her shine and stuck, fluid and frozen, aspects.
- Align with shine; mirror stuck.
  - What is the intelligence in the situation?

CULTIVATING UNBIASED PERCEPTION AND ENERGETIC EXCHANGE

Do this longer version in a small group with a presenter, a timekeeper, and others in exchange, or with a partner, with one person presenting and the other in exchange and keep-

ing time. Everyone studies the three modes in advance and picks a person whom they would like to present. Significant others could present each other. Work creatively, like creating a character in a novel. The more precise you are, the more the person comes to life. He or she becomes vivid like a hologram. Presentations are confidential, and a made-up name can be used.

PURPOSES

- To see another person more clearly and improve your relationship with him or her
- To invite the person being presented into the room
  - The relationship of the presenter and the person being presented also becomes present.
  - The experience of the presenter and of the listener/group members is included.
- To facilitate exchange and the arising of maitri and karuna
  - Exchange: direct, unobstructed sharing of energy and experience of another (other words for exchange: *oscillation, resonance, psychophysical barometer*)
  - Maitri: unconditional love, wishing happiness for all
  - Karuna: compassion: wanting to ease the suffering of others

PRESENTER

- Describe someone in terms of the three modes. Take forty-five minutes, fifteen minutes for each section. It is important not to use the three modes list so you can truly "create" the person on the spot.

- Use the discipline of description to evoke the presence of your person.
  - Bring him or her to life, like a hologram or a character in a novel.
- Say everything you know about the person.
  - Tell what is noticed, what stands out.
  - The more precision there is, the more vividly the person comes to life.
  - Give details, nuances, and examples.
- Step into the other person's shoes; put yourself in his or her place.
  - Consider the person's interests, views, dilemmas, issues.
  - Feel the predicaments of his or her life.
  - Feel the person's pain or problems as well as his or her intelligence or sanity.
- Talk from personal experience.
  - Avoid preconception, interpretation, and projection.
  - Avoid history or story line unless vitally important to the present.
- Whatever is not remembered is good information. You might see ways in which you don't notice the person.

FACILITATOR/LISTENER(S)

- Keep track of time and interject process comments.
  - Remind the presenter to stay with the discipline of description.
- Create a container of maitri.
  - Practice authentic presence and exchange.
- Intervene to remind the presenter of various aspects of the description if needed.

- Have the list by your side to help keep things on track, if needed.
- Focus on moment-to-moment experience.
  - Stay with the process, without solidifying or fixating.
  - Do not get caught in digressions and extraneous preoccupations.
  - Notice when you distance mentally and go out of your heart.
- Anything and everything that arises from the listener or group is relevant.
- At the end of each section, ask clarifying questions.

THE LISTENER OR LISTENERS EXPRESS THE ENERGETIC EXCHANGE

- Open your heart and pay attention to the felt sense in your body.
- Say how you feel, perhaps in your body, using "I" statements.
  - You could use imagery or show how you feel with a body gesture or movement.
- It is important not to offer opinions or solutions, try to fix what has been presented in any way, or get caught in speculation and projection.
- Offer an aspiration, which allows the exchange to simmer and go deeper.

THE QUALITY AND ACTION ARISE FROM THE BSM DESCRIPTION

- Quality is one of the five energies with their unique combinations.
- Action is the activity that arises from the energies.

CREATIVE EXPRESSION OF THE PRESENTATION AND EXCHANGE

This can be done right after the presentation or later with a partner. Allow fifteen to thirty minutes.

- Both people color the energy of the person presented.
- Each shows the other, with the presenter going first.
  - Say how it feels in your body.
  - Possibly demonstrate with a body posture, movement, and/or sound.
- Name which energies, sane and neurotic, are present in the person. Also name his or her wisdom activity.
- Reverse roles, allowing fifteen to thirty minutes.
- If working with a group, have a discussion. Allow thirty minutes.

Aligning with Sanity through Appreciative Inquiry

This is the fruition of working with your relationship. Do this with a partner.

- The presenter responds to the following questions asked by their partner, who is taking notes. Allow fifteen minutes. Then switch roles.
- For each question, name the energies.
  1. When in the relationship do you feel the best?
  2. What external conditions make that possible?
  3. What qualities in you make that possible?
  4. What aspirations do you have for the relationship?
  5. What conditions or circumstances will make that possible?
- If working with a group, everyone reports for the person he or she interviewed. Give a quick feel for the person.

Knowing What to Do

- Say how you see the sanity and intelligence in the relationship or situation.
- What agreements are needed to take the next step?
  - What do you need from the other person to feel good about the relationship?
  - What are you willing to do to meet the person more authentically?

The following exercises work with BSMQA, exchange, and perception.

FIVE MODES TO CREATE A CHARACTER

Do this extended sensualization (using all the senses) on your own or with a facilitator. Allow your creativity to fully express itself.

- With eyes closed, allow your mind to go blank. Then let a colored dot arise spontaneously in the distance. Think of the dot as the essence of the character you will be creating. (You can also choose to create an animal.)
- Slowly progress through the three modes to develop your character.
- Quality and action are the way the character/animal would express itself: stance, gesture, movement, sound.

- End by shrinking the character/animal to one inch.
  - Flip it around so it faces the same direction as you and have it jump into your heart.
  - Let it grow inside you so that you completely embody it.
- If you are in a group, characters could then interact, have brief encounters.
- What did you discover about yourself?

FIVE MODES TO CREATE A SELF-PORTRAIT

Do this with a partner.
- Presenter: describe yourself to your partner through the five modes.
- Listener: stay present, in exchange.
- At the end, both say how you feel and what energies are present.

MIRRORING NEUROSIS AND ALIGNING WITH SANITY

In small groups of four or five, stand in a circle.
- Arouse a sense of unconditional friendliness in the group.
- One person presents someone with movement, words, and/or sounds, exaggerating the neurotic aspect to make it more vivid.
- Group members mirror the neurosis back to the presenter, also exaggerated.
- Then the group sits, breathes in the neurosis, and breathes out the sanity.
  - Then all embody the sanity.
- Discuss your experience in the group.

EXCHANGE AND UNBIASED PERCEPTION IN RECOGNIZING STYLE

Do this with partner, one person acting as an expresser and the other acting as a listener, as if you were a client and a coach/therapist.
- The expresser presents himself or herself as:
  - Unaware: expectations, projections, story lines
  - Personal, immediate, unresolved pain, hooked in, stuck
- The listener puts himself or herself into the other's world, yet does not get enmeshed. The listener:
  - Has compassionate presence: is spacious, warm, receptive.
  - Does energetic exchange: joins with the other person, gives him or her a sense of being met.
  - Has clear seeing: active listening, letting the person present himself or herself.
  - Holds his or her seat: rests, allows a gap between listening and responding.
  - Reflects back to the other: says how the body feels and which energies are present.
  - Aligns with sanity and mirrors the neurosis.
- Switch roles and repeat.

In a group discuss the experience, focusing on the process versus the content.

MOCK DIALOGUE

Do this with a partner, one person taking the stuck role and the other the shine role.

- Try to be convincing in your roles.
- What happens?

SIGNIFICANT RELATIONSHIPS CONSTELLATION

(Adapted from Bert Hellinger, psychotherapist in Systemic Family Solutions)

The purpose of this exercise is to engender the ability to appreciate significant others and understand their interconnectedness. Do this exercise for your relationships with family, friends, or work colleagues.

- The presenter:
  - Places people in a configuration that visually shows their relationship.
  - With a few words, says whom they portray.
- The participants:
  - Each person gets into the quality of the person he or she is portraying.

- There could be a gesture or movement and an interaction among people.
- See the dynamics of the relationships.
  - Move from stuck energy to fluid energy.
  - See the intelligence present.
- Come to a new configuration that expresses the sanity.
  - See the basic goodness that was present all along.

PRIMARY PARTNERS

1. Jot down a constellation of your mix of colors.
2. Do an appreciative inquiry and jot down the constellation of the relationship.
3. Color or make a collage of the constellation of the relationship.
   - Be aware of the confusion and intelligence present.

II

Engaging Effectively

WHEN WE GO DOWN the path of cultivating authenticity in ourselves and our relationships, we find that our interactions with the people with whom we live, work, and play are much easier and infinitely more enjoyable. We have put people first. Next we need some skillful ways of engaging with them to be more effective in the world. This chapter is full of ways to work with others that could apply to many aspects of our personal and professional lives. Regardless of whether we are working with people who are motivated to engage in the following ways, we can set our own standards, though we cannot necessarily expect the same from others. Most important, we can be proactive and lead the way.

The Five Wisdoms approach is complementary to contemporary modalities in working with others. This reciprocal relationship between ancient wisdom and ever-evolving new skill sets—and new professions—makes a potent combination. We can weave our understanding of the Five Wisdoms into the topics in this chapter, often bringing out greater depth, either for personal reflection or to have a common language.

Most of us spend the major part of our day on the job. The demands on our time and energy are often out of proportion to what we can handle. We are all multitasking, meeting piling on meeting, and task on task. There is a seemingly infinite amount of work to cram into a finite time. Preoccupied by what went before and what lies ahead, we cannot stay in the present moment. Technology is advancing so rapidly and being utilized so universally that we are left with two choices: either learn to swim through its complexities or slowly drown in the technological tsunami. Surely more people are morphing into the walking dead at their desks than were killed in the 2004 tsunami in Southeast Asia.

As a result of all this, we live with a sense of oppression, feeling victimized, trapped. The more data we have to manage and the more times we are personally dealt with aggressively, the more this sense of oppression deepens. We are also stressed from being confined in not-so-human-friendly organizations and environments. Our institutions are not unlike prisons: enclosed spaces in which we must adhere to a fixed schedule while confined with people we do not trust.

An August 2004 article on meditation in *Business-Week Online* stated that there is a $200 billion loss annually in "absenteeism, subpar performance, tardiness and workers' compensation claims related to stress. In fact, stress-related ailments account for upward of 60% of all doctor visits, according to the Mind/Body Medical Institute at Harvard University."

To add to the stress of overwhelm and speed, faulty leadership roles, poor internal relationships, and managerial blind spots create a never-ending drama, whether openly acknowledged or tacitly sensed, giving our workday an undercurrent of tension. In that kind of environment, how to move forward is very confusing.

MAKING A LIFE, NOT A LIVING

The good news is that there are people out there turning this around.

Your Dream Job

Beezwax aims to be the best place you'll ever work. We pride ourselves on building a sustainable, friendly workplace that empowers staff members to be fulfilled both at work and in their lives beyond. This isn't just a mantra: it's a primary reason the company exists. . . . This means that in addition to competitive compensation, we offer significant flexibility in work schedule. The Beezwax management style is based on democratic values and transparency. We welcome diverse viewpoints and reward initiative. For instance, developers are encouraged to work on projects that interest them (in fact, all of our products and tools have come from this curious exploration). . . . We seek out super smart people with excellent communication skills and proven rock-solid reliability. Non-traditional backgrounds are welcome. We believe that an engaged, empowered team of happy and intelligent professionals can produce great results.

—Beezwax Datatools Web site

I have had the good fortune to work for many years in the Netherlands, where I have noticed several things. The Dutch have a commitment to ongoing learning that is supported, in many cases, at the government level. For instance, for five years, I was a trainer to the trainers at the National Institute of School Development. More recently, I have been invited by the Ministry of Justice to create and deliver a training for Buddhist chaplains and those in the service of others. The Dutch also have more vacation time than any other country. How good is that? One of the reasons this can happen is that it is a small country, so, like smaller companies that are not top-heavy with bureaucracy, it can be more creative.

Axialent is a consulting company dedicated to the development of disciplined individuals, teams and organizations. Our mission is to enable the economic success of our clients through the behavioral, emotional, cognitive, moral and spiritual development of its people. We help individuals achieve their full potential as they express their creative passion at work. We help teams grow into communities of excellence, where people cooperate with dignity, authenticity and respect. . . . It is the "people factor" that will make or break a company. The only way to generate enduring success is to build a work environment that attracts, focuses and develops talented employees to achieve their highest potential.

—Axialent Web site

MAKING A LIFE, NOT A LIVING

If we are going to spend so much of our time at work, let's do a proper job of it. Let's live our deepest values and celebrate this good life as we produce results.

SUMMARY OF FIVE WISDOMS @ WORK

Self

- Recognize and utilize the five basic energetic qualities.
- See the unique ways we display energy and interact with the world.
- Celebrate our strengths and work with our weaknesses.

Relationship

- Improve our ability to understand others and work with their mix of colors.
- Appreciate diverse styles as assets, not obstacles to communication.

Task

- With fresh energy, move from passive involvement to our full potential.

Environment

- Tune in to how energy manifests in the environment as inspiration or obstacle.
- Create enlivened environments.

FIVE STYLES IN HUMAN DYNAMICS

As a language to express the dynamics in personality styles, the Five Wisdoms give us an invaluable understanding. We know what we can expect from people at their best and where they will get stuck. We can also be aware of what they lack the capacity to do, at least at this time. Someone's hardwiring is what it is: Judith can't balance her checkbook and Ricardo gets totally flustered in the company of women. We might feel that people should be manifesting more of a certain energy and get frustrated that they are not. Being more skillful, we could simply see them for who they are and find in ourselves the flexibility to work with them. As irritating as someone might be, if we take the attitude that everyone is trying to do his or her best, we can appreciate others rather than criticize them. This is where unconditional kindness plays a big part.

[Buddha:] It is important in this role to be open, spacious, relaxed, ready for anyone to come through the door and present a question, concern, problem, or idea . . . the ability to be accommodating and open, but not reactive. . . . It is very important for people to feel heard—and actually be heard—without judgment.

[Vajra:] To determine what *is* required in any given situation requires a unique combination of clear seeing and discernment. . . . I can use it to create important boundaries and to counter my tendency to want to please people and be loved. This energy is a cooling, refreshing, invigorating experience for me.

[Padma:] My predominant padma energy will be essential . . . as I will work with others with a sense of warmth, kindness, and inquisitiveness. . . . I have learned to harness this energy in such a way that I can now ride it rather than it riding me. I am able to use discriminating awareness wisdom as a way to understand and appreciate others.

[Ratna:] …the nurturing quality of ratna is something I would cultivate . . . to work with others with a sense of equanimity, caring and supporting without a sense of favoritism.

[Karma:] . . . I didn't embrace my karma energy because it doesn't fit certain ideas I have about myself. . . . I have to come to see that it is a powerful force in my experience and that when channeled properly, allows me to accomplish a tremendous amount and feel really good and inspired. . . . It entails a focus and motivation that I don't always let in, but when I do, it is quite remarkable—and enjoyable!

—Dan Glenn's application for director
of programs at Karmê Chöling,
a Shambhala retreat center

In any endeavor our results are better when our primary focus is not only the task but also our colleagues, our most powerful resource. Lack of this kind of awareness creates misunderstanding, conflict, and failure rather than enabling everyone to achieve their highest potential. An environment where the emphasis is on people who recognize, respect, and understand one another enables us to make better connections in order to work together. As well, a shared vision creates an environment of mutual respect and common larger purpose.

We're a talented team that truly enjoys working together. We've created Beezwax collaboratively, as an environment where our work lives are fully engaging and satisfying. . . . We've supported a distributed workforce as an essential part of honoring each individual "bee." . . . It demands initiative and professionalism from everyone. The result is an effective team for whom work is a natural self-expression. We bring that enthusiasm to our clients, with the hope of not just building great software for them, but helping them build great workplaces as well.

—Beezwax Datatools Web site

A primary reason we have trouble working with others is that we are unaware of differing personality dynamics. At their best, diverse styles are an asset; at their worst, they block communication. Our relationships can be either complementary or clashing. That is why the good work of energetic exchange, unbiased perception, and knowing another's energy style is so important. It is the only way we really, truly understand each person's unique contribution, whether in intimate or public relationships.

The energies reveal that we all have different ways to process information, communicate, learn, and solve problems. When comfortable in our style, we have the flexibility to change gears and manifest in other styles. Using just one energy is unskillful. Sometimes changing gears can be very subtle: a simple choice of words. We can also be more sensitive to the words and phrases common to each style. What is said is not always what is heard.

When engaged in over a period of time, the Five Wisdoms work brings out our full human potential in working with others. When we both embody the Five Wisdoms in a sane way and recognize them in others, we will be able to resonate with others, enjoy one another

FIVE WISDOMS IN ACTION

WISDOM/ ELEMENT	SEE/ UNDERSTAND	COMMUNICATION NEEDS	CAPACITY/ FUNCTION	WORK POINTS/ GROWTH AREAS
VAJRA WATER	overview, big picture structure strategic plan details elegant environments	objective clear direct precise respectful	pacifying, insightful create cohesive overview give meaning, relevance evaluate objectively articulate principles goal of excellence	overly conceptual convoluted logic hold all the information angry, defensive critical, impatient distant, cold, rigid
RATNA EARTH	people's potential diversity what is needed rich environments	personable generous contribute tirelessly give and receive care for others	inclusive team builder community maker create opportunities resourceful goal of cooperation	feeling inadequate, inferior low self-esteem, needy need to be needed arrogant, overbearing greedy, never enough claiming territory
PADMA FIRE	people relational dynamics enjoyment arts elegant environments	connect personally speak from the heart listen deeply warm, share openly inspire others playful	intuitive, empathetic take feelings into account process-oriented lubricate situations artistic, imaginative, creative goal of enjoyment	overly self-absorbed overly emotional taking things personally superficial jealous around relationships manipulative
KARMA AIR/WIND	when to act what to do when to end skills needed functional enviroments	goal oriented direct, straightforward detailed, factual want facts dependable methodical	organize time management create systems make things happen practical goal of accomplishment	driven taking control, manipulative not delegating aggresive domination paranoia, lack trust jealousy around power
BUDDHA SPACE	simplicity value just being simple presence	spacious think it over alone	dependable letting situations unfold acceptance	denial overwhelm inability to deal, lazy blind, deaf, dumb

more, and be more effective. We move from a passive involvement in our life and work to realizing our creative potential and manifesting fully.

WORKING WITH THE GROWTH AREAS

We can work with another's stuckness and help him or her grow by offering qualities of other energies.

- Offer vajra's stuckness:
  - space to see himself or herself

- richness to work with dry intellect
- warmth and charm to work with up-tightness
- activity to overcome conceptual preoccupation
- Offer ratna's stuckness:
  - insight into his or her own self-existing richness
  - space to feel that richness
  - a warm, caring heart to work with low self-esteem
  - activity to overcome heaviness
- Offer padma's stuckness:

- spacious engagement to relax obsessive passion
- clarity to penetrate confusing emotions
- richness and depth to work with superficiality
- activity to overcome moodiness

• Offer karma's stuckness:
- space to allow room to move
- intention so energy has direction
- resourcefulness to expand horizons
- inspiration to give joy to hard work

• Offer buddha's stuckness:
- motivation to work with his or her laziness
- resourcefulness to open him or her to possibility
- inspiration to enliven his or her dullness
- activity to get him or her moving

Adapted from Sebo Ebbens, senior trainer at the National Institute for School Development, the Netherlands.

CHECKING IN

Checking in is a good way to begin engaging with others. It allows us to see what is below the surface and get on the same wavelength. It can be very brief. There are various possibilities, depending on the context of the relationship(s). In personal relationships, we want an emotional connection (padma and ratna); in work relationships, the connection is more around the task (vajra and karma). The rule of thumb is that it is better to communicate than to ignore whatever is going on, as the subtext inevitably affects relationships. When aware of one another's thinking and feeling, we can make individual and collective adjustments to improve the process. Making everyone aware of what is happening keeps things from getting confusing.

CHECK-IN POSSIBILITIES

1. To begin working together in a group, state your name and one thing about yourself, perhaps where you are from or your profession.

2. If you feel it would be good to share more, check in around these questions:
   • Who are you?
   • What do you do?
   • What do you care about?
   • What makes you happy?

3. Check in by presenting yourselves using an image to show the sense of your energy: " I am a very ripe melon." Or "I am a road runner." When beginning a training on emotional energy, we might check in with an emotion. To make it more vivid, we exaggerate it.

4. If living with people, a primary partner or others, schedule a periodic check-in, before there is a crisis, or spontaneously if you feel someone is getting into closed energy. If things come up that need further communication, you could set a check-in time that is mutually convenient.

5. Later in the process of working together, you could ask these questions:
   • How do you feel about yourself, others in the group, and the process?

- Are you successfully fulfilling your role? If not, why?
- What can you do to contribute more fully?
- What can you do to facilitate the functioning of others?

At the end of a meeting or any encounter, it is also good to check out, to close the meeting. The checkout at an inner and outer level gives us a sense of what people will be taking away with them. It helps to seal the exchange, thereby creating a bond. No matter whether it is the annual board meeting or a short talk with a fellow employee in the hall, there could be a beginning, middle, and end. Record the main points so when you speak with the other(s) again, you will know where you are.

BEGINNING, MIDDLE, AND END

In any communication have a sense of:
- Beginning: setting the agenda
- Middle: discussing the topics
- End: a clear summary, focusing on action items, which seals the meeting

REACTIVITY VERSUS RESPONSIBILITY

We react emotionally and act impulsively when someone or something presses our button. Habitually, we take the defensive position of a coward, adopt a powerless-victim mentality, feel trapped in a situation not of our own making, and blame others. Instead, we could be a player, a warrior. The victim comes from a self-protec-

tive place, wrapped up in emotional logic; the player has a transpersonal outlook. When we are convinced of our story line, we see only our side; when we see the bigger picture, we realize that everyone has played a part and no one is to blame. Becoming aware of this, we can cultivate the ability to be a warrior in the world. We can challenge the self-pitying coward and align with the wisdom warrior.

When constantly caught in a reactive mode, we sabotage our best interests: the freedom to choose how to be. We just give ourselves over to the tide of external factors. Merely because our phone rings does not mean that, like a robot, we must answer it. What happens happens. We need not capitulate to seeming demands. The stimulus is just information about our world. With awareness, and based on our style, we can choose an appropriate response. Then we are a player, a warrior.

Here is an example: Justin was in negotiation around a very large contract at a major corporation. He saw that the draft contract was skewed to benefit the other party in a number of ways. He asked for modifications and was given a flat no. He chose not to sign. He lost money by this decision but kept his sense of integrity.

We can take unconditional responsibility in all we say and do: be response-able. When we feel we have the freedom to choose our response, we empower ourselves. Freedom to choose, in any situation, gives us the possibility of being consistent with our goals and values. We are accountable for our behavior, taking ownership of both our actions and their consequences. Challenges and adversity can be an opportunity to manifest our values. When we trust ourselves, we inspire others to trust in themselves.

Otherwise, we are unconsciously reacting to situations from a mentality of powerlessness. We cannot necessarily do anything about the external factors and situations, life's constraints, but we *can* do something about our inner workings. This is not obvious, especially when situations trigger strong emotions in us. We automatically go into reactive mode, regarding the external circumstances as beyond our control. This is why it is so important to bring the dark corners of our unexamined selves into the light of day. When the particular way we get stuck is brought to awareness, we are no longer stuck. We have the freedom to choose to be either a coward or a warrior.

> The chance to act with dignity is absolutely basic and inalienable. Dignity, like responsibility, is as unconditional as the human being's humanity. . . . It is precisely in difficult times that scruples become vital. It is when the world threatens to pull us away from our center and wreck us against the rocks of unconsciousness, that our true nature is most clearly exposed.
>
> —FRED KOFMAN

THE VICTIM AND THE PLAYER (ADAPTED FROM FRED KOFMAN)

Do this on your own or with a partner.

• Think about an unsatisfactory situation in the past or present.

• First, look at the situation from a victim's perspective.

  – Take on the role completely, feeling absolutely irresponsible.

  – If with a partner, let him or her help you complain: "I can't believe they did that to you." "It is so unfair." "You shouldn't be treated like this." "They are so mean." "Poor thing, you don't deserve this."

• Explore these questions:

  – What happened to you? Who hurt you or had a negative impact on you? What has this person (or group) done to you? How do you feel about that? What should that person (or group) have done? What should that person (or group) do to repair the damage? How would it affect you if this person (or group) carries on with the behavior?

  – How do you feel in the victim's place?

• Next look at your own behavior and ask these questions:

  – What challenge did you face? How did you choose to respond to the situation? What was your goal? What values and principles would you like to guide your actions? What were the (negative) consequences of your behavior? Can you think of any alternative action that might have been more effective to reach your goals (success)? Can you think of any alternative action that would have been more consistent with your values (integrity)? Is there anything you can do now to minimize or repair the damage of the original situation? Can you learn something from the experience that will help you behave with more effectiveness and integrity in the future?

  – How do you feel as a player (a warrior)?

MEASURING SUCCESS

When the result of our efforts is consistent with our objectives, we feel successful. If we work to earn money and get a monthly paycheck, we feel satisfied. However, such success is conditional because it depends on outside factors beyond our control. We could lose our job in a flash. When our objectives come from a deeper place, we measure our success in a different way. Acting in accord with our inner values gives us success that is unconditional because it is based on our free will. This success is ultimately more rewarding: it generates an inner peace and happiness that transcend external factors. Even if the external results are not what we want, we know we have acted with integrity. We can feel disappointed and successful at the same time. We can dissolve the dichotomy between success and integrity; we can act effectively without compromising our principles.

> Success is truly an inside job. . . . It is within the reach of almost everyone.
>
> —ALICE WALKER

We tend to focus on the outcomes we want. But focusing on the end result, a product goal, makes us dependent on others to fulfill our wishes. If we are interested in working with others, a process goal, we drop our agenda, at least initially. Only then can we stay open to the process. We need to spend as much time inquiring about others' understanding and asking questions as we do stating our own views. We might find that while we empathize with and understand those with whom we are working, we don't necessarily agree with or support them. We could also find that even if our particular agenda is not fulfilled, we have had the opportunity to relate to others' ideas. This is not about winning but aligning with others to make things happen.

ENGAGING IN AN OPEN WAY

Try this with someone with whom you are working or living:

- Pick a topic of contention.
- Inquire about his or her side of it.
  - Really try to understand the other person and thus help the other express his or her view.
  - Listen deeply and check your understanding.
  - Find the truth in what the other is saying, even if it seems toxic at first.
  - Ask for both the other's reasoning and his or her feelings.
  - Ask for a proposal, if appropriate.
  - Ask for permission to counter what the other has said.
- Express your view.
  - What: Present your opinions with humility and "I" statements.
  - Why: Ground your opinions with facts, examples, a logical reason, precedents.
  - Make a suggestion or an offer.
  - Invite questions and counterarguments.
- Are you finding ways to align with, rather than oppose, the other person?

To work with others, we must have a shared vision, a common intention. Without an initial alignment, we could go off in very different directions. This is where everything could break down. Once we have a shared vision, everyone has something uniquely theirs to offer. We might be in the position of asking others what they would like to contribute. Guiding people to bring out their best colors is very rewarding for everyone.

> We've experienced great trials before, and with every test, each generation has found the capacity to not only endure, but to prosper—to discover great opportunity in the midst of great crisis. That is what we can and must do today. And I am absolutely confident that is what we will do.
>
> —President Barack Obama

We often feel overwhelmed by circumstances and have no effective response, thinking, "Life is a terminal disease for which there exists no known cure." All we are guaranteed is the chance to play honorably: that is the fundamental difference between success and integrity. It is possible to act with integrity and still fail. It is also possible to triumph without dignity. Success involves accomplishing a goal, whereas integrity involves playing fair. We can't always be successful, but we can always live and act aligned with our highest values.

Our work, whatever it is, can be a source of meaning in our life: we are doing something useful, regardless of whether it seems as if we are just a cog in a machine. When our work is aligned with a vision, we can feel that what we do makes a difference. When it is aligned with the idea that we are serving others, or a common good, we feel the fullness of belonging.

MoveOn, a grassroots organization in the United States, endeavors to have the voice of the people heard. It has been an inspiration. It is largely responsible for creating a major shift in U.S. politics and was very instrumental in getting Barack Obama elected to the presidency. This organization galvanized millions of people into action because it aligns them with deeper values and stands for what is truly important: peace, ecological integrity, and affordable health care, education, and housing. Obama will always be successful because his actions are based on integrity, not just external results. People are hungry for this kind of leadership.

FRED KOFMAN STATES FOUR WAYS TO BE SUCCESSFUL

1. Have unconditional responsibility or accountability for all your decisions. Avoid the victim mentality of powerlessness.
2. Have a purpose beyond the next big deal.
3. Learn how to have difficult conversations. Disentangle your emotional response from events.
4. The secret is to have humility.

MAKING DECISIONS

Although making decisions is probably one of the most challenging endeavors we all face, making decisions is not enough; we must then act. If personal decisions are hard for us, they are infinitely harder when working with others. As Fred Kofman says, "It is a wonder that anything ever happens at Chrysler; that any cars are produced is a miracle, proof of the existence of god!"

DECISIONS ARE NOT SUFFICIENT: WE MUST ACT

Five frogs are on a log. Four decide to jump. How many are left? . . . Five.

When using the five energies, we see that decision making comes not only from the head but also from the felt sense. When we pay attention to energy, we have an experiential sense of what to do. It is like divination, a traditional way of arriving at a decision in several cultures. We can be our own divining rod in making decisions.

DOWSING TO MAKE DECISIONS

When you are making a decision, weigh your options by doing the following:
- Stand and immerse yourself totally in one of your options, getting the felt sense of it.
  - What is the physical, emotional/energetic, and mental environment?
  - How does it feel?
  - Does your body lean forward to affirm it as a good choice or lean back to negate it?
- Now stand in another place and immerse yourself totally in another of your options.
  - Repeat what you did for the first choice.
- Do you have some clarity as to what to do?
  - If not, let some time pass and try the process again.

– Given enough time, the answer will arise.

DECISION MAKING IN FIVE COLORS

I worked with a training participant who had been teetering on the edge of a decision: to stay in or leave her marriage. Near the end of the process, she was leaning toward leaving, so we checked in with her mix of colors. I would ask, "Is vajra ready to go?" After a few moments of reflection, she would say, "Yes." Then we would proceed to each of the remaining energies in turn. This brought out the intelligence of all aspects of herself. This can be done in a group, with everyone contemplating the situation in five energies.

When we have to make a decision as a group that will affect everyone, there is more at stake and the decision-making process is more complex. People want different things. They have personal preferences and perhaps hidden agendas. How can all parties get what they want? Going deeper, moving to another level, to more basic concerns, is helpful. Then we avoid getting trapped into thinking that we must have a particular thing. If we make decisions from our deeper values, like serving others or having a passion for creating something together, we see that aligning with others is easier. If we want two different things, both can be possible when everyone is aligned with a bigger view. In negotiation based on common interests rather than external factors, everyone is more amenable.

Think of a specific thing (outcome) that you want.

- Answer these questions:
  - Why is it important to you to get the particular thing (vacation, job) that you want?
  - What is more important than the thing itself?
- Move to progressively deeper levels.
  - What is the life experience that the thing you want will give you?
  - What fundamental quality is it you are seeking?
- What is the felt sense of what you want at a deeper level?
- Decision making with a team could look like this:
  - What is more important than a particular decision's going this way or that?
  - Is being part of the team more important than the result of that decision?
  - Can you let go of your own agenda to join with others?
  - Can you feel at one with all members of the team?

At one point, my personal experience with this process was quite profound. I started by saying I wanted to be in a relationship. What was deeper? A sense of joining with another, having physical intimacy. What was deeper than that? The pleasure and enjoyment of padma energy, which can manifest in many ways. And then? Bliss emptiness that I experience at times on the meditation cushion.

SKILLFUL COMMUNICATION

Though learning to employ tools for skillful communication can be extremely helpful in all our interactions, we need to remember that we ourselves are the most important tool. The more we rely on our own insight and intuition, the more creative and appropriate our responses will be.

TOOLS FOR SKILLFUL
COMMUNICATION

- Letting go of self-referencing and seeing only your own side
- Energetic exchange or resonance
- Insight: seeing clearly, seeing it the other person's way, seeing him or her
- Intuition: a felt sense, knowing what to say or do with your whole being
- Using the language of the Five Wisdoms to see personality styles and relationships

One of the most straightforward and effective models for skillful communication comes from Marshall Rosenberg, founder of Nonviolent Communication (NVC). For her fieldwork project in the Five Wisdoms @ Work training, Lotte Paans, in collaboration with Peter Slenders, created a model called Heart Communication. This model merges Five Wisdoms and NVC. In keeping with the emphasis put on body awareness and the energetic dimension in Five Wisdoms work, they include that as an important tool to create greater emotional awareness. As Lotte says, "In our training we don't only practice verbal communication but also physical and energetic communication." Inspired by what they had done, I went a little further by adding the buddha energy. This model follows the natural order of the Five Wisdoms cycle, except that ratna and padma are reversed. We have trained in these steps in previous chapters.

FIVE WISDOMS IN SKILLFUL COMMUNICATION

1. *Just being: buddha.* Take your seat with authentic presence. Synchronize body, speech, and mind with good posture, easy breathing, and an open mind. Be aware of your surroundings. (See chapter 6, "A Quiet Presence.")

2. *Observation / unbiased perception: vajra.* See clearly without projections. (See chapter 10, "Unbiased Perception.")

3. *Emotional connection: padma.* Use energetic exchange to break down the barrier between us and come into the emotional aspect of communication. (See chapter 9, "Energetic Exchange.")

4. *Awareness of unmet needs: ratna.* Here we must make an important distinction: needs based on our shortcomings versus needs based on holding a big mind. (See the two paragraphs following step 5.)

5. *Making a request: karma.* If we have been skillful in steps 1 to 4, we can make a request based on the sanity we feel is present.

The wounds of childhood, deep within us, create chronic needs. We carry them around like little time bombs, ready to explode when triggered. With those, our work must be primarily with our inner world of emotions. Needing someone or something to provide what we see as lacking in ourselves perpetuates the misunderstanding that our needs can be met by another. It creates dependent relationships that have a lot of hidden agendas and manipulation. We can take all the relationship trainings that exist, but if these deep wounds are not addressed, they will surface at inappropriate times.

When we are able to drop personal referencing, our needs could be a way of enhancing our sanity and acting in the service of others. It is important to note that we can present our own request without making another person wrong. The most skillful way to ask for what we need is to clearly state our aspiration with no ax to grind. Just let it float in the space. We could hold that desire as our own without needing a request for action. If the request is basically good, it will magnetize others. Our requests then lead to a conversation with another to commit to some action. When we feel that the result is satisfactory, we have completed the cycle of skillful communication.

FOUR WISDOM ACTIONS OR POWERS

The four wisdom actions or powers allow our actions to come from a deeper place, as they are sourced in wisdom. They operate somewhat sequentially but not strictly so. We can cycle through them continually to reengage, communicate, feel the particular situation, and tune in to the totality of the environment.

FIVE WISDOMS AND FOUR WISDOM ACTIONS IN COMMUNICATION

BUDDHA: WISDOM OF ALL-ENCOMPASSING SPACE; WISDOM ACTION: PACIFYING

- Have an unyielding, immovable quality.
  - An attitude of big mind sees there is fundamentally no problem.
  - Embrace nonjudgmental openness.
- In the medium of big space, anything can happen.
  - Boundaries are not solid, so everything can be accepted.
  - Problem areas simply reveal themselves without justifications or defensiveness.
- Our intelligence comes out spontaneously.
  - If our suggestions are not infused with space, we could push our own agenda too strongly.
- Note how your psychophysical being shifts when you go to this place.

VAJRA: MIRRORLIKE WISDOM; WISDOM ACTION: PACIFYING

- Hold a mirrorlike quality of reflecting things as they are.
  - Clarify the situation, the context, with unbiased perception.
  - Hold a bigger perspective.
- Continually return to calmness and evenness that cuts emotional upheaval.
  - Be solid and dependable, unflustered by emotionality.
- Defuse the sense of struggle and conflict.
  - When we see another's perspective, we are not so combative.

- The issue initially presented is usually not the real issue.
  - Penetrating, insightful questions allow us to go deeper.
- Ask, "Is this familiar to you?" to draw out the sense of history present in the moment.
- Do a brief BSMQA assessment of the person, relationship, or situation to get a full-picture.
- Non-violent Communication (NVC): observation

RATNA: WISDOM OF EQUANIMITY; WISDOM ACTION: ENRICHING

- Provide the generosity of your presence.
  - Nurture and support so others feel a sense of self-worth.
- Appreciate others in a genuine way.
  - Share their world.
  - See and communicate their richness and beauty.
  - Recognize that everyone has something of value to offer.
- Appreciate the wisdom and intelligence present.
  - Pick up on and highlight others' sanity.
  - Also see the richness of confusion and neurosis present.
- Be resourceful in a creative way.
  - There are endless possibilities when we think outside the box.
  - Offer richness, skills, talents.
- Ask, "What do you need right now? Where in your body are you feeling it? What does the feeling say?"
- NVC: need

Padma: Discriminating Awareness Wisdom; Wisdom Action: Magnetizing, Attracting

- Inspire others by your presence; draw people to you.
  - On the ground of intrinsic goodness, be open, warm, and friendly.
  - Understand, empathize, and communicate in a heartfelt way.
  - Embrace them with a soft, warm, non-threatening, inviting quality.
- Create an environment in which people are willing to share their private world.
  - Have real curiosity about others' world.
  - Invite them to share by doing so yourself.
  - Uncover their mask, what they hide, don't talk about.
  - Invite them to drop their defensiveness and make a connection.
- Establish a feeling of connectedness that allows compassion.
  - Break down their sense of isolation.
  - Help them see that they are not alone with their problems.
- Have a willingness to experience whatever arises.
  - The more we open to exchange, the more clarity we have about the other person.
- Ask, "What is the felt sense? Are you feeling the other person in your heart?"
- NVC: feeling

Karma: Wisdom of All-Accomplishing Action; Wisdom Action: Subduing

- Penetrate and cut fixation, solidification, and habitual patterns.
  - Refresh the situation, get it moving again.
  - Achieve a sense of actualizing or fulfilling.
- Skillful interventions and appropriate actions arise spontaneously, in response to a common ground of experience.
  - What to say and do depends on what is appropriate to the particular situation.
  - Effectiveness has everything to do with the right timing.
- Join compassion and clarity, so you know what to say and do.
  - There is no need to convince someone with logic.
- Being present and listening is very powerful.
  - Alternate between being in the immediacy of the moment and intervening.
  - Holding your seat in difficult situations is the ultimate skillful action.
  - Be genuine, fearless, and dignified.
- Acknowledge a tendency to push through stuckness.
  - See how you might act prematurely because you really want to help.
  - Stay with feeling stuck fully, then opening naturally occurs.
  - Out of that, creative action becomes possible.
- Ask, "What could cut through the stuckness and provide more wakefulness?"
- NVC: request

Closing: Letting Go and Grounding the Energy

- Go back to space, back to buddha.
  - Don't hold the situation in a fixed way.
  - Give up all hope of results.

- Transmit a sense of ease and relaxation.
- Don't beat yourself up for seeming failures.
  - This process requires patience with its many ups and downs.
- Close by grounding in basic being.
  - Then return to joining, with reduced energy.

SUMMARY

- Pacify to create open ground, come to clarity.
- Enrich by appreciating the richness present.
- Magnetize by communicating.
- Subdue or cut by touching and letting go.
- Dissolve into space.

DIALOGUE, ADVOCACY, AND INQUIRY

The principles of dialogue have emerged as a way to have skillful and effective conversations. In contrast to discussion, in which we hold to our views, dialogue has to do with coming collectively to a shared understanding. The heart of dialogue is a capacity to listen rather than expound our own views. In listening we move from the stance of "I know," based on our sense of expertise, to "I am open." The language of an expert revolves around one's competence; the language of an open person is inquisitive, questioning, wanting to learn.

Conversations can change our beliefs, perceptions, and actions. When we converse skillfully, we can help each other to expand our thinking, act more compassionately and wisely, and learn more deeply. When we converse unskillfully, we can wound, confuse, manipulate, and dehumanize each other.

—SUSAN SKJEI

SHIFTING TOWARD
LEARNING CONVERSATIONS
(FROM SUSAN SKJEI)

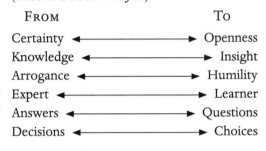

FROM	To
Certainty ⟷	Openness
Knowledge ⟷	Insight
Arrogance ⟷	Humility
Expert ⟷	Learner
Answers ⟷	Questions
Decisions ⟷	Choices

Using advocacy and inquiry in dialogue is a way of broadening our awareness: we can clearly state our position and at the same time be receptive to others' views. With advocacy we have a voice and reveal what is true for us no matter what anyone else thinks. With inquiry we are actively listening and inquisitive about another's world. As we have seen, fully understanding another person requires a big leap. However, it is only when we do, that we can move forward with a shared vision in an unbiased way. Our habitual pattern in any given situation is to infer, project, make assumptions. From there we draw conclusions and swing into action. Using advocacy and inquiry as a discipline can reorient us to a more expansive way of having conversations. When we have practiced being fully present with all our colors and receptive to others' energies, we know, collectively, what to do. Consensus emerges.

ADVOCACY AND INQUIRY (FROM SUSAN SKJEI)

ADVOCACY

- State your view.
- Say what you think.
- Provide data to support your view.
- Give an example, if possible.
- Invite others to test your thinking.

INQUIRY

- Ask questions with open curiosity.
- Ask for examples.
- Ask what others mean and how they feel.
- Ask for data and standards.

  - your mental models based on inference
  - your opinions, data, standards, values, concerns
- The silent partner listens deeply with the attitude: "I want to understand you."
  - Checks what you said by summarizing: "You think that . . ."
  - Asks you to explain giving facts and reasons: "Why do you think . . . ?"
- Keep the dialogue going until you have more shared understanding.

Within this way of conversing, many things arise. We could oppose another, clearly expressing our differences, inquire into others' logic and feelings, and test our ability to go beyond our own way of looking at things.

Dialogue is about expanding our capacity for attention, awareness and learning with and from each other. It is about exploring the frontiers of what it means to be human, in relationship to each other and our world.

—GLENNA GERARD, The Dialogue Group

PRACTICING DIALOGUE

Do this with a partner or in a small group.

- Pick a topic about which you and your partner could take strongly opposing views.
- Take turns advocating your positions. Expose:

REFLECTION CIRCLES

In the Five Wisdoms @ Work training, we use reflection circles to have peer-level communication about both the content and process of the training. It is an opportunity to integrate the learning journey both individually and as a group. Reflection circles are an integral part of the training and a key element in creating a community.

Because the tone of the circle is inviting and warm, people feel they can be themselves, relaxed and open. A field of awareness invites inquiry and fresh insight. Having openness toward everyone and being in exchange allow group members to go deeper with their experience. The group sits in a circle and begins and ends each session with a few minutes of meditation practice.

The position of leader is rotated so everyone has an opportunity. At an outer or body level, the leader organizes the time, place, and people in advance, and keeps track of time in the session. On an inner level, the leader makes sure everyone is participating and has a voice and that people are using the "Six Points of Mindful Speech" and/or "Circle Practice" (below). The idea is to resist providing "answers" and instead allow questions to percolate. On a mind level, the leader reminds people to bring themselves back to simple awareness.

SIX POINTS OF MINDFUL SPEECH

1. *Precision:* Enunciate your words clearly.
2. *Simplicity:* Choose your words well.
3. *Pace:* Speak slowly, without speed or aggression.
4. *Silence:* Regard silence as an important part of speech.
5. *Others:* Listen to the words, texture, and quality of others' speech.
6. *Self:* Be mindful of your own speech.

CIRCLE PRACTICE (FROM THE PEACEMAKER ORDER)

1. Listen from the heart.
2. Speak from the heart.
3. Be spontaneous.
4. Be lean on words.
5. Keep confidentiality.
6. Keep the sacredness of what has been shared.

THE CAFÉ

The café is an excellent form for large groups to engage with a specific topic. This is an adapted version using the five energies.

- Divide into small groups, with each person in each group representing a different energy.
- Discuss the topic from the perspective of your energy.
- Rotate to a new group, keeping your energy.
- In the large group discuss what you have learned.

COMMUNITY COUNCIL

We have used the following format in Five Wisdoms @ Work to bring group mind to an issue within the group or as a way of working with issues outside the group, as in a case presentation. The same format can be used between two peers.

- Someone presents a situation using the three-modes format.
  - The situation could involve several people in a particular context.
  - The group can ask clarifying questions at any point.
- When the presenter has finished, group members note the energies present.
  - Always express appreciation first, aligning with sanity.
  - Then point out the stuck place, the growth area.
- Group members then make suggestions for how to work with the situation.
  - The basic point is to see the intelligence within the confusion.
- Group members should not speak about the issues outside the format.

- Doing so will dilute the power of what has occurred.
- If the issues remain potent, another council could be held.

TEAMS

A new paradigm is emerging from the world of science: the evolution of any species has not always come about by the survival of the fittest but rather through collaboration and cooperation. Our psychological fixation that we must perpetually defend ourselves, our kin, our clan, our nation, has distorted what happens very simply in nature. When a species needs to adapt to meet change or threat, it collectively, nonconceptually, finds a fresh strategy.

My favorite example of collective cooperation involves amoebas living in a swamp, able to access both water and sunlight. When conditions are good, they multiply and so create a dense population. Huddled together, some do not get the the sun's rays and others can not reach the water. What to do? They don't kill one another off. Through osmosis, they bring sun energy to the lower ones and water to the top. They take care of one another. Such friendly little amoebas.

By teams, I mean any people living or working together who are relating consciously and communicating regularly. Our biggest challenge, as we have seen, is to let go of self-referencing—the me, myself, and I team. Practicing advocacy and inquiry is helpful: we know when to state our views and when to put our agenda aside. Not being biased creates a certain dignity.

When we are confident and warm, we shine and can offer our best. Also, the more we employ our full mix of colors, the more useful we will be. We can change gears: "What's needed? OK, got it. I'll be blue." My daughter, after a congenial padma/ratna outing at a restaurant with a group of friends, finds she is often the one who decides to change gears. What's needed? Someone must put on his or her blue hat to divide up the check.

We can consciously create teams of mixed personality styles to have a balance of energies, like instruments in an orchestra. Diversity offers us the opportunity for complementary teamwork. We can use one another's gifts and affinities: each of us has our unique intelligence to offer. We can also be aware of the weak points and what causes stress in each style. Our team could have more cohesion based on mutual respect for everyone's styles. The colors also act like checks and balances, so no one color or personality dominates. Five equally valuable points of view can work synergistically in a collective process, which is generative.

When my son, James, was in kindergarten, I was asked to coach his soccer team. Not knowing much about the game, I invited Mike Xu to coach with me. He agreed if given the role of senior coach. After Adam Artebury scored our team's first goal with a kick of over twenty yards, Mike pulled Adam out of the game and asked him to name the two members of his team who were closer to the goal than he was. Adam was benched for much of the game until he could remember the names of the players. It was in the first game that the principle of assist became embedded in the minds and hearts of these young children. Over the next several years, the teams coached by the mantra "An assist is as good as a goal" . . . were unbeatable!

—John J. Gardiner

Good teamwork is rare. The kind of openness described here could be scary. The less control we have, the more vulnerable we feel. That is the main reason teamwork does not happen. It breaks down the conventional hierarchical norms that keep people safe by giving them a defined role. More collaborative work gives rise to many issues: letting go of control, being pushed into areas that feel foreign, and so forth. However, natural order, which is innately present in the intelligence of the group, can emerge. Though teamwork can seem chaotic at first, we begin to see the flow of things and how people work together.

Mutual learning and collaborative creation make us cocreators of any situation rather than one person having unilateral control. We can let things happen, stand back and allow the situation to evolve. Then we can see how we can contribute in a way that is actually needed. This kind of interdependence and interconnectedness creates a win-win situation. However, sometimes there is intelligence in not being a team player. We may stick out because we are not going along with the others, but it could be because we are seeing something that others are not. Undoubtedly we will make ourselves unpopular by doing this. However, a good team would be able to see the intelligence in the criticism.

WHO HAS THE POWER AND HOW IT AFFECTS US

- Authority, as in a hierarchical organization
  - We let those in power, the higher-ups, make the decisions.
  - This will get compliance but not necessarily commitment from others.
  - More commitment comes when the vision is shared.
- Compromise: a mutual agreement taking into account all parties' needs
  - All parties accept somewhat less than they aspire to or need.
- Consensus: Everyone reaches agreement.
  - Generally some method is needed to achieve consensus.
- Agree to disagree: All parties hold whatever opinions they want.

The Energetic Constellation in Your Team or Workplace

Do this in a group with a facilitator. After working with your energetic constellation (chapter 4), apply it to your workplace in order to:

- find out if your personal power or intelligence is aligned with your work
- bring your whole being into your workplace or living situation
- create an opportunity to see friends and colleagues more fully
- permit more effective teamwork, as each person's full potential is brought out
- enable people to communicate on more levels, with more colors
- help see the energetic makeup of the organization and environment

- permit greater cohesion based on mutual respect and teamwork
- enable participants to create a more harmoniously functioning organization or living situation

FORMAT

- Lay out the directions of the mandala on the floor.
- Do three rounds, as follows, which may or may not take you into different energies:
  - Go to where your work energy is.
  - Go to the energy where you feel your personal power or intelligence.
  - Go to the energy where you experience your power at work.
- For each round, note with whom you communicate most often.
  - Say how you experience the energy of the relationship.
  - Say what aspirations you have for that relationship.

In a group discussion of the experience, ask:

- Is where you shine aligned with your role or work?
- Are communication lines open?
- What is missing in the energetic matrix of the group?

FLOW ISSUES

In project management and problem solving, it is helpful to have the diverse perspectives of the five energies within a shared vision. To move into action, we could harness different energies to accomplish particular tasks and at different points of a project. Some people will be good at envisioning an outcome, others at making it happen, and still others at relating to people. We can be aware of energy dynamics and flow issues, seeing where the process is blocked and where it is functioning smoothly. We could regularly check in with the team, acknowledging successful accomplishments to encourage the sanity present and flushing out what remains stuck.

Tina's fieldwork project for the Five Wisdoms @ Work training focused on having all the energies present. She works as a research and development manager at an aeronautics company. Her task had been to promote WebEx meetings. Her personal motivation was to travel less, be less exhausted, and be more environmentally friendly. The company's motivation was to reduce costs. The project focused on a one-day meeting with around fifteen participants from two to seven different places.

Tina saw that the dominant qualities at work, vajra and karma, became even stronger at the WebEx meetings as people were so focused on the screen. Buddha, ratna, and padma (space, earth, fire) were virtually missing. So the primary intent was to bring in those energies as well as cultivate a sane relationship to vajra and karma.

Several things became evident: Tina learned that if people have never met, it is better to have a face-to-face meeting first, that the WebEx option is best for half-day meetings, and that it is more appropriate for certain phases of projects.

To bring in padma, she talked with each

colleague by phone before a meeting and also came in a little early to use the "chat" function. This created a lighter atmosphere. To her delight, she saw that the "bugs" that often occurred in the WebEx process would prompt jokes. She says, "I have been fortunate to work on projects dealing with the development of more ecological technologies. Whenever the discussion is getting too flat, reminding people of their passion (technology and/or ecology) brings back liveliness." People also suggested having their photos on the screen. Buddha space was created with coffee breaks. However, experience showed that this kind of meeting is very sensitive to space and that the space could become "cold" very quickly. If the breaks last more than fifteen minutes, it is difficult to regain the "connection" among the participants.

Tina observed, "The simple fact of choosing this topic as a project brought a lot more awareness and mindfulness into my activities related to the meetings and all our projects. Important changes stemmed from this: On physical and mental levels, I have been less exhausted after meetings. The whole game made work more playful and hence more enjoyable. Work has been more integrated into my spiritual practice. Seeing my working environment as an opportunity to practice also makes a big difference. Carefully setting the appropriate agenda has increased the efficiency of the discussions, though this was not the primary goal. More clarity about what is suitable for this kind of meeting came out. With time, I have felt that applying some of the ideas above has put more red

into the picture. However, no major change has been observed regarding ratna."

TASK ACCOMPLISHMENT

Time management and getting organized (karma) are basic skills we need in order to keep up with ourselves. How can we remember all the things we are responsible for? We can't. We must all find our own ways to get organized and follow some simple disciplines.

GET ORGANIZED

There are many ways to get organized, from computer programs to just having a few basic tricks. I simply have a page called "Action," which I keep on the side of my computer screen, with headers: "Now," "Soon," "Later," and perhaps some special project. I use the label "A . . ." for file folders that I am currently relating to. "A" is at the top, easy to find. File folders that are out of date but that I don't want to discard I label "Z Old. . . ." "Z" is at the bottom, so I don't have to keep stumbling over them.

GROUP ENERGY IN PROJECT MANAGEMENT

This exercise is most effective when a situation is current and has some charge to it. Sit in a circle.

- One person briefly describes the situation.
- Everyone then entertains the following questions:
  - What energies do you bring to the situation? Stuck? Open?

- How could you contribute more? shine more?
- What do you need from others to make that happen?
- Discuss the experience as a group and ask:
  - What happened?
  - What did you learn?
  - What should happen next?

THE CREATIVE CYCLE

Creativity is not reserved for artists. Any group of people are more successful when they feel creative, feel their juices flowing. When we live fully, there is a natural fullness of being that we experience and want to express. When we inspire creativity, we bring out the best in people; they flower. When we work creatively in sync with others, we move from being passively involved to expressing our full potential.

Paying attention to the quality of our process will naturally generate qualitative results. Being able to stay on our edge between certainty and uncertainty allows others to stay on their edge. Then we can tap into our collective creativity. The process is empowering; the end product arises naturally. When every voice is heard, every way of being is respected, and the gifts of each personality style are used, people's experience is deeply satisfying and enjoyable. Whatever the endeavor, it is more likely to bear fruit because every member is invested and wants to do the utmost to see it fulfilled. It also builds a reservoir of trust that is the foundation for future collaboration.

Without a qualitative process, people may see short-term results but pay a high price in stress, dissatisfaction, lack of trust, hidden agendas, reluctance to collaborate, and depleted energy. This issue is mostly overlooked in the rush to reach the goal. So the question is how to achieve bottom-line results while fostering trust and collaboration. There are no simple solutions, but first we must value the quality of the process.

The natural order of the Five Wisdoms is a creative cycle. When we use each wisdom in turn, they foster a naturally evolving engagement with whatever our endeavor is and ensure that the intelligence of all five energies is present. They provide a process and are also present in the product. Different energy styles will be better at one phase of the creative project than another: some will be more resourceful, others better at implementing, and so forth.

THE CREATIVE CYCLE

- Allow a space of mind for inspiration and insight to arise.
- Get clarity, a general vision or outline.
- Be resourceful, bring in resources, delve into the rich possibilities.
- Engage deeply and passionately, then express it.
- Act, make it happen.

FIVE WISDOMS IN PROJECT DEVELOPMENT

1. Opening to the moment
   - Have a sense of all-accommodating space, open mind.
   - See space as full of all possibilities with no reference point.

2. Allowing inspiration to arise
   - Have a sense of inquisitiveness and clarity.
   - Let inspiration arise spontaneously, without strategy.
   - Brainstorm. The key rule is that every proposal is acceptable.
   - Create a long list of possibilities, including even crazy ones.
   - What arises depends on who you are, where you are, what your energy is, and what you are trying to create.
3. Grounding your inspiration
   - Have a sense of richness and possibility.
   - Elaborate on, develop, and embellish the first idea.
   - Use all your skills and resources.
   - Make the vision full-blown; bring the essence of the idea, the seed, to flower.
4. Adding a personal touch
   - Have a sense of detail and refinement.
   - Be in tune with your personal energy, unique manner of expression.
   - Bring definition and shape to your creation.
   - Enjoy the human element: playful, humorous, magnetizing.
5. Finishing
   - Have a sense of action, making it happen.
   - Bring all the elements together.
   - Work in an efficient and timely manner.

CONFLICT

Conflict is inevitable. We see things differently from everyone else. Our stance is always based on our values (vajra), needs (ratna), desires (padma), a focus on getting the job done (karma), or any combination of these. If we could have whatever we wanted without depending on another—as in the self-sufficiency of buddha—there would be no conflict. More commonly, every relationship has issues of identity, self-esteem, and relative power.

So if conflict is inevitable, we need to know how to work with it. The first thing is to acknowledge that there is a conflict. We tend to deny it exists and avoid facing up to it. The primary instruction is to start by working with our own internal conflict. Only when we have somewhat pacified our own turmoil can we truly be ready to deal with interpersonal conflict. It also helps to see that everyone is entitled to his or her own views and ways of doing things. So it is not necessarily about resolving an issue with another but dissolving it within ourselves. Working with the Five Wisdoms also enables us to see that there need be no deep conflict, only differences of tastes and opinions. Different people simply have different points of view and wishes.

Interpersonal conflicts involving an outcome that will lead to action are the most challenging. Assertions about who is right, together with many justifications to support those assertions, just exacerbate the divisiveness. We can only see the opposing views as wrong. This gets us nowhere; we have to work with ourselves first. How do we contribute to making this a difficult situation? What has become solidified in us? What is a sane expression of ourselves?

Working with energetic exchange and unbiased perception, we try to see what the other person really wants/requires. What are the emotional and practical needs of everyone involved? If we skip this part and go straight to negotiating the external situation, we miss the inner aspect, which is bound to affect the outcome. In human affairs, the shortest route is not always the fastest or most effective. When we have done the work on this personal level, we might simply have become more accepting of the situation. It is what it is.

As we saw with making decisions, going to a deeper level also applies here. What we want may be more a state of mind, such as equanimity or joy, which no one can give us but ourselves. If we want something like this, there is no scarcity, no constraint. It is available and infinitely abundant, and up to us to attain it. We could find that the more superficial desire—getting the promotion, having the project go our way, or keeping the house the way I want it—creates too much stress. It is easier to focus on universal truths, values that transcend a specific object of desire. Could we have a win-win negotiation? Is it possible to get what we want without its conflicting with what he or she wants? If yes, talk about what that outcome would look like. If no, we can agree to begin a process. The spirit of negotiation empowers us to get what we want.

CONFLICT RESOLUTION PROCESS

First do some preparation on your own.

- Ask what your true needs and desires are. Look at your own position, emotionally and practically.
- Consider your situation, evaluating the differences you have with another.

To begin the process:

- Take a minute to check in with your emotional state and come to just being.
- Say that you want to resolve the conflict/tension in a creative way.
- Ask if the other person is willing to go through a process to do so.

Take turns addressing these questions:

1. How do you see yourself in the situation? What is happening?
2. How do you see the other person in the situation?
3. How do you think he or she sees you?
4. What is your vision of a healthy outcome? (A good relationship, for example.)

Then take turns addressing these questions:

1. How have you experienced violation of trust or expectations?
2. What do you need from the other person to regain trust?
3. What do you need the other person to do (more of, less of, the same of) toward a healthy outcome?
4. What are you willing to do to support the other person in working toward a healthy outcome?
5. What agreements do you need in order to take the next step?

If this exercise goes well, it has a great effect on the emotional dimension of our relationship. It encourages us to express our emotions and ideas authentically, directly, and respectfully. When another's truth is heard and validated, our emotions lose their intensity and we can have much more reasonable and productive conversations. By raising our understanding and lowering our defensiveness, we can discover new information and perhaps modify our position. None of us possesses the full truth, so it is a way to pool knowledge, increase creative energy, and sharpen our ideas. Being emotionally and creatively involved with others is a way to go beyond our expectations of what could happen.

EVALUATION AND ASSESSMENT

What is often missed in working with others is periodically evaluating how we are doing. It is best to assume that all parties are doing their best given their understanding, experience, capabilities, and circumstances. However, from a human dynamics perspective, there are many issues that could need attention: the job and the person may not be a good match, someone may be burned out, or two people's energies may not be synchronized. The Five Wisdoms are useful in assessing people, the work at hand, and the environment. Using the intelligence of the energies, we could find out what is and is not working—and why.

Once the fire has consumed your neurosis, you can go anywhere and do anything, as long as it is connected with what is needed.

—adapted from a Buddhist text

12

Creating Our World

To REVIEW, we have looked at how work with ourselves creates personal authenticity, conscious relating creates authentic relationships, and skillful interactions creates effective action. Here we are going to look at how affecting our surrounding creates enlivened environments.

The environment in which we live and work has a great impact on us. As well, we can also impact our environment. Creating enlivened spaces, whether at home or in the workplace, can affect human dynamics. We can lift people's spirits and help to bring out their best. Becoming more sensitive to environmental energy facilitates this.

THE ENERGY OF OUR ENVIRONMENT

- We are perpetually affected by the environments we inhabit.
- When we are unaware of our environment, it can gain the upper hand.
- When we are aware of our environment, we are empowered by it.
- We can appreciate enlivened environments through working with our sense perceptions and psychophysical barometer.
- We can create enlivened environments by using the Five Wisdoms to work with space, visual order, richness, invitation, efficiency.

It is simply true that some environments give us a sense of upliftedness—expansive and cheerful—and others make us feel uncomfortable because they are chaotic or confining. We can tune in to how energy manifests in the environment as inspiration or obstacle. As people aware of these truths, we can take on the practice of creating what Trungpa called "environments of sanity" or "uplifted" environments.

We could think of our everyday life as a work of art: the art of living our life, doing everything with a sense of precision and delight. This is a practice of ultimate mindfulness. When we open to ourselves most fully, we are also opening to our world most fully. Our relationship with the phenomenal world could be uncomplicated. Everything could be done with a sense of appreciating the quality of life. The way my fingers touch my keyboard—the oh-so-smooth surface of the MacBook keys—brings me out of these endless words I am weaving to the immediacy of a tactile experience. A small pleasure, but I could have missed it.

As a young adult, I visited Agamemnon's palace in the Peloponnesus in Greece. No one was there but me. It is a starkly bold setting. The ruins of the palace sprawl across a rugged hilltop overlooking the blue, blue Mediterranean. The power of the place lies in the harsh terrain, the vast expanse of sea, the cloudless blue sky, and the brilliant sun. The next time I visited this place whose magical power had been haunting me, there were sixteen tourist buses and crowds of people. Greek teenagers, their ghetto blasters at full volume, were hanging out and smoking. They were being introduced to a profoundly powerful site yet seemed to have no connection to it whatsoever. It was painful to see this place of primal power so violated.

The power of even a small gesture put into the environment can be very vivid. A psychiatrist friend of mine was working with a disturbed young woman whose life was in turmoil. At the end of a session one day, he suggested that she buy herself some flowers. She did and went home and put them on the mantelpiece. That gesture inspired her to clean up her whole apartment.

When we understand the significance of the reciprocity between ourselves and our environment, we can pay more attention to everything in our outer world. The environmental aspect could be the strongest statement of anything we say or do. In many ways, it is the strongest aspect of contemplative training. It is modeling rather than

saying, a way of working from the outside in. It is a way to both express who we are and also, with good intention, have an effect on others.

This comes down to how we dress and how we arrange our living and work spaces. Feeling our body and its relationship to the environment, being part of the whole situation, is a healthy relationship. When we split off from our environment, we are out of sync and become confused. We are no longer in tune with the total power and strength of our surroundings, which makes us uncomfortable and eventually leads to mental and/or physical illness. So our very health is grounded in the environment. This is quite vivid in these times of ecological and political struggle. We see how our survival instinct and our being part of the environment are two aspects of a single expression.

We have tremendous power to affect the world. In creating environments—especially environments in which an awakened state of mind can flourish—we take on a social responsibility. Both Chögyam Trungpa Rinpoche and Sakyong Mipham Rinpoche recognize arts and culture and encourage them to flourish. As well, the vision of creating an enlightened society has a lineage; people have done this before us. When we have the confidence to align with our vision (what others might regard as lofty ideals), then we can bring it to earth in a practical way. We need to combine the freedom of immense potentiality with the pragmatics. This is the basis of creating a good society.

ENLIVENED ENVIRONMENTS

We can use the environment as our ally to come into the wisdom aspect of the energies. For this to happen, each of the energies must somehow be present: spaciousness, visual order, richness, invitation, and efficiency.

FIVE WISDOMS IN YOUR ENVIRONMENT

Take some time to reenvision either a living or work space using these guidelines.

Spaciousness and the Power of Pacifying

To create an all-accommodating environment simplicity is the key.
- Clear out any unnecessary objects with the idea of there being "enough."
- Pay attention to your personal appearance.
- Hold an upright but very natural and relaxed posture.
- Pay attention to your deportment.
- Dress in a simple way, not imposing your self but giving space for others.
- To much space or spaciousness feels sparse or barren.
- This is the power of pacifying through spaciousness.

Clarity and the Power of Pacifying

To capture someone's mind and wake him or her up, order is the key.
- Pay attention to both the overall look and the details.
- Place objects and furniture with a sense of both spaciousness and visual order.
- Make things clean and neat, with clear boundaries.

- Cluster things together, usually in groups of three.
- Have eye-catching objects, like paintings, sculptures, flowers, rocks, or crystals, paying attention to their shape and texture.
- Place symbols that have meaning for you in prominent places.
- Wear blue with clean lines and silver accents. This can provoke inquisitiveness and intelligence.
- Too many bold colors, sharp lines, and metallic textures feels cold.
- This is the power of pacifying through clarity.

Richness and the Power of Enriching

To invoke a sense of abundance, use rich, permeated colors, lush textures, and living things.
- Use colorful fabrics and warm, indirect lighting.
- Have plants, flower arrangements, an aquarium, pets.
- Women can wear bright, warm colors, with floral designs and gold jewelry; men can wear casual, more colorful clothes.
- If this approach is overdone, it feels indulgent. Just enough is when you feel richness but are not overwhelmed by it.
- This is the power of enriching through feeling your resourcefulness.

Invitation and the Power of Magnetizing

To create an inviting space that promises pleasure and intimacy, use gentle curves and soft textures.

- Use soft contours, warm colors, and subtle lighting.
- Decorate with pillows, candles, flowers, artwork.
- Wear clothes that make you feel attractive. Women can wear something more flashy that draws attention to the natural curves of the body; men can feel good-spirited by wearing a colorful shirt or tie.
- If not overdone, the space invites us to be together in more intimate ways.
- This is the power of magnetizing through being attractive.

WORKABILITY AND THE POWER OF SUBDUING

To create an environment that is efficient, focus on how the space will be used.
- Organize it so it functions for its intended purpose, depending on what is to happen in the space.
- Set up whatever work spaces and tools will be needed to accomplish things.
- Wear clothes suited to the job.
- This is the power of subduing through aligning with the energy of the moment.

These five powers have a sense of being layered rather than sequential. The total effect will have aspects of all five qualities.

When I was training the trainers at the National Institute for School Development in the Netherlands, during the part of the training that involved working with the environment, it was discovered that the institute's main office building had no expression of either buddha or ratna energy. What to do? For buddha, a seldom-used upstairs room was turned into a quiet place where people could meditate or just be quiet. For ratna, a corner of the cafeteria was rearranged and plants were brought in.

I was always delighted to visit my tax accountant, Felice Owens, and my mortgage broker, Suter DuBose, in Boulder, Colorado. Felice's office was in a building whose entire second floor was arranged around an interior Zen garden designed by Trungpa Rinpoche. It took your breath away to come into it. Behind Suter's desk, on most of the wall, was a photo of a Japanese landscape with red cherry trees in full bloom. Both these environments allowed the mind to relax, even though the numbers in each case could be challenging.

13

Professional Arenas

WORKING IN SEVERAL professional arenas has led me to see a deeper resonance among them: I have been a bridge builder, seeing the differences in orientation as well as the deep correspondences. In particular, each professional arena has both an inner and outer journey, the inner journey being key to a sane manifestation of the outer journey. In seeing the common ground among various disciplines, I have come to regard my work as generic: we all can cultivate more personal awareness, conscious relationships, and effectiveness at work. My contribution is to enhance professional work by offering a deeper understanding through the Five Wisdoms. The Five Wisdoms can be applied anywhere. Here we are going to look at two professions where they have had the greatest impact: education and health care.

FIRST-PERSON LEARNING

Contemplative education, espoused at Naropa University but also modeled elsewhere, aspires to educate a full human being, which is greatly enhanced by working with the five wisdom energies. By being curious about the uniqueness of each person's journey, we educate the whole person. While we are interested in students' educational development, we are equally interested in students as people. their full array of colors. There is an allegiance to inherent well-being that creates friendliness and a ground of trust among fellow learners. Students are encouraged to work creatively on their own rather than sit in front of someone who is downloading information to them. This puts the teacher in the role of guide, albeit with sufficient understanding about a particular body of knowledge. So the focus is on process as much as content, on being as much as doing, on embodied knowing as much as accumulated knowledge.

Emphasizing the Five Wisdoms creates a balance between mastering specific disciplines and enhancing personal growth. We could think of them as "five ways of knowing." When Naropa was applying for accreditation, we referred to the Five Wisdoms as "the five qualities of a fully educated person" and put them as such in our brochure.

THE FIVE QUALITIES OF A FULLY EDUCATED PERSON, OR FIVE WAYS OF KNOWING

(adapted from a previous Naropa University brochure)

Openness and respect for immediate experience. This quality acknowledges our direct perception of the present moment, including ambiguity and uncertainty, chaos and confusion, both in ourselves and in the environment. It involves developing a clear, accurate, and open-ended relationship to experience. In order to act with intelligence and confidence, we must proceed from a foundation of ongoing awareness and curiosity.

Intellect and insight. This has to do with passion and curiosity for learning. Intelligence includes critical thinking, analysis, and sharpening insight. It facilitates understanding the world and ourselves and enables us to articulate it in precise and creative ways. This quality involves proficiency in understanding principles, structures, logic, and relationships. It is the willingness to maintain a larger view and to regard situations beyond our own self-interest, including being able to take another's perspective.

Resourcefulness and appreciation of the richness of the world. By increasing our knowledge and appreciation of the world in its diversity, creativity and resourcefulness are evoked. We can tap the resources we have and cultivate hidden inner talents—intellectual, emotional, and pragmatic. This qual-ity involves developing our ability to respect the many modes of human expression, experiences, creativity, and cultural backgrounds.

Interpersonal and communication skills. This is the ability to relate and communicate effectively with people. It begins with valuing the experiences of others and allowing them to teach us about themselves. From this follows work on the various modes of interpersonal communication—effective reading, writing, speaking, and listening skills. It includes communication through nonverbal artistic media like music, movement, and visual arts. This quality also includes an ability to connect with others empathetically, and an interest and curiosity about other people's lives. It is the ability to give and receive feedback skillfully.

Effective action. This is the ability to apply our learning and insight effectively in the world, putting openness, insights, knowledge, and communicative capacities into action. It involves becoming organized, responding effectively to demands, sustaining interest, and being committed to carrying projects through to completion.

The Five Qualities enhance an educational setting in several ways. Teachers understand their own and their students' styles. They see the ways they manifest, present material, and relate to others. They can access styles appropriate to each student and situation, so are more available to students and show them greater understanding. They are more equipped to evaluate and guide each student's educational journey. Students find that each energy quality is necessary in the learning process. They see the qualities as a foundation for ongoing learning, understanding, and creativity throughout life. As well, administrators understand the energetic makeup of students, teachers, staff, and the board. They see what is needed to create a more harmoniously functioning educational environment.

> This work is a vehicle for building something more profound in education, a fundamental approach. Learning is only possible in an open and free, "here and now" environment.
>
> —Johan Hamstra, National Institute for School Development, the Netherlands

The paradigm of integrative education through Five Wisdoms is powerful and effective. It helps to ground the education process deeply in a meditative model that brings out the whole person. The Five Wisdoms model encourages us to see that meditative intelligence is not an "add-on" to the education process, but is its very core.

> —Ashok Gangadean, Haverford College philosophy professor, cofounder of Global Dialogue Institute, and host of *Philly LIVE*

Dr. Shoshana Simons at the California Institute for Integral Studies was inspired by the Five Wisdoms in teaching leadership principles. Her course description for Resonant Leadership read like this: "We will explore ways we can nurture our own and others' capacity for resonant leadership in relation to some of the key literature in the field. . . . We will use Irini Rockwell's (Rockwell, 2002) exposition of the Buddhist system of the Five Wisdom Energies as a key organizing tool. To this end, the 'classroom space' has been divided into five rooms each one corresponding to one of the Five Wisdom Energies. These energies are associated with the five Buddha families and each in turn relates to a core learning objective for this class."

LEARNING STYLES

- Vajra—intellectual; using analysis, abstractions, and general principles
- Ratna—amassing information, doing research
- Padma—intuitive, creative, and empathetic
- Karma—by doing, trial and error
- Buddha—repetition using simple, basic concepts; sleeping on it; osmosis

DEVELOPING TEACHING MATERIALS WITH THE FIVE QUALITIES

- Design a course, a class, or a presentation with the five energies present
- Example: Present a subject bringing in all five energies:
  - *space:* silence, ground in sitting and breathing
  - *clarity:* the pith instructions on the material to be presented
  - *resources:* where to find more information, a larger context
  - *communication:* dialogue time to see if the material is being communicated

- *action:* some activity that brings the material home to the students
- *space:* Come back to this from time to time and to close.

FIVE QUALITIES FOR EVALUATION AND ASSESSMENT

- Design an evaluation form employing the five qualities, for use by:
  - teachers to evaluate students' participation
  - students to evaluate themselves, the material presented, and the teachers
- The form could be pithy or more elaborate, depending on the students' level.

Only a learning environment that enhances the many aspects of who we are can foster a sense of personal integration. Creating a learning community with a healthy environment allows a dialogue, which both sharpens intellect and melts hearts. Different points of view can rub up against one another within an openhearted, accepting context. Everyone can be involved in creating an atmosphere that is gentle, dignified, and committed to intellectual, artistic, and spiritual development. This atmosphere instills a sense that learning is omnipresent and lifelong, a way of being that takes us into the world, open, inquisitive, resourceful, communicative, and willing to act. Then we are better able to meet the diverse demands of our world.

I look at my world with different eyes, have become more mild and accepting, and use this new type of consciousness in my leadership and in my coaching and training.

—INGRID VERHEGGEN, director,
National Institute for School
Development, Netherlands

Several trainers I was working with at the National Institute for School Development were instrumental in creating De Nieuwste School (The New School), an alternative high school in the Netherlands. They used the Five Wisdoms as a foundational model to design the school environment, train teachers to teach and coach students, and enliven the students' learning journey.

I visited the school almost five years after its inception and was quite curious as to what I might find. Two major things stood out: the sense of first-person learning and the environment. Annemarieke Schepers, my main contact person, and three students gave me a tour. In only one out of six classrooms we visited was there a teacher up front downloading information via PowerPoint. In all the other classrooms, everyone was deep into some project.

Classrooms are called living rooms and are arranged accordingly, with comfortable sofas in addition to the computer tables and chairs. Color and plants are everywhere. Posters with inspiring slogans display the school's main themes, primarily student-centered learning. The preponderance of computers, I found out, is because the school uses online digital material rather than books, so sources are more flexible. It was heartening to see how much could be done with a simple paradigm shift.

Over a period of time, David Marshall was

in consultation with me while working with a team at Evergreen College to develop a learning rubric. Though other influences and modalities were discussed, the college settled on the five qualities to be utilized for structuring, guiding, and assessing student work. The five qualities were renamed: view, appreciation, communication, method, and presence. Marshall says, "Part of what this rubric is promoting is a broader view of thinking that adds feeling, perception and intuition to conceptual cognition. . . . By organizing the elements in this way, I have hoped to produce a tool that will have general utility for assessing student work and for providing a framework for teachers and students to consider aspects of learning and demonstrations of learning."

Here's how Five Wisdoms @ Work graduate Berry Trip explained to his children what Dad and Mom were doing with Irini for all those long hours: "I had to find a child's perspective with words and examples. I started by asking them what feelings and thoughts they have when seeing the different colors. Then I told them my interpretation, and together we tried to find real-life examples. Their examples were TV personalities, teachers, *Avatar*, neighbors, and friends, then their surroundings, like rooms and the garden.

Recognizing the wisdom within the neuroses became the next step. It was surprisingly easy. After summer holidays my daughter Iki had a new, more conservative teacher. I asked her about her teacher's colors: "Blue! Like ice!" "OK, what do you like about blue when you think about it?" "It's clear like the sky or like the water when you can look to the bottom of the sea." A conversation started about turbulent and calm water. Eventually I asked her what she really wanted to say to her teacher. Iki: "It isn't nice when she is like that. I can't hear what she is trying to say. I know she is right about what she tries to say, but I can't listen when she is so angry." We talked about her colors again, and she said that shiny red and blue are needed. The next day she wrote a note and gave it to her teacher. The teacher then invited her for a talk, she shed a tear, and thanked her for her open heart and clarity."

Five Wisdoms @ Work graduate Marlies Hallingse (Berry's wife and Iki's mother) organized a karate weekend for the youth of Kenkon Integral Life and Training Center. She was interested in deepening her understanding of karate by focusing on each quality. What follows is a good example of how you could approach any mind/body discipline.

WISDOM AND NEUROSES IN A KARATE TRAINING

VAJRA

Wisdom: You are accurate, sharp, precise. You have a desire to know the technique and do it to the best of your ability. You are curious and interested in the material and want to teach it others. You have an overview of the basic principles and integrity in following them. You are on time.

Neurosis: You are critical; nothing is ever good enough. You are stiff and do the movements without feeling. You get angry when things don't go your way. You are overly analytical, become authoritarian, and blame others or yourself. You are very critical in choosing a partner to practice with. You have no fun and see the practice as a duty.

Ratna

Wisdom: You see a lot of variety in the technique and are resourceful in trying combinations. You are deeply satisfied during the lesson and generous to the others.

Neurosis: You want too many different things and never get enough. You are concerned only with yourself, are arrogant, and exaggerate the movements. You are preoccupied with pleasing your teacher and partner. You are constantly telling others what is best for them.

Padma

Wisdom: You enjoy the connection with your partner and are friendly and honest. You like the companionship of the group and communicate in an easy way. You have a good time and really enjoy the experience.

Neurosis: You want a lot of attention and need to be confirmed. You try to do the movements well when the teacher is looking. You are insecure and thus get giggly and look for fun as a distraction. You become overly emotional when somebody kicks you.

Karma

Wisdom: You are very effective and efficient, skilful and practical. You are timely and ap-

propriate, doing neither more nor less than is necessary to reach your goal. You are full of positive energy, so you inspire others.

Neurosis: You are too speedy and restless. You want to be the top dog, dominant, and get jealous when somebody else gets a compliment or prize. You don't care about your partner but about your desired goal. You are clumsy, rude, and unmannerly. You are very focused on being the best.

Buddha

Wisdom: You give space to your partner, are present and awake in the moment, and stay relaxed and peaceful. You are easygoing, not stressed, and hold your seat.

Neurosis: You are easily distracted, lazy, humorless, and stubborn. You ignore what the teacher is saying. You arrive late and are always the last to find a new partner.

A working group was formed to develop an articulation of contemplative administration at Naropa University that could serve as a foundation for hiring, staff orientation, training, community building, and evaluation. They collected much data through interviews with students, faculty, staff, and trustees. "After spending time with our data, attempting to sort it and make sense of it in many different ways, we ended up coming back to the Five Qualities [which were already in Naropa's mission statement]. It became clear that the Qualities were implicit in the themes that had emerged . . . and could provide a framework for a model of Contemplative Administration."

IN THE SERVICE OF OTHERS: HEALTH CARE

Though my father was a third-generation missionary and a doctor, I did not come to understand service to others until much later in life. First, I wanted to dance! Later, as a teacher, adviser, and meditation instructor to dance students at Naropa University, and by then following a Buddhist path, I came to feel that I was more interested in others as people than as dancers. Moving from a primary interest in the arts to a profession in service to others was a major shift. This simple truth dawned on me: these people think of others! It was a breath of fresh air. We genuinely feel better when we are doing something for someone else rather than being perpetually preoccupied with ourselves. Why? Our heart is open. There are many ways to be of service to others, but what stands out primarily is that those who focus their work around people have a different sensibility.

I don't teach dance; I teach people.

—MARY WHITEHOUSE, dancer and one of the founders of dance therapy

Contemplative approaches to working with others, originally sourced in the Contemplative Psychotherapy Department at Naropa University, have proved to be the touchstone, the criterion and standard for working with others. The power of this training is that it brings contemplative practice and a Buddhist understanding of the process of mind to the immediacy of an interpersonal practice. The premise is that the more we work with ourselves, the more we can work with others. As we have discussed, too often we are caught in projections and fail to see who the other person is and what he or she brings to us. So the primary training is to plumb the depths of our own psychology through direct experience. It takes a certain fearlessness to look at ourselves without self-protecting ploys. Instead, we could become extremely inquisitive. We integrate our personal practices with the interpersonal practices of psychotherapy, counseling, and coaching. Our success in working with others depends on how deeply we know ourselves.

If you have patience with people, they will slowly change. You do have some effect on them if you radiate your sanity.

—CHÖGYAM TRUNGPA

Cultivating an authentic presence and practicing energetic exchange and unbiased perception makes us available to track and guide another's journey. We fully enter the other's world and appreciate his or her situation for what it is. Within a container of intrinsic sanity, maitri, and compassion, insights about the other arise. This way of working is in contrast to most Western psychiatry, which works primarily with diagnosing and curing pathology. Focusing on pathology undermines sanity whereas aligning with sanity makes it a most powerful healing agent: we stay open to whatever arises as workable. So Five Wisdoms training for psychotherapists is the most in-depth. When people have firsthand experience of their own psychological process and energetic makeup, they become better prepared to tune in to others' states of mind. This approach takes courage and daring. It is powerful because it is a shared exploration. Ultimately, we cultivate a friendship, a genuine connection based on mutual appreciation.

> The feedback I get from people being cared for by someone practicing mindfulness is that they feel seen as people, apart from the medical or mental problem. . . . Mindful caregivers are able to listen more, talk less, and utilize a more sophisticated understanding of non-verbal communication.
>
> —JUDITH LIEF, author of
> *Making Friends with Death*

At the time my sister was put under the care of San Diego Hospice, Dr. Charles Lewis, a meditator, was on her team. He is the medical director of both the Inpatient Care Center and their Institute for Palliative Care. I was present at the intake interview. He radiated a calm presence and, from his questions, you felt that he was seeing a whole person. In the two hours he spent with her and later in my conversations with him, he was attentive to every nuance my sister displayed. He created a healing environment not only for my sister, but also her caregiver, Jenna, and myself.

> My working definition of healing is coming to terms with things as they are. That's very different from curing. With curing there is the expectation that things will be restored to the way they were before.
>
> —JON KABAT-ZINN, PhD, Center for
> Mindfulness in Medicine, Health Care, and Society
> at the University of Massachusetts

As we have seen, the most fundamental principle is that all human beings have inherent sanity, are fundamentally good, and naturally possess dignity and intelligence. Inherent sanity is a genuine experience that is simple and direct. It is close to us: we can experience it, touch into it, all the time. Once recognized, it can be encouraged and cultivated. Feeling our lives fully and thoroughly, we appreciate that we are genuine, true human beings. Then we can develop the ability to recognize intrinsic sanity in others. With this approach, our neurosis and confusion become more superficial issues and less of a problem.

HIGHLIGHTS OF THE CONTEMPLATIVE APPROACH TO WORKING WITH OTHERS

- Make ongoing work with yourself the ground for working with others.
- Cultivate the warmth of an open heart to fully appreciate another human being.
- Willingly enter someone's world as the first step in helping him or her.
- Practice energetic exchange and unbiased perception.
- Align yourself with the basic goodness and sanity in everyone.
- Take action based on clarity and benevolence.

> I find it easier to coach people. Principles like honesty, straightforwardness, opening up, and compassion are increasingly important to me.
>
> —ANKE DE GRAAF, National Institute for School
> Development, Netherlands

As the five wisdom energies acknowledge the inherent inseparability of confusion and sanity, they are at the heart of this approach. The emphasis is on seeing any state of mind as workable, just as it is, including ordinary suffering and major illness. When we allow intensified confused energy to be present without judgment, that powerful energy transmutes into not just ordinary sanity but brilliant sanity. The goal is not to change people but to see them more fully as they are. In seeing them fully, we see them as workable. Our job is to bring out the best in all people by having an unconditional positive regard for them.

Dr. Nguyen Thi le Dung, a Five Wisdoms @ Work graduate and osteopath, did her fieldwork project to deepen her understanding of her profession by taking the perspective of the Five Wisdoms. She says, "Cranial biodynamic osteopathy uses our hands to appreciate the movement of the internal forces of healing that are already present in the patient without adding forces, direction, or intention. Those healing forces are the forces of growth and development from the embryo and sustain us through our life. So there is always a movement toward "normal" to keep us in balance called "homeostasis." In order to engage our relationship with those embryonic forces called Primary Respiration, we learn to let the Health transmute our consciousness. In order to see the Health, which is a sweet, warm transparency, we have to practice Wisdom and Being. In order to communicate, we go to a "meeting place" called Contemplation where our consciousness will be shifted: "Be still and know."

During the session we stay empty, still, present, and aware of what's happening inside the patient. We are also aware of the space around us, from the room to the horizon and beyond. We make the diagnosis with our hands. We are simply present and contemplate, not doing anything else. In this communication we create a space of love and compassion, generosity and openness, in which the patient feels secure and can let go. They let their physical and emotional blockages rise up, and if they feel confident enough, will talk about it.

In summary, in the "ideal session" with the "ideal patient," I am in buddha energy all through the session, mixed with vajra for diagnosis and seeing how the therapeutic process goes. There is no karma energy intervention. It is done in an atmosphere of trust, security, and warm welcome: padma and ratna energies.

FIVE WISDOMS COACHING

It is good to have a guide. Our blind spots are more obvious to others and often most hidden from ourselves. There are many possible guides, depending on where we want to focus. To name a few: a counselor or therapist guides us in deep personal work; a teacher or mentor guides our learning; a spiritual teacher guides our spiritual path. For me all these come together in what I call Five Wisdoms coaching.

I have worked with several coaching models and adapted them to the Five Wisdoms and contemplative approaches to working with others. A coach can help us see where we are, where we would like to be, and what is necessary to get there. We may have no idea where this journey will take us. A coach creates an environment of unconditional positive regard and appreciation for who we are. This establishes a ground of trust in working with our more challenging aspects, the parts of ourselves we like the least, and allows the best of us to emerge. The coach supports our innate abilities to move toward what is best for us.

If we are working with others, it is good to get coaching, supervision, or therapy ourselves. If we are stuck in coaching someone, the chances are that that is the place where we are stuck as well.

HOW FIVE WISDOMS COACHING ENHANCES YOUR ABILITIES

Five Wisdoms coaching helps you to
- See where you perform the best and how you limit yourself.
- See your current situation more clearly.
- Gain insight about how to manage your life more productively.

- See new possibilities for generating deeper meaning and fulfillment in your life.
- Connect with your priorities, purpose, and deeply held principles and values.
- Take more informed, better, and smarter decisions and actions based on your personal definition of what it means to live and work.

CONTEMPLATIVE SUPERVISION

Do this in a small group.
- The presenter says why a particular person/situation is being presented.
  - He or she does a short, unbiased perception presentation with the three modes.
  - Group members stay in energetic exchange during this.
- Group members express their felt sense and intuitive understanding.
  - They bring out what is healthy and intelligent in the situation.
  - Then they see where the constriction is.

Chögyam Trungpa would say, "Be who you are," and going further we can say, "Be the best of who you are." It's more fun! Inevitably it includes others. In fact, the more we enjoy ourselves, the more others are drawn into a genuine sense of well-being. With this kind of attitude, we can enjoy our work, our friends, our life. We can have our daily diet of Five Wisdoms and make our daily contribution to fit into the big picture.

14

No Ending

LIFE HAS NO SCRIPT, only options. We have a choice: our same old, same old life or the lively journey of becoming our best self . . . which leads to transcending our self. When we open to the moment, we make a fresh start and open to vast possibilities. If our intentions are good and we are connected to what is happening, we can trust the situation. We can ride the coincidence of the moment. It is exquisitely fresh and exhilaratingly groundless.

A SUMMARY OF THE FIVE WISDOMS APPROACH IN THREE SLOGANS

1. Be who you are: enjoy your energies and they will dawn as wisdoms.
2. Ride the coincidence of the moment.
3. Align the best of who you are with whatever is needed.

INVOKING THE FIVE WISDOMS

This is a contemplation to raise confidence in our innate wisdoms: to rouse a field of power and radiate our wisdom as authentic presence. Do it sitting or standing. You can use one or more aspects and vary your practice from time to time. The sounds reflect the first elemental sounds of the particular energy arising from vast primordial space.

1. Invoke the energetic essence of buddha.
   - Say the elemental sound: AH.
   - Visualize the color: white in the top and back of your head.
   - Mentally name the key words: *wakefulness, spaciousness.* (You can use your own.)
   - Contemplate the element: space.
   - Contemplate the sense perception: mind.
   - Do a personal hand gesture or movement.
2. Invoke the energetic essence of vajra.
   - Say the elemental sound: EE.
   - Visualize the color: blue in your forehead (third eye) and chest.
   - Mentally name the key words: *clarity, visioning.* (You can use your own.)
   - Contemplate the element: water.
   - Contemplate the sense perception: seeing.
   - Do a personal hand gesture or movement.

3. Invoke the energetic essence of ratna.
   - Say the elemental sound: UH.
   - Visualize the color: golden yellow in your solar plexus and belly.
   - Mentally name the key words: *richness, abundance.* (You can use your own.)
   - Contemplate the element: earth.
   - Contemplate the sense perception: smelling/tasting/touching.
   - Do a personal hand gesture or movement.
4. Invoke the energetic essence of padma.
   - Say the elemental sound: EH.
   - Visualize the color: glowing red in your throat, heart, and genitals.
   - Mentally name the key words: *joining, relating.* (You can use your own.)
   - Contemplate the element: fire.
   - Contemplate the sense perception: hearing.
   - Do a personal hand gesture or movement.
5. Invoke the energetic essence of karma.
   - Say the elemental sound: O.
   - Visualize the color: green in your limbs.
   - Mentally name the key words: *acting, doing.* (You can use your own.)
   - Contemplate the element: wind.
   - Contemplate the sense perception: functional touch.
   - Do a personal hand gesture or movement.

There is no end. A published book is merely a decision to stop editing: adding, deleting, embellishing, honing. But life goes on. After the words, there is only experience. And experience is ultimately ephemeral.

Resources

BOOKS

Berliner, Helen. *Enlightened by Design*. Boston: Shambhala Publications, 1999.

Blake, William. *The Marriage of Heaven and Hell*. 1793.

Bohm, David. *Wholeness and the Implicit Order*. London: Routledge, 1980.

Brown, H. Jackson. *Life's Little Instruction Book*. Nashville, Tenn.: Rutledge Hill Press, 1991.

Heckler, Richard. *Crossings*. Boston: Harcourt Brace and Company, 1998.

Hoffer, Eric. *The True Believer*. New York: Harper and Row, 1951.

King, Martin Luther, Jr. "Drum Major Instinct." www.ijourney.org/index.php?tid=364.

Kneen, Cynthia. *Awake Mind, Open Heart*. Cambridge, Mass.: Marlowe and Company, 2002.

Kofman, Fred. *Conscious Business*. Audiobook. Louisville, Colo.: Sounds True, 2006.

Lief, Judith. *Making Friends with Death*. Boston: Shambhala Publications, 2001.

Senge, Peter, et al. *The Fifth Discipline*. New York: Doubleday. 1990.

Spears, Larry C. *Insights on Leadership*. New York: Wiley, 1998.

Spretnak, Charlene. *The Resurgence of the Real*. London: Routledge, 1999.

Suzuki Roshi, Shunryu. *Zen Mind, Beginners Mind*. Boston: Weatherhill, 1973.

Trungpa, Chögyam. *Cutting Through Spiritual Materialism*. Boston: Shambhala Publications, 1987.

———. *Orderly Chaos*. Boston: Shambhala Publications, 1991.

———. *Secret beyond Thought*. Halifax, N.S., Canada: Vajradhatu Publications, 1991.

———. *Transcending Madness*. Boston: Shambhala Publications, 1992.

———. *The Lion's Roar*. Boston: Shambhala Publications, 1992.

———. *Dharma Art*. Boston: Shambhala Publications, 1996.

———. *The Myth of Freedom and the Way of Meditation*. Boston: Shambhala Publications, 1998.

———. *Journey without Goal*. Boston: Shambhala Publications, 2000.

———. *True Perception: the Path of Dharma Art*. Boston: Shambhala Publications, 2008.

Varela, Francisco. "Three Gestures of Becoming Aware." Interview with Claus Otto Scharmer. January 12, 2000. Paris. www.presencing.com/dol/interviews/Varela-2000.shtml.

Wegela, Karen Kissel. *What Really Helps.* Revised edition of *How to Be a Help Instead of a Nuisance.* Boston: Shambhala Publications, 1996, 2010.

Wilbur, Ken. *The Integral Vision.* Boston: Shambhala Publications, 2007.

WEB SITES

Authentic Movement—BodySoul Center, founded by Mary Whitehouse: www.authenticmovement-bodysoul.com/amcenter.html

Bonnie Bainbridge Cohen's Web site: www.bodymindcentering.com

Ashok Gangadean's Web site: awakeningmind.org

Robert Greenleaf's Web site: www.greenleaf.org

The Web site for the Center for Mindfulness in Medicine, Health Care, and Society, founded by Jon Kabat-Zinn: www.umassmed.edu/cfm/home/index.aspx

Parker J. Palmer's profile at the Center for Courage and Renewal: www.couragerenewal.org/parker

Peter Senge's profile at the Encyclopedia of Informal Education: www.infed.org/thinkers/senge.htm

Shoshana Simons's profile at the California Institute of Integral Studies: www.ciis.edu/Academics/Faculty/Shoshana_Simons_Bio.html

Index

Page numbers followed by the letter *f* indicate the term appears inside a figure.

emotional dilemma, 113

emotional/expressive mode, 130. *See also* modes, five

emotions

    managing, 112–15 (*see also* reactivity vs. responsibility)

    projecting onto an object, 38

    See also projections

empathy, 117

energetic constellation

    discovering your, 62–63

    See also colors

energetic exchange, 117–18

    cultivating, 132–34

    exchange encounters, 124

    experiences with, 121–22

    moving with, 123–24

    practicing, 124

    in recognizing style, 135

    as a tool, 125

    ways we block, 119–20

    working with, 122–23

energetic makeup, understanding your, 57, 57f

energetic mix, 53

energetic qualities, expressing full range of, 10–11

energetic resonance, 12–13

energetic wisdom, 70

energies

    becoming familiar with our, 54–58

    exploring them in relation to each other, 50–51

    recognizing your dominant, 56

    slogans to bring us back to the wisdom of each energy, 62

energy

    defined, 12–13

    dynamic world of, 12

    grounding, 151–52

    open vs. closed, 70–71

    reading, and knowing someone fully, 128–29

    tuning up your psychophysical barometer, 120–21

    understanding your psychophysical barometer, 13

energy patterns, 53–54

enhancement energy, 54

environment(s), 163–64

    energy of our, 163

    enlivened, 164–65

    five wisdoms in your, 165–66

evaluation and assessment, 162

    five qualities for, 170

exchange. *See* energetic exchange

experience

    opening to vs. closing off, 37

    openness and respect for immediate, 168

fear, 96

fire. *See* padma energy

five modes. *See* modes, five

five wisdom skits, 50

five wisdoms, 10

    in action, 141f

    dynamic play of, 59–62

    experiencing how each is layered in an object, 40

    exploring the energies of, 44–51

    invoking, 177–78

    overview, 9–10

    as path to becoming the best of who you are, 74–75

    practical uses of, 13–14

    practice of, 73–75

    where are they, 11

    See also specific topics

About the Author

Irini Rockwell, MA, is director and principal trainer at the Five Wisdoms Institute. She is author of *The Five Wisdom Energies: A Buddhist Way of Understanding Personalities, Emotions, and Relationships*. Wisdoms@Work is the signature training series of the institute, engaging people in the personal work needed to genuinely serve others. Irini has created customized trainings for the National Institute for School Development in the Netherlands, Karuna Training in Germany, and the EastWind Institute in Canada. Irini holds a master's degree in contemplative psychotherapy and a certificate in authentic leadership from Naropa University, where she was director of dance and dance therapy. A senior teacher in the Shambhala community and at Naropa University, she is a longtime student of Chögyam Trungpa Rinpoche. Her website is at www.fivewisdomsinstitute.com.